THE
RENAISSANCE VILLA
IN BRITAIN 1500–1700

Spire Books, the editors and authors gratefully acknowledge the financial support of English Heritage and the Society of Architectural Historians of Great Britain in the publication of this book.

THE
RENAISSANCE VILLA
IN BRITAIN 1500–1700

Malcolm Airs and Geoffrey Tyack

Spire Books Ltd

PO Box 2336. Reading RG4 5WJ
www.spirebooks.com

Spire Books Ltd
PO Box 2336
Reading RG4 5WJ
www.spirebooks.com

CIP data:
A catalogue record for this book is available
from the British Library
ISBN 978-1-904965-13-8

Designed and produced by John Elliott
Text set in Adobe Bembo

Printed by Hobbs the Printers Ltd
Totton, Hampshire

Cover illustration: The Queen's House, Greenwich, by Inigo Jones, begun in 1616 for Queen Anne of Denmark and completed in the late 1630s for Queen Henrietta Maria. The colonnade was added in 1809-11 (*Geoff Brandwood*).

CONTENTS

PREFACE

The ideal of the villa – a fusion of urban sophistication and rural simplicity – has haunted western man ever since classical antiquity, and it still beguiles British commuters, Russian dacha-owners and holidaymakers in Tuscany or the Algarve. Interest in the history of the villa, both as a cultural phenomenon and as a type of building, has grown greatly in recent years. Yet, while shelves groan with books on the villas of the Veneto and on the English country house, relatively little research on the architectural history of the villa in Britain has appeared in print, at least in book form,[1] and virtually none on its origins and early history.[2]

This volume grew out of a conference sponsored by Oxford University's Department for Continuing Education and held at Rewley House, Oxford, on 5-7 January 2005 under the title of 'The 16th and 17th Century Villa in Britain'. Since 1994 annual conferences have been held at Rewley House on aspects of British domestic architecture, starting with the Great House, moving on to the Town House, and concluding with the Villa. Each conference has presented new and often unpublished academic research to an audience comprising both scholars and interested amateurs (in the best sense of that word), and it is with the intention of offering some of that research to a wider public that this volume has been compiled. It consists of edited versions of all the conference papers arranged in two sections, the first tracing the history of the villa in Britain in the 16th and 17th centuries, the second looking more closely at individual houses and groups of houses in the London area.

Our main debt of gratitude is to the contributors, all of whom generously agreed to allow publication of their papers. We are also grateful to the loyal band of participants at successive conferences, whose comments and questions have helped make them such intellectually stimulating events. Publication would not have been

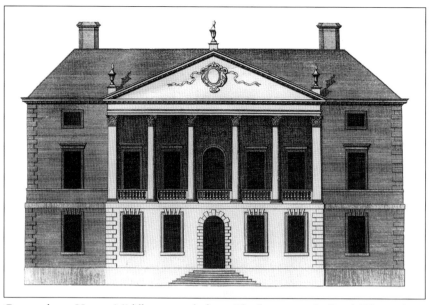

Gunnersbury House, Middlesex, south front. The house was built *c*.1658 to *c*.1663 to designs by John Webb for Sir John Maynard, law advisor to Charles II. It was demolished in 1801 (*Colen Campbell,* Vitruvius Britannicus, *vol. 1, 1715*).

possible without the generous financial assistance given by English Heritage, and we are also extremely grateful to the Society of Architectural Historians of Great Britain for the award of a Dorothy Stroud Bursary to enable us to use colour for some of the illustrations. Finally, the Department for Continuing Education deserves thanks for helping to maintain Oxford's reputation as a nursery for scholarship in the history of British architecture.

Malcolm Airs
Geoffrey Tyack

Oxford, February 2007

1

The English Villa: Sources, Forms and Functions

Nicholas Cooper

Many years ago, my mother used to take a small, fat, green magazine called *The Countryman*. It was full of anecdotes of country life, farmhouse recipes, photographs of different kinds of farm gates, and other such things to show what an enjoyable and interesting place the countryside was. But what puzzled me was the motto on the front cover, which read 'O more than happy countryman, If he but knew his good fortune'. At the age of ten, I did not know that this was a quotation from Virgil; I had probably never heard of Virgil, and all I knew was that it seemed odd that somebody should be happy without knowing it. It is, after all, an idea that is both sophisticated and patronising. It is a comforting belief for the world-weary townsman; it may not be what you really think if you are a Roman slave weeding a vineyard, or an English cowman getting up for milking at five o'clock on a January morning. But it is a very persistent belief, and the villa is its architectural expression.

The villa may be defined by both form and function. Functionally, it relates to both town and country. In its out-of-town location it is a place of escape and relaxation, where selected delights of rural life can be enjoyed in fulfilment of the townsman's dreams, but there is no large estate attached to it with its troublesome responsibilities, and its owner can ignore those aspects of real country life that he finds uncongenial. At the same time, through its proximity to the city its owner can enjoy the sophistication of urban culture and access to urban pleasures. As a place of entertainment, he can justify extravagance, while as a place of relaxation he need not be unduly restrained by protocol. In its form and amenities its builder can indulge his invention. The villa is almost inevitably the house of a rich man, because culture and comfort, space and a pleasant location are seldom cheap. And until the term lost its exclusive cachet in the 19th century, the villa was often not the owner's only house. If he was a businessman, he probably had a house in town where the serious part of his life was transacted; if he was an aristocrat, he probably had not only a town house but a country estate as well where the serious business of a landowner's life was carried on.

The importance of the Palladian model for the design of the Georgian country house has often led to the impression that Palladio invented the villa and that Campbell and Burlington introduced it into England, mature and fully developed, in the 18th century. Yet the term was already well understood in 1700 when Timothy Nourse wrote of the villa as

> a little House of Pleasure and Retreat, where Gentlemen and Citizens betake themselves in Summer for their private Diversion, there to pass an Evening or two, or perhaps a Week, in the Conversation of a Friend or two, in some neat little House amid a Vinyard or a Garden, sequestered from the Noise of a City, and the Embarrass or Distraction of Busines, or perhaps the anxious and servile Attendance of a Court.[1]

The definition is similar to that by Roger North a few years before, who described what he called the 'suburb villa' as being like a lodge, with a garden, to retire to for sleep and enjoyment away from the crowds.[2] The section on the villa that John Evelyn wrote in his great unpublished work on gardening, *Elysium Britanniae*, is lost, but in 1672 he wrote of Ham as 'indeede inferiour to few of the best villas of Italy itself',[3] presumably because of its idyllic setting, its location with respect to London itself and the quality of its lavish interiors. Evelyn had already applied the word to similar houses in Italy and France.[4] Its earliest English use to describe a modern house may be by Thomas Coryat in 1611 who, recording his experiences in Italy, wrote of 'a Gentleman called Bassano, who … lived in a villa that he had in the country, as many Gentlemen of Padua and other Cities of Italy doe in the Summer time'.[5] From Coryat's description this was evidently a house of considerable sophistication.

However, in the early 17th century Englishmen would have been more familiar with the accounts of villa life contained in the classics. These writings are of several kinds. There are those like Virgil in the *Georgics*, Horace and Martial, who praise the simple life as an escape from the corruptions of town and the troubles of public affairs, and for whom a life of improving retirement was the only path to virtue. There are those like the younger Pliny, for whom the country life represented escape from the tumult of the city, but who themselves owned villas of great sophistication. The Romans made the distinction between the often elaborate *villa urbana* and the simple *villa rustica*, the house with a working farm, but when in the course of the 15th century villas began to appear in the countryside around many Italian cities – notably, Rome, Florence and Venice – they were built by the rich and the great, in search generally of temporary retirement in cultivated surroundings.

The power of Roman and Italian models in formulating our notion of the villa – and in giving us the word itself – is such that even now it is difficult to visualise the type without some idea of these prototypes. But the house of retirement has been invented independently in many times and places. Even in the later middle ages many London citizens owned country property in addition to their town houses. Out of 882 London citizen freeholders assessed for the 1412 Lay Subsidy at over £5 on land and rent, some 15 per cent owned property outside the City.[6] Some of this will have been inherited and might be far afield, while property in the home counties was often bought as investment or as a negotiable asset that might be used as business security. But although much detailed work would be needed to establish how many of these men made personal use of houses on their country estates when these were within easy reach of the City, there is at least anecdotal evidence that they did.

In 1497 Robert Hardyng, a retired goldsmith, leased his Surrey property to a local yeoman, retaining the north wing of his manor house, the orchard, garden and stable 'with all sportyng places there' which he reserved for visits by himself and his guests. Another goldsmith, Thomas Wood, in 1503 bequeathed his leasehold interest in a country property to members of his family 'for their recreation,'[7] implying that they lived elsewhere, presumably in town. In 1579 possession of a house of retirement was evidently established practice among the higher classes. 'The manner of most gentlemen, and noblemen also,' wrote an anonymous writer,

> is to house themselves (if possibly they may) in the suburbs of the city, because the place is healthy, and through the distance from the body of the town, the noise not much: Also for commodity we find many lodgings, both spacious and roomy, with gardens and orchards very dilectable.[8]

In 1593 John Norden described Middlesex as having 'many fair and comely buildings, especially of the merchants of London … which also they have cunningly contrived, curiously beautified, with diverse devices, neatly decked with fair inventions.'[9] In 1618 the chaplain to the Venetian ambassador wrote of 'the villages … around London, being situated in the midst of meadows and woods, and here and there we see pleasure residences belonging to the merchants and to the gentry, with such delights as flowers and fruit gardens and orchards'.[10] Citizens and gentlemen both built villas, and the villa itself may be seen either as a rich townsman's house transported to the country, or as an aristocratic house of pleasure built conveniently close to the city – in any case as an instance of the increasingly close relations and the increasing convergence of behaviour, in the early modern period, between aristocracy and mercantile wealth.

In the early 17th century the village of Tottenham, five miles from the City of London, was just such a place as those described by the Venetian ambassador's chaplain. In 1631 William Bedwell, the parson, wrote of his parishioners that there were 'many of no mean quality. I have heard called at a Court there held [i.e. the Tottenham Manor Court] four Noblemen, as many Knights, and divers Gentlemen and Esquires.'[11] The village contained no large estates, but in 1662 there were nine houses in the parish with thirteen or more hearths rated for the Hearth Tax. The only survivor in 2005 is Bruce Castle, probably built around 1570 for Lord Compton, whose principal seat was Compton Wynyates in Warwickshire. It is traditional in form and plan, but the precocious symmetry of its façade at this early date is

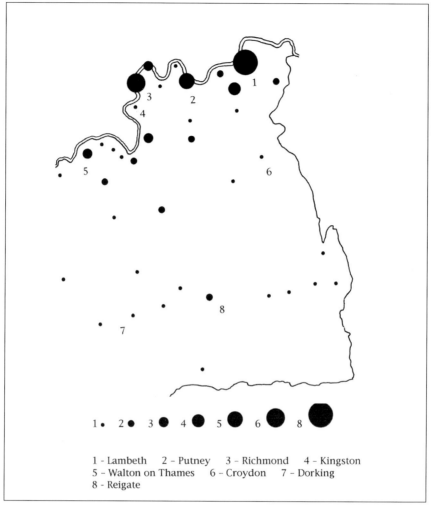

Map 1. Eastern Surrey: parishes containing houses with more then 20 hearths in 1664.

typical of the sophistication of the villa. In the 1660s, when tax was paid on eighteen hearths, it was the suburban house of a minor aristocrat of intellectual tastes, Lord Coleraine, whose country house was Longford Castle in Wiltshire.

The anecdotal impression can be confirmed from figures for the Hearth Tax returns for eastern Surrey. The first map shows parishes that contained houses with more than twenty hearths; the next one the houses of men and women of title. The esquires are scattered throughout the Surrey villages, but those of higher rank are

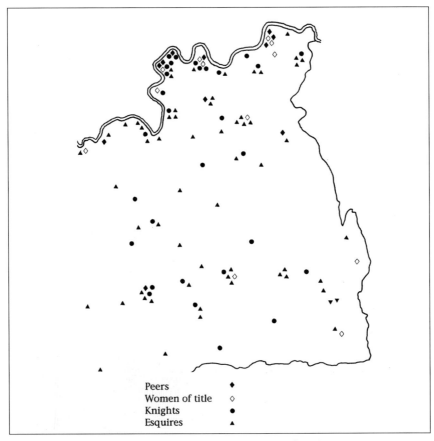

Map 2. Eastern Surrey: titled inhabitants in 1664 (*Hearth Tax*).

significantly concentrated along the river. Otherwise, these houses broadly group themselves into two bands – the suburban villages along the Thames corridor, and a smaller band immediately below the North Downs which was already easily accessible from London. This southern band would have been about three or four hours' ride from the City – too far to go home for the night, but a pleasant place for one's family to spend the summer and where one would visit them oneself whenever one could spare the time. It is reasonable to suppose that it is the proximity of London that is responsible at least in part for both of these groups. Ham, for example – described as a villa by John Evelyn – is in the northern band, while in the southern band, at Bletchingley, is Pendell House (see p. 49-51) – an obviously villa-like house of 1636 in the most advanced style of London building. Richard Glyd, the builder of Pendell House, was Master of the Tallow Chandlers' Company and a member of the Common Council of the City during the Civil War – typical posts for a leading citizen, and the City remained at the centre of his life.

The third map shows houses with more than ten hearths owned by men designated 'Mr' – a lesser honorific and one used less consistently (the absence of the title in the Richmond and Kingston returns is notable) but a designation often applied to the higher citizenry. There is a broad correspondence between all three maps, but in the case of the 'Mr's there is a contrast with the distribution of men and women of higher title, the esquires in particular, strongly suggesting that the map indicates the presence of London citizens who had chosen north–eastern Surrey as a place of retreat or retirement.

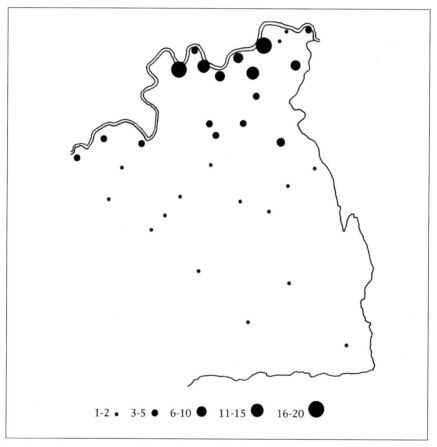

Map 3. Eastern Surrey: inhabitants designated 'Mr' with more than ten hearths in 1664.

15

The Middlesex bank of the river was equally attractive, and is shown in detail in Moses Glover's 1635 map of the hundred of Isleworth.[12] Glover names the leading occupants or owners, providing a graphic illustration of the density of upper-class housing. Names at Isleworth include a peer and four knights, at Richmond Ferry two countesses and another knight, and at Twickenham a peeress, the Lord Steward, a knight's widow, and the Bishop of Norwich. And there are numerous named gentlemen, who include both members of the landed gentry and wealthy men from the City.

One of the more tantalising of the images in Glover's map is of Twickenham Park, built by Francis Bacon, Lord Verulam. What this seems to show is a long, narrow building with a tower at each end – a strange form which it is difficult to parallel. But Bacon indulged in architectural fantasy elsewhere, in a scheme for a geometrical fishing

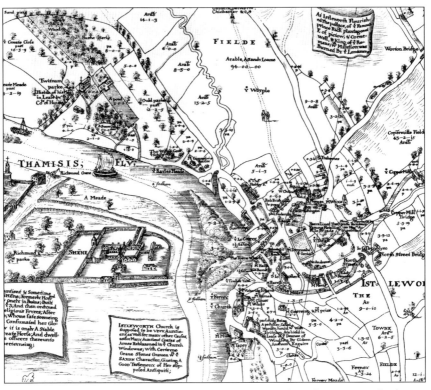

Isleworth and Twickenham Park in 1665. The houses of Lord Grey, Sir Charles Overbury, the Countess of Home and other members of the upper classes are identified. Reproduced from an anonymous 19th-century engraving of Moses Glover's map of Isleworth Hundred (*Society of Antiquaries of London*).

pavilion and at the elaborate Verulam Lodge near his principal seat at Gorhambury, and Twickenham Park may have been another of his *jeux d'esprit* – it was there that Bacon took refuge in 1592 from a fever outbreak at Gray's Inn, a further use for these suburban retreats. Twickenham Park was demolished, much altered, in 1817, but its many changes of owners illustrates a further aspect of the London villa which contemporaries remarked on: the frequency with which these houses changed hands. Between Bacon and its demolition it belonged successively to the Countess of Bedford, Sir William Harrington, the Countess of Home, Lord Berkeley of Stratton, the Earl of Cardigan, the Earl of Albemarle, Thomas Vernon, the Earl of Mountrath, the Duchess of Newcastle, the Duchess of Montrose and Lord Frederick Cavendish – eleven different owners in two hundred years – and it is not surprising that in 1797 it was said that little remained recognisable of Francis Bacon's original building.[13]

There is an obvious connection between the fashionable amenities of these houses and the frequency with which they were bought and sold. Such houses seem seldom to have been regarded as part of the principal estate even of such aristocrats as these, and hence not entailed and easily disposed of. The absence of any significant amount of land attached to them probably made for a lack not only of legal but also, perhaps, of emotional commitment on behalf of the families who owned them. In any case, many of these houses belonged to men from the City, whose ambitions did not extend to the lordship of ancestral acres. Other short-term occupants were rich widows, women whose connections linked them to the social life of the town but who preferred to live somewhere more relaxing. Owners or executors who decided to dispose of such a house were not betraying a family inheritance: such houses were expensive, but one could always buy or build another, perhaps one more fashionable than before. The continuing demand for houses that were both fashionable and comfortable meant that when they ceased to be either they were modernised or pulled down, while if the neighbourhood itself ceased to be attractive they could be demolished and something more profitable built on the site. All these are reasons why so few of these houses now survive, while their frequent change of ownership is why so many are undocumented.

The apparently unprecedented forms of London suburban houses in the early 17th century, and the subsequent widespread adoption of a novel, four-square, hipped-roof form of house that Roger North characterised as 'suburban,' have encouraged the idea that formally the villa was a novel type at that date. But this may be a false impression, the result of so few 16th- and even 17th-century houses surviving the pressures of novelty and fashion. Southampton House, north of Holborn, shown in the so-called Agas map of the mid-16th century, seems to be a conventional, hall-and-cross-wings house standing within a moat. But by contrast there is the house in Hackney, built in 1520 for Christopher Urswick, rector of Hackney and retired diplomatist.[14] The footprint so closely resembles that of a group of drawings by John Thorpe that it must have had an identical, double-pile plan with flanking towers. It is hard to believe that such inventiveness was unique, and one of Thorpe's plans of this type is titled 'Potters Bar, 1595'.

No compact houses of this kind now survive in the London area from before 1600, but away from the pressures of fashion and the land market there are earlier examples of this characteristic, compact, double-pile plan. These include Beckington Castle in Somerset (*c*.1570) and Whitehall in Shropshire (1578) (see p. 40), built on the

The Church House, Hackney, in the early 19th century. Dated 1520, and a very early instance of a double-pile house built in a suburban location (*Society of Antiquaries of London*).

fringes of medieval towns for members of local elites. In the Royal Fort area of Bristol, a pleasant hillside not far from the city centre, a number of merchants in the 17th century had built themselves pleasant houses of two sorts – either proper houses standing in their own grounds or what were described as garden houses, small buildings of two or three rooms, with their own gardens, where it would be pleasant to stay in hot weather or to spend a summer Sunday. The garden houses of Bristol may well be similar to those described by John Stow in his *Survey of London* (1598) as 'fair summer houses … some of them like mid-summer pageants, with towers, turrets and chimney tops, not so much for use or profit as for show and pleasure,'[15] while the Bristol buildings seem comparable in function and location to those shown in Hollar's map of the St Giles's Fields and Holborn areas around 1660: detached, villa-like houses as well as many smaller buildings in gardens secluded from the noise and bustle of the street.

In function both of these groups correspond closely to what Alberti described as *horti* – a subordinate type of villa, close enough to the town for the transaction of daily business. Probably neither Stow nor the merchants of Bristol were familiar with Alberti, but Alberti had written that whereas a town house should be of a sober character: 'in a villa the allures of license and delight are allowed.'[16] In granting these garden houses the status of villas, one must recognise that few people have the space or the money to build the perfect house or to lead the perfect life, and that in practice the extent to which people can indulge their architectural tastes and protect themselves from the less pleasant aspects of town or country is largely a matter of cash.

No doubt one reason for the multiplication of suburban houses was the rapid growth of London from the late 16th century, and the increasing unpleasantness of living there: the stinking drains, the sulphurous coal that already blackened buildings and rotted furnishings, the overcrowding, the crime and disorder. London was widely represented, too, as a sink of vice and extravagance. But opposed to the pressures for dispersal there were countervailing attractions. The pressure on space was in part the result of the upper classes crowding into London, to go to Court, to go to law and to do business, or just to enjoy themselves and because everyone else did.

Although the net effect of these conflicting forces cannot be quantified, both revulsion from the City and attraction to it probably led growing numbers of people to compromise with a suburban retreat.

It is clear that houses with many of the functions of villas, and perhaps with forms that anticipated the villa of the later 17th and 18th centuries, were in existence around London and elsewhere for a long time before the word villa was adopted to describe them. Nor was London the only city whose citizens owned suburban villas. By 1600 half the aldermen of Gloucester had houses in the country round about, and more than half of the magistrates of Norwich.[17] But words are adopted in response to a need. It may not be a coincidence that this apparently new awareness of the villa as a concept coincided with changing views of the countryside, views that were themselves responses to real economic and social changes. These changes were deep-seated and fundamental. Some were ideological in origin: a sense of English nationhood, growing with a successful defiance of Catholic Europe and pride in a patriotic monarchy, was developing into a new consciousness of the land of England itself. Other changes were economic and social, and more tangible. These included the massive redistribution of former monastic and Crown lands into the hands of new owners, population growth, price inflation and a century-long decline in rural living standards, the substitution of leases and rack rents for old tenurial relationships, enclosure, a decline in the ancient, communal administration of the agrarian community, an increase in specialist production, and a new concern with the techniques and economics of agricultural improvement. Broadly, rural society and relationships were evolving from being founded on custom to being based on statute and legal agreements, and the notion of ownership was itself being transformed from property based upon rights and obligations to property based on capital. Economic individualism was emerging as a force as powerful in the country as it was in the town. It was natural that images of the countryside should have required adjustment to accommodate these new conditions.

These new mental images were expressed in a number of ways. What all had in common was evidence of a new interest in the land, in property and its owners, in its physical character and its productions, in its description and depiction, and in how land could be used and enjoyed. The late 16th century saw the emergence of the professional land surveyor. Expert in tenurial law and in the exact measurement of land, he also provided maps and plans in which the owner could see his property and all its assets graphically set down for him to contemplate and enjoy. The period also saw the birth of topography – of what was termed at the time chorography. Chorography combined physical and historical description with a celebration of the productivity of the English countryside, and an acknowledgement of the goodness of Providence in granting such blessings for man's use. Among its first and most successful productions was Camden's *Britannia* of which the slim first edition appeared in 1586 and the huge sixth edition only twenty years later. A substantial number of local studies rapidly followed, some published, some circulating in manuscript, and evolving in the course of the 17th century into a greater interest in the history of property and the genealogies of its owners. Together, the work of the surveyors and the work of the chorographers served a new concern with the facts of landowning and the pleasures of ownership.

But the creation of a new image of the land went further than chorography and survey – the representation, albeit in a favourable light, of actual facts about the countryside. The imaginative literature of an age may tell one more about its mental climate than such factual accounts as these, and in the literature of the period there is a corresponding change in how land is described that parallels these factual accounts. 16th-century descriptions of the countryside had drawn largely on classical conventions of pastoral. 'Pastoral' describes ideal landscapes and ideal relationships, and although it contains rich potential for allegory and metaphor, it is only at the very end of the 16th century that English pastoral begins to contain references to real landscape or particular places. One may contrast two prose descriptions to illustrate the development of perceptions, though one is taken from a pastoral romance and the other from a work of chorography. Each describes a countryside with an agreeable, sociable scatter of houses, and though one is an imagined ideal and the other an idealised actuality, there is a clear relationship between them. Philip Sidney's *Arcadia* of 1579 is conceived through recourse to a catalogue of stock images: there are pleasant hills, stately trees, meadows enamelled with flowers, well-tuned birds, peaceful flocks and contented shepherds, while 'as for the houses of the country, they were all scattered, no two being one by the other, and yet not so far off so that it barred mutual succour: a show, as it were, of an accompanable solitariness, and of a civil wildness.'[18] William Webb's Cheshire, described in the 1620s, has fertile fields, fat beasts, fruitful woods and orchards and teeming rivers, and is 'on every side so garnished and adorned with the seats and habitations of Baronets, Knights and Gentlemen, as scarce to be seen … so far remote from Great and Populous Cities.'[19] Webb idealises the Cheshire landscape, but it is a real landscape that he idealises rather than an imagined one like Sidney's which is an ideal in itself. And significantly from our point of view, it is the countryside in the neighbourhood of the great city that Webb takes as his model.

In Webb's Cheshire and in many other writings, pastoral informs chorography; in turn, chorography informed pastoral, and in the decades after 1600 there is a similar shift in the poetry of country life from the description of ideal countryside and of ideal peasants to a celebration of real places and of real people. These too are often idealised; places can be mythologised as in Michael Drayton's great poetic description of England, *Poly-Olbion* of 1613, and peasants can be perfected as Drayton does when in his ninth Eclogue of 1606 he turns Cotswold shepherds into Virgilian ones. But real landscape features more and more, and Herrick, Denham, Carew and many other poets in the early 17th century produce poems that present a view of the bountiful and fertile countryside that is similar to that of the chorographers.

Royalist poets saw the bountiful countryside as emblematic of benevolent government, by which the perfection of the natural order paralleled the political. For such writers, retirement could be seen as a good in itself. Perhaps the clearest illustration of the new taste is the extraordinary outburst after around 1620 of English translations of the works of the most important of classical writers on the theme of retirement. Ben Jonson translated Martial's *Epigram 47* of his Tenth Book – a text which has been described as 'the key poem of English literary classicism.'[20] Jonson's translation begins:

> The things that make the happier life, are these,
> Most pleasant Martial; Substance got with ease,

Not labour'd for, but left thee by thy sire;
A soyle not barren; a continewall fire;
Never at Law; seldom in office gown'd;
A quiet mind; free powers; and body sound;[21]

And so forth: in other words, a life of modest retirement on ancestral acres. Abraham Cowley stated his wishes explicitly, writing that 'I never had any desire so strong ... that I might be master at last of a small house and a large garden, and there dedicate the remainder of my life only to them and the study of Nature.'[22] Not everyone could own a simple house on ancestral acres, but it is difficult to believe that the popularity of the genre – beginning well before the troubles of the 1640s which drove many royalists to opt out of public life for hard, practical reasons – did not find a resonance in some people's actual behaviour.

But on the other side of the ideological coin the countryside could be recommended by a wise engagement with it. The Georgic tradition, deriving like pastoral largely from Virgil, could evolve into a providential image that conformed closely to protestant ethics: to the notion that God had given the fruits of nature for man's use, but that as a consequence of the Fall and of human sinfulness, man must work to make best use of them: to exploit these resources through his own diligence and hard work and thus to make himself worthy of God's blessings. In such a view, land was an asset not simply to be enjoyed but to be made use of, but such exploitation did not rule out its enjoyment: enjoyment was to be earned, but once earned, it brought consciousness of virtue with it.

These literary images are necessarily the views of sophisticated writers, and their readers are presumably also men and women of sophistication. The view of the countryside that these writers purvey is a slanted one: a place of bounty and of beauty, and even in those 17th-century poems that describe real landscape almost everything that actually *happens* in the country, as James Turner remarks in his book *The Politics of Landscape*, is taboo. Turner suggests that 'Stuart culture was courtly and metropolitan, though its wealth was based on country estates. To resolve this contradiction, the rural element of the gentleman's life must be identified as exceptional, a *villegiatura* or rustic episode in which the real business of life is left behind'.[23] If literary distillations of the countryside were one means of resolving this dissociation, the villa, a house that mediated between town and country and excluded all that was unpleasing of either, was another. Perhaps too it is no coincidence that the first use in English of the word 'villa' occurs only a few years later than the first occurrence of the word 'landscape'. Both terms refer to a rural ideal safely remote from reality – in the one case, the allurements of rural existence as seen from a house where one can be insulated from the often sordid realities of country life, in the other the beauty of the countryside contemplated in the safety of the closet or gallery. Landscape painting is virtually unknown in England in the 16th century; in the course of the 17th it rapidly grew in popularity, initially following models developed in France, Italy and the Low Countries. As with poetry, English taste in landscape soon evolved from ideal foreign views to pictures that showed real English houses, fields and woods. These painted landscapes, with their idealisation of the real countryside, connect the factual visual images made by the surveyors with the literary descriptions made by the poets.

If early-17th-century England was depicted by these chorographers and poets as a happy place, in point of fact it was not. It was of course a time of unprecedented contention – religious, economic and political, and these conflicts too find their reflections in contemporary literature. But there is a common theme, as there is in most revolutionary situations where passions are aroused, and this is a yearning for the good life: for a life of peace, prosperity and justice. Webb's ideal description of Cheshire – a productive landscape scattered with pleasant houses – can be seen as expressing a similar viewpoint to Inigo Jones's royal masques, described by Kevin Sharpe as '[uniting] poetry and architecture as the arts that civilise man, regulate nature and serve government.'[24] What was questioned in the 17th century, in literature no less than in politics, was what form paradise on earth should take and how it was to be achieved. The literature that celebrated the country life and rural virtues – whether those of innocent retirement or of productive engagement – may suggest that the mental climate of the age was particularly favourable to the ideal that the villa represented, and that a new consciousness of its potential may have developed as a result.

2

A Place to 'Cultivate The Soul': the Idea of the Villa in the Sixteenth and Early-Seventeenth Centuries[1]

Paula Henderson

Our idea of a villa is conditioned by the long history of the building type: the villas of the ancients: of Renaissance grandees, particularly in Florence and the Veneto; of 18th-century gentlemen; of 19th-century middle class suburbanites; and, most recently, of package tour holiday-makers. The plans, design and function of all these have varied dramatically and we must be careful not to transfer our modern ideas of the form to English builders of the 16th and early 17th centuries. What must be determined is what Englishmen knew about villas in the Tudor and early Stuart periods, whether they actually tried to build them and for what purpose.

The idea of the villa

According to the *Oxford English Dictionary*, the first appearance of the word 'villa' was in 1611 in Thomas Coryate's *Crudities*: 'A certaine Gentleman called Bassano … lived at a villa that he had in the country'.[2] A few years later George Sandys, in his *Travels*, noted 'Passing by Ciceros Villa, even at this day so called, where yet do remaine the ruines of his Academy'.[3] The first reference is to a contemporary Italian villa and the second to a well-known ancient one. These are not the first English references to a villa, though, as the word appeared almost sixty years earlier in the writings of William

Thomas, a Welshman who published the first history of Italy written in the English language (*History of Italy*, 1549) as well as the first Italian grammar (*Principal rules of the Italian grammar with a dictionarie for the better understanding of Boccace, Petrarcha, and Dante /gathered into this tongue by William Thomas*, 1550). Thomas had left England in 1545, after being caught embezzling money from his patron. Although his reasons for going abroad were hardly educational, he did put his time to good use. Travelling on horseback through Italy, he wrote with enthusiasm about much he saw, including the *Villa* Imperiale in Pesaro (italics mine), which

> standeth on the side of an hill and hath prospect both to the city and to all the valley; it hath ... excellent fair fountains. But that which most of all pleased mine eye was that, being of a great height, you may out of the highest garden ride about on the top of the house, which is very fair paved with brick and railed on both sides, with fine pillars and rails of white marble.[4]

In Florence, Thomas admired the 'small houses' (here he did not use the word 'villa') he visited near Florence, where grandees would 'go for a month or two, or three, where under the fresh arbors, hedges, and boughs, amongst the delicate fruits, they triumph in as much pleasure as can be imagined'.[5] Of one in particular, he wrote,

> the Duke hath made a garden at a little house that was his fathers. Wherin is a laberinth or maze of boxe full of cypre trees, having in the middest one of the fairest conduite of white marble, that ever I saw: besides that it hath dyvers other conduites, and such conveighances, that in maner every flowre is served with renning water: and al the chanels are of white marble so fayre, that it is in my judgement at this presente, one of the excellentest thynges in all Europe.[6]

Thomas's accounts were full of praise for these 'small houses', their fine gardens, views, roof-top terraces and other pleasures.

In 1605, another British traveller, Sir Robert Dallington, published an account of his visit to Italy in the 1590s as *A Survey of the Great Dukes State of Tuscany* and wrote of 'the exquisite and rare invention of the Water-workes' at Pratolino, at that time the most famous of all Medici villas.[7] A few years later, Fynes Moryson visited what he called the 'pallace' of Pratolino and also Castello (similarly, a 'pallace'). His lengthy and vivid accounts, published in 1617, remain among the most important contemporary descriptions of these splendid villas and their gardens.[8]

It is clear, then, that builders had opportunities to read about contemporary Italian villas from those who had seen them at first hand from as early as the mid-16th century. Equally accessible was the idea of the villa in antique literature – in the works of Virgil, Varro, Horace and Vitruvius (and reiterated in the more contemporary publications of Alberti) – much of it familiar to the educated, building elite. To these classical writers, the countryside was superior to the city and the villa, or country house, offered a haven from the corruption, disease and strife of urban life. Such ideas permeated Renaissance thought and architectural models for villas were found in archaeological remains, such as Hadrian's Villa, and were eloquently and quite explicitly expressed in the letters of Pliny the Younger, written late in the first century A.D. Pliny had two villas, one for summer, at the foot of the Appenines in Tuscany, and the other, for winter, at Laurentum, overlooking the sea near Rome. His fondness for these retreats – with their numerous rooms, courtyards, loggias, terraces, gardens, pools and expansive views – is fully expressed in the letters. At Laurentum he had a suite of rooms (*diaeta*) with parlours and bedrooms at the end of a long terrace, where there were splendid views over the sea and surrounding landscape. Most importantly, here he found privacy and peace: 'a bedroom for use at night which neither the voices of my young slaves, the sea's murmur nor the noise of a storm can penetrate'. 'When I retire to this suite', he wrote, 'I feel as if I have left my house altogether and much enjoy the sensation: especially during the Saturnalia ... for I am not disturbing my household's merrymaking nor they my work'.[9]

Such ideas influenced builders of Renaissance villas. Among the earliest and most important were the famous villas built by the wealthy and powerful Medici family around Florence, some of which were mentioned in 16th-century English accounts cited above. Although many villas were associated with farms and agricultural production, others were clearly meant for more intellectual pursuits, such as the relatively modest villa at Careggi, an old castle remodelled for Cosimo de Medici by Michelozzo di Bartolommeo between

1420-59. This is made eminently clear when in 1462, Cosimo wrote to Marsilio Ficino, the Neo-Platonist philosopher: 'I came to the villa of Careggi, not to cultivate my fields but my soul. Come to us, Marsilio, as soon as possible. Bring with you our Plato's *De summo bono*… I desire nothing more ardently than to know the route that leads most conveniently to happiness'.[10] Cosimo also built a villa in Fiesole, again designed by Michelozzo between 1458-61 and built on a virgin site, chosen especially for its magnificent views over the Arno Valley. Like Pliny's villas, the house at Fiesole had open loggias and its gardens faced outward over the landscape. Within an easy ride from Florence, it was here that Cosimo's grandson, Lorenzo il Magnifico, created his 'academy' for learned discussions, poetic readings and private meditation. It may well have been the 'small house' that was described with such enthusiasm by William Thomas in the 1540s.

It is clear, then, that an accurate idea of the villa could have been in the Tudor mind well before model plans and elevations were available in printed form. Yet it was not until the late-17th century that an Englishman attempted to define the characteristics of a villa, when Roger North wrote that a villa was 'quasy a lodge, for the sake of a garden, to retire to injoy and sleep, without pretence of enterteinement of many persons'.[11] All of this conforms to the Renaissance idea of the villa, but put into contemporary context. The choice of the word 'lodge' ('a small house or dwelling') is also interesting, for it is exactly this type of building that would first fulfil the idea of the villa in England.

The Tudor 'country house' and the lodge

Like ancient Romans and comparable contemporary builders across Europe, courtiers and wealthy men and women in England had a number of houses, each serving a different purpose. William Cecil, Lord Burghley, for example, had a large London house, situated on the Strand to provide access to both the financial centre of London – in the City – and to the court at Whitehall.[12] He owned a suburban house at Chelsea, shown in a drawing attributed to William Spicer, and endorsed by Lord Burghley, which had large gardens and orchards, presumably to provide provisions for the London house. He rebuilt his family seat, Burghley House, on the Northamptonshire/Lincolnshire border, and erected another house at

Theobalds in Hertfordshire, which he made grand enough to entertain the Queen and also to serve as the future home of his younger son Robert, whom he hoped would inherit his political power and position. Although the last two houses were in the country, they were in no way an escape from the pressures of the Lord Treasurer's life: they were built for business and for the display of his wealth and power. But Burghley did have an escape, according to his biographer, who wrote: 'For, if he might ride privately in his garden upon his little mule or lie a day or two at his little lodge at Theobalds retired from business or too much company, he thought it his greatest and only happiness'.[13]

Little is known specifically about Lord Burghley's 'little lodge' at Theobalds, but lodges were common in the period and used in a variety of ways. Hunting lodges, of course, were the most abundant. Some of these were only large enough for an afternoon of hunting: the building known as 'Queen Elizabeth's hunting lodge' in Fairmead Park in the ancient Forest of Essex (Epping Forest), but built earlier and known originally as Henry VIII's 'Great Standing' and completed

Detail of a map of Cranborne Manor, Dorset, by John Norden, c.1610. The medieval royal hunting lodge was modernised by Robert Cecil in the early 17th century and surrounded by fine gardens, terraces and walks (© *The Marquess of Salisbury*).

in 1543, is a rare survival.[14] Three storeys in height, the upper floor was originally open to provide an elevated platform for viewing the hunt. The rooms below might have been used for banqueting, but an overnight stay would have been unlikely. As suggested by its original name, then, this lodge was more a 'standing', or viewing platform, than a place for a prolonged visit.

In contrast, Cranborne Manor in Dorset, given by James I to Robert Cecil early in the 17th century, is a far more substantial building with a hall, parlours and bedchambers. The medieval lodge was adjacent to Cranborne Chase, the grandest of all royal hunting parks (over 250,000 acres), and Cecil immediately improved both the house and the enclosed private park in anticipation of visits from the king. That this was more than just a standing or temporary residence for hunting parties is suggested by the elaborate gardens that were created around it, shown in two estate maps of *c.*1610, one of these by John Norden.[15] Furthermore, within the private hunting park (clearly shown with its enclosure walls) were fine tree-lined walks, one of which led to a little lodge on a hill: 'at this lodge the whole park is discovered' is inscribed alongside it. Here, Robert Cecil and his guests could gather to look down over the wildness of the park where, no doubt like the duke in Shakespeare's *As You Like It*, they would find 'woods … more free from peril than the envious court' and 'good in everything': a classic Arcadian trope.[16]

Another type of lodge was the 'secret house', from the medieval practice of the master retiring from the main house with a reduced retinue during the annual audit.[17] In 1512, for example, the fifth Earl of Northumberland went with his family to a lodge about a mile from the castle at Leconfield, a building that Leland referred to as a 'fair tower of brick' and contained, according to an inventory, a number of rooms, including a chapel. Similarly, the retreat in the park of Woodstock Palace, Oxfordshire, known as 'Rosamund's Bower' because it was said to have been built by Henry II in the late 12th century for clandestine meetings with his mistress Rosamund Clifford, had a cloister, king's high great chamber, queen's chamber, chapel, kitchen and wine cellar. This well-equipped lodge was set into a walled enclosure, protected by a gatehouse and ornamented with ponds and gardens, all sketched by John Aubrey in the 17th century.[18] There were other examples as well, including Henry V's 'fair

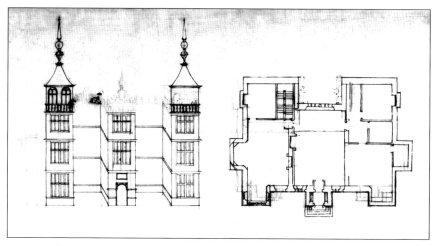

Drawing by John Thorpe of the elevation and plan of the banqueting house at Holdenby, Northamptonshire, erected in the 1580s by Sir Christopher Hatton. The axial hall was unusual in England at the time but was similar to plans by Palladio as copied by Thorpe (*The Trustees of Sir John Soane's Museum, London: photograph, Conway Library, Courtauld Institute of Art*).

Pleasaunce' at Kenilworth, Warwickshire, a timber-framed banqueting house set on a double-moated island. This isolated retreat could only be approached by boat across the great 'mere' or pool. All of these were places of retirement, privacy and pleasure and, most importantly, they were equipped with all the basic services and lodgings necessary for an extended visit.

Some, if not all, these medieval lodges and retreats were known to the early Tudors. Henry VIII apparently wanted such escapes to be built even closer to the house: he had the banqueting house from the Pleasaunce at Kenilworth moved into the castle precinct; he built a number of large lodges in the tilt-yard at Hampton Court (1520-8); and he erected a spacious banqueting house on a raised mount in the gardens at Nonsuch, Surrey.[19] In so doing, he established a precedent for erecting very large garden buildings near the house, a practice that would culminate in the late 16th and early 17th centuries.

In the 1580s, for example, Sir Christopher Hatton built a large banqueting house in the gardens at Holdenby, Northamptonshire, then the largest private house in England. The building is shown standing in the corner of the entrance court, overlooking the terraced gardens to the south in Ralph Treswell's estate map of 1587, but not in the earlier map of 1570, giving an approximate date of construction.[20] John Thorpe recorded the banqueting house in an elevation and plan: a tall, compact three-storeyed building with an unusual axial hall, the latter significantly a characteristic of the Palladian villa plans copied by Thorpe.[21] The exceptional size of this building, erected so near the house, suggests that the bachelor Hatton may have found it more economical and comfortable than the palatial house in whose shadow it stood.

John Thorpe also recorded Wothorpe Lodge, erected by Lord Burghley's eldest son Thomas Cecil, first Earl of Exeter, about a mile from Burghley House.[22] According to Thomas Fuller, Wothorpe was where Thomas retired to 'out of the dust, whilst his great house of Burghley was asweeping', suggesting the practice of keeping a 'secret house' survived well beyond the medieval period.[23] Wothorpe is now a ruin, missing its projecting tower ranges, but Thorpe's plan shows that it contained all the rooms necessary for a nobleman's escape: hall, kitchen, lodgings, parlours, cellar and services. Furthermore, Thorpe placed the cruciform plan into a circular 'gardin', a symbolic 'conceit' or 'device', typical of the period. It is possible that Thorpe was indulging his own interest in symbolic plans, for a later estate map

The ruins of Wothorpe Lodge, Northamptonshire, erected by Thomas Cecil, 1st Earl of Exeter, early in the 17th century as an escape from the great house at Burghley (*Author*).

The remains of Sir Thomas Tresham's garden lodge at Lyveden, Northamptonshire, begun in 1594 and left incomplete at his death in 1605. The lodge, cruciform in plan, with signs of Christ's Passion in the metopes of the frieze, was about half a mile from the house and set in its own enclosure, visible from the mounts at the end of the water garden (*Author*).

shows the house in far more expansive and elaborate gardens, cut through by a canal in a zig-zag or chevron pattern that was much admired by his younger half-brother Robert, 1st Earl of Salisbury.[24] The relationship between Burghley House and the lodge at Wothorpe is typical of a number of late-16th- and early-17th-century houses. In some other cases, these lodges were built further from the house; elsewhere, they were remarkably close: the lodge (now called 'Turret House') at Sheffield Manor, Yorkshire, was built in what appears to be the forecourt, as it was at Holdenby.[25] The lodge has two rooms in each of the three storeys, some with exceptionally fine plasterwork ceilings and chimneypieces. A stairway leads to a broad walk on the roof, providing a vantage point over the dramatic landscape of the hunting park below.

Sir Thomas Tresham's 'garden lodge' at Lyveden, Northamptonshire, lies about a half mile from the main house, approached through the elaborate terraced and moated gardens. Begun in 1594, the lodge was placed in its own enclosure, surrounded by a 'deepe allye' which would 'serve to walk round about in' and by hedges, suggesting that Tresham wished to conceal views of the lodge. Although left incomplete at Tresham's death in 1605, the quality of the stonework and detail attests the importance of the building and, like Tresham's other lodge – the warrener's lodge or Triangular Lodge in the park at Rushton – the plan and ornament of the building is a testament to Tresham's Catholic faith with symbols of Christ's passion in the metopes of the Doric frieze and inscriptions honouring the Virgin Mary above. Thorpe's plan of Lyveden shows all three floors as they might have been completed, again with kitchen and services in the basement, hall and parlour in the raised ground floor and great chamber and bedchambers above.[26]

Culmination: the early Stuart lodge

Like so many aspects of Tudor architecture, the 'villa lodge' reached its apogee in the early 17th century, evident especially in three very important buildings: Inigo Jones's Queen's House at Greenwich (a garden lodge); Charles and William Cavendish's Bolsover Castle, Derbyshire (a 'secret house'); and Francis Bacon's Verulam House at Gorhambury, Hertfordshire (a combination of both).

In 1616 Inigo Jones was commissioned to build a 'house of delight' at Greenwich Palace for Anne of Denmark, who had already begun to improve the gardens there. The Queen's House, as it would come to be known, was built over the main road from Deptford to Woolwich so that it would link the garden with Greenwich park. This 'curious device' was built on an H-plan with the bridge across the road forming the linking range and, with the Banqueting House at Whitehall, is among the earliest English buildings fully modelled on the work of Andrea Palladio. When completed in the 1630s, by then for Henrietta Maria, the building contained a fine cubical hall, bedchambers, cabinets and a splendid cantilevered stair that led to a broad platform on the roof. Although the internal configuration and functions of the rooms are not fully understood, it is possible that the cellar was meant to include kitchens and services.[27] The Queen's House, then, conforms to the category of garden lodge found at Lyveden and Holdenby, a retreat for privacy and pleasure.

Bolsover Castle was begun by Charles Cavendish and completed by his son William, later Earl then Duke of Newcastle, as an escape from their main seat at Welbeck Abbey, Nottinghamshire, a short ride away. Its fantastic, romantic silhouette is complemented by a fine walled garden, with sunken bath and garden rooms hidden in the thickness of the wall, and by its complex, sometimes erotic, interior decoration. This was not just a comfortable haven from the rigours of aristocratic life, but a sensual destination for entertainment and pleasure. Again, all the necessary rooms are found here (kitchens, hall, great chamber and bed chambers), further enhanced by carefully orchestrated sequences of rooms and ornament. Its form and purpose suggests that it was the early Stuart equivalent of the medieval 'secret house'.

These buildings also correspond to the definition of the villa given in the most authoritative recent study, James Ackerman's *The Villa: Form and Ideology of Country Houses* (1990). In addition to the characteristics already considered, Ackerman asserts that villas have traditionally been 'highly imaginative and assertively modern'.[28] This is certainly true of many of the buildings discussed here: the precocious axial hall in the banqueting house at Holdenby; the symbolic forms of both Lyveden and Wothorpe; the romantic medievalism of Bolsover; and the emphatic Palladianism of the Queen's House, Greenwich. All may be seen as testing grounds for radical changes in building practices and a number were deemed 'curious' or 'ingenious' by contemporaries. In the context of British culture of the period, they also may be seen as the architectural equivalents of the portrait miniature and the sonnet. Just as the 'villa lodge' was a smaller, more compact version of the great house, miniatures and sonnets were little versions of the full-sized painting and the epic poem respectively. Lodges, miniatures and sonnets all reached their height of popularity in the late 16th and early 17th centuries and all were intended for private, intimate pleasures. They were also often highly complex in form and meaning. Just as miniatures frequently had mysterious inscriptions and sonnets their hidden texts, a number of these buildings were symbolic in form or decoration, engaging the intellect and requiring decoding.

One last building must be considered in this context, one that most completely satisfies the definition of a villa: Francis Bacon's Verulam House at Gorhambury. On the death of his elder brother in 1601, Bacon inherited his father's house in Hertfordshire, which already had quite magnificent gardens, including a 'wilderness' near the house itself.[29] In 1608, Bacon began thinking about a 'place of pleasure', an elaborate water garden, described in a memo intended for his cousin, Robert Cecil, Earl of Salisbury.[30] The water garden would consist of a lake with islands, upon which he would erect a 'house for freshness' with an open gallery, terraces, a dining room, music room, bedchamber, cabinet and its own garden. The similarity to Pliny's descriptions are obvious and there may have also been some attempt to replicate the well-known Canopus (a pleasure house on an island) at Hadrian's Villa at Tivoli. Other islands would have had mounts, grottoes, arbours and statues. The gardens he eventually created are shown in an estate map of 1634 in the Hertfordshire Record Office as a series of ponds about a mile northeast of the house (probably the site of the original medieval fishponds) and approached down a long tree-lined avenue.[31] They were also described by John Aubrey, who visited in 1656 and noted 'a curious banqueting house of Roman architecture ... paved with black and white marble', standing in the 'middle of the middlemost pond'.[32]

Even grander was Verulam House, built to overlook the ponds, which Aubrey wrote was 'his Lordship's Summer-house: for he sayes (in his essay) one should have seates for Summer and winter as well as Cloathes', an idea straight from classical authorities. Aubrey went on to hail Verulam House as 'the most ingeniously contrived little pile, that ever I saw...' and suggested that 'his Lordship was the chiefest Architect'. His coloured sketch of it (**Plate 1**) shows a square, three-storey building of brick with a lively roof-line of curved gables, a balustraded platform and a lantern, remarkably prescient of later houses like Coleshill. The lantern provided light for the fine stairway at the centre of the house, which had newel posts carved with figures of 'a grave divine' and 'a mendicant friar'. The chambers in the upper storeys were painted with figures of Roman gods and goddesses 'all bigger than life and donne by an excellent hand'. The roof itself, reached via the 'delicate staircase of wood, curiously carved', was 'very well leaded' and had a 'lovely prospect to the ponds'.

Bacon chose to call his summer house Verulam House to celebrate the antiquity of his property, on which stood some remains of the Roman Verulamium (present day St Albans): a site-specific classical reference that was common in Italy – as in the relationship between Villa d'Este and Hadrian's Villa at Tivoli – but probably unique in England. His admiration for antiquity so evident in his writings is also obvious in the similarities between his 'place of pleasure' and Pliny's descriptions of his two villas with their terraces, parlours, dining rooms, bedchambers, expansive views and, perhaps most important, the peace and privacy they provided. In addition to the two well-known letters mentioned above, some of Pliny's other letters also praise villa life in general. For example, he wrote to Caninius Rufus about his 'lovely house outside the town with its colonnade where it is always springtime, and … the stream with its sparkling greenish water flowing into the lake below …'.[33] In another, addressed to Minicius Fundanus, he inveighed against the trivialities and wasted time involved in duties:

> I always realize this when I am at Laurentum, reading and writing and finding time to take the exercise which keeps my mind fit for work … no one disturbs me with malicious gossip, and I have no one to blame − but myself − when writing doesn't come easily. Hopes and fears do not worry me, and I am not bothered by idle talk; I share my thoughts with myself and my books. It is a good life and a genuine one, a seclusion which is happy and honourable, more rewarding than almost any 'business' can be. The sea and shore are truly my private Helicon, an endless source of inspiration.[34]

These words must have rung especially true to Bacon when, having been dismissed from service at court following charges of bribery and corruption, he retreated to Verulam House to work on the essays and philosophical works for which he would be remembered.

Although rarely reliant on the specific contemporary plans of villas that are associated with the form − Thorpe's plan for Holdenby and Jones's Queen's House being the possible exceptions − English builders of the 16th and early 17th centuries did erect 'small houses' where they might go for a short period − to relax, to enjoy nature and to escape the burdens and stresses of their lives. Men like the Cecils and Christopher Hatton sought refuge from the demands of court office; Thomas Tresham, a place to contemplate the mysteries of his religion; and Francis Bacon, a place to study and write. While the word villa was not yet commonly used, these lodges and large garden buildings conform to the spirit of the villa, as it was understood then: 'quasy a lodge, for the sake of a garden, to retire to injoy and sleep …'; or, as some might have preferred, 'a place to cultivate the soul'.

3

Halls into Vestibules

Andor Gomme

'A villa is a building in the country designed for its owner's enjoyment and relaxation'.[1] So James Ackerman defines his field in *The Villa* – too broadly, one might think, and also too narrowly? A summer-house is surely not a villa, nor is a garden pavilion; and what about a lodge? Is Lodge Park, Gloucestershire, a villa? It is undoubtedly a building in the country, and was designed explicitly to enable its owner to relax and enjoy his favourite sport of gambling on deer-coursing. But it has no bedrooms; so perhaps it is really a grandstand. What about Worksop Manor Lodge, Nottinghamshire? Again undeniably built for enjoyment; and here there are bedrooms in which doubtless relaxation of a kind was envisaged. Still, not everyone's idea of a villa. What about the Red Lodge, high up in the back garden of Sir John Younge's house in downtown Bristol? It is the merest stone's throw from the house, yet with a once wonderful view and so sumptuously equipped that it really does look like a house to move out to from the turmoil of life in the city. I do not think that Ackerman considered the possibility of any English villas before Chiswick: everything before that was either a country house or – something else.

'Something else' in this case is a large field, encompassing the lodges and secondary seats of the aristocracy and the smaller country houses of the gentry and the commercial classes. Who made up the 'commercial classes'? Merchants and industrialists certainly: did their habitations necessarily count as country houses? That Sir Francis Willoughby's fortune derived from nearby coalmines does not make Wollaton the headquarters of an industrial concern; but people with lesser social ambitions did stay close to their works. There were other professionals – lawyers, especially – who would not have liked to be classed as 'commercial': they were certainly gentry, but their fortunes did not derive from ancestrally owned land. And some of them were in the van of the development – starting in the late 16th century and initially far away from centres of influence – of a peculiarly English compact 'villa-like' plan which, within fifty years or so, sprinkled England with examples in a wide variety of architectural styles. The type, which we have dubbed the 'Square Ideal', is one which Alison Maguire and I studied closely as part of our research for a book to be published shortly by Yale University Press; the groundwork of this paper has been essentially a joint process.

Two hundred years earlier still the Square Ideal had a marvellous and totally unconnected forerunner: with some trepidation I propose that the first English villa is the tower house of Warkworth Castle in Northumberland, built, as is now generally agreed, in the 1390s. The great Percy stronghold was a few miles to the north at Alnwick: they had gained Warkworth in 1332, and it quickly became the Percys' favoured residence. When the Norman keep was replaced, what took its place was essentially a remarkably compact country house, in itself only slenderly fortified (though within the *enceinte* of a large castle): it has all the necessary equipment of a self-contained medieval lord's house – great hall, chamber, solar, chapel, kitchens and service rooms – tucked with great ingenuity into a 74-foot square. It was plainly designed for comfortable living away from the military rigours of fortified Alnwick, which was repeatedly attacked and burnt by the Scots. Relaxation can hardly have been the rule of life at Warkworth; but the preference for a relatively small establishment with, one supposes, less of the pomp as well as of the obvious military presence of Alnwick, suggests an anticipation of what in more peaceful times villa life might become.

In truth the outline and moderate scale are really all that Warkworth has in common with the square ideal of the 16th and 17th centuries. Even if it was a place to escape to, Warkworth still had to crowd into its limited volume most of the ceremony that accompanied a powerful aristocratic family. What are now to be discussed are the houses of men well below that level of ceremony, who have no need of a great hall, whose hall in fact is not always easy to distinguish from other rooms on the ground floor except as the one which visitors will enter first. What the visitor *first* enters however, through a door in the middle of the main front, is not a room at all, but a passage. Not a passage of the medieval kind with offices to one side and a screen to the hall on the other: this type is designed to give direct access to all rooms on the ground floor and, by leading straight to the main (or only) stair at its far end, to those directly above: ready access and an easy flow through the house are the characteristic marks of the planning of houses of this type. The prototype is Whitehall, Shrewsbury: prototype, however, only in the sense of coming first, for it sprang like Athene from Zeus's head and at one go established the ideal template for houses of this kind. There is nothing in the least tentative about the house begun in 1578 by Richard Prynce, burgess, lawyer of the Middle Temple, MP for

Whitehall, Shrewsbury, built 1578-82 for a local lawyer, Richard Prynce. The fully-developed prototype of the square-plan house (*Malcolm Airs*).

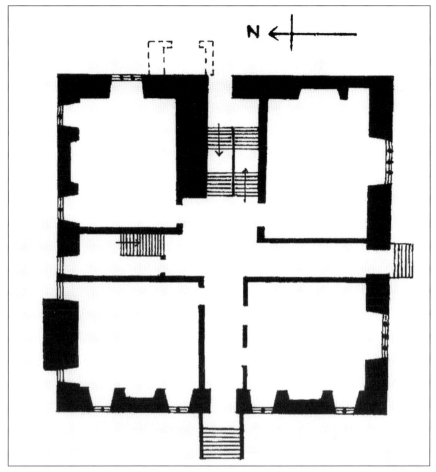

Whitehall, Shrewsbury. The original ground-floor plan as reconstructed (*Susan and Andor Gomme*).

Bridgnorth and feodary of Shropshire: it stands in former monastic land a short distance across the river from the walls of the medieval town: essentially therefore the suburban house of an upwardly mobile professional gentleman (his father was a shoemaker) who, while he established himself as a considerable landowner in the surrounding country, needed to keep closely in touch with the county town, who took out a grant of arms but no more and whose immediate domestic needs could be answered by a hall and two parlours and an office on the ground floor, four chambers with closets above, and an attic probably given over to servants' rooms and a nursery, though there may have been a miniature gallery; kitchens and offices were all in the basement. The original symmetrical layout allowed for a hall no larger than the front parlour, but Prynce's younger son, another Richard, who inherited Whitehall in 1615, wanted a grander one and shifted the entrance northwards via a new off-centre porch. Even as enlarged the hall was very unlike a medieval one.

Whitehall's compact planning suggests that tightness of site was an important factor in settling its innovative design, though Prynce's holding in the Foregate was substantial. Its exterior character was certainly not unique; but a comparison with the outwardly somewhat similar cuboid of Beckington Castle, near Frome, Somerset, also suburban but archaic in plan, illuminates the significant novelty of Whitehall's. Yet the first and closest of Whitehall's imitators was built on the top of a steep hill and in the midst of a large estate fifteen miles south of Shrewsbury, where space-saving cannot have been a priority. Acton Scott Hall is actually dug into the side of the hill, so that on two sides it is a full four storeys high and the kitchen can be included within a wholly exposed basement. The plans of the two Shropshire

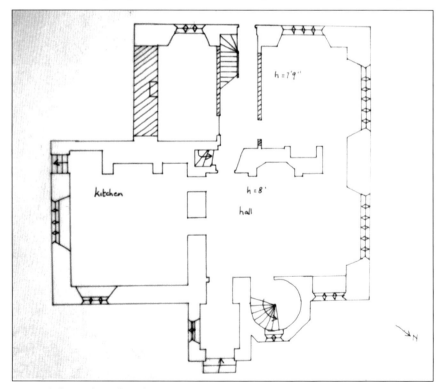

Ground-floor plan of Beckington Castle, Somerset (*Author*).

houses are (or were) to all intents and purposes identical, and the similarity of the elevations suggests that Walter Hancock (responsible for the Shrewsbury market hall and probably for much of the masonry at Condover Hall) may have been in charge of both houses, though except for the basement Acton Scott is of brick – an early instance in Shropshire. In both, however, all the internal divisions are stud partitions, which suggests that one of the numerous Shrewsbury carpenters must have taken a large hand.

Acton Scott was one of the numerous houses of a widespread Shropshire family, who may have farmed the estate from the house. At Wharton Court, two miles outside Leominster in Herefordshire, 17th-century farm buildings show that this was certainly the case, though the house is said to have been built in 1604 by a London merchant named Richard Whitehall, who had apparently been High Sheriff of the county. The porch is an addition of 1659, which is probably also the date of the hipped double-roof, an unlikely feature

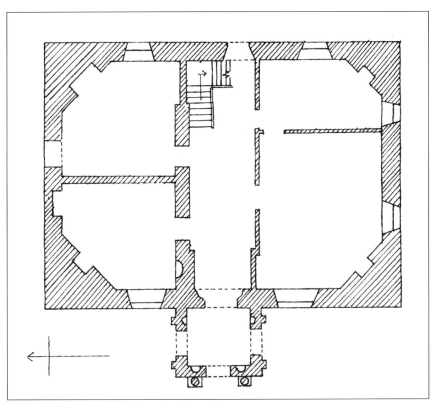

Plan of Wharton Court, Herefordshire (*Author*).

in Herefordshire at the start of the 17th century. The plan explains Wharton Court's curious external appearance with its prominent corner chimneys and windows crowded into the middle fifty per cent of each elevation: on each floor all the hearths are angled across the outer corners of the rooms – designed presumably to throw heat into the middle of squarish spaces. The transverse passage is a little wider than at Whitehall – wide enough to contain the handsome staircase which, unlike Whitehall's, has a narrow open well: staircases, rather than being mere utilities, were becoming notable features within the entertainment suite of houses great and smaller, linking the hall and best parlour with the best chamber above. Entertainment cannot have been on a great scale at Wharton, but even here there is a clear distinction – in this case right to left – between an upper or polite side and the offices and family rooms.

Burton Hall, near Tarvin in Cheshire, is a smaller and somewhat rustic variation on the theme, also making much of corner hearths: it has four rooms per floor arranged around a central lobby and a full complement of services within its well-windowed sandstone plinth. It was built, apparently soon after 1600, by a Chester lawyer named

Red Hall, Bourne, Lincolnshire, built *c*.1610. A neat suburban house for Gilbert Fisher, only just above yeoman status (*Author*).

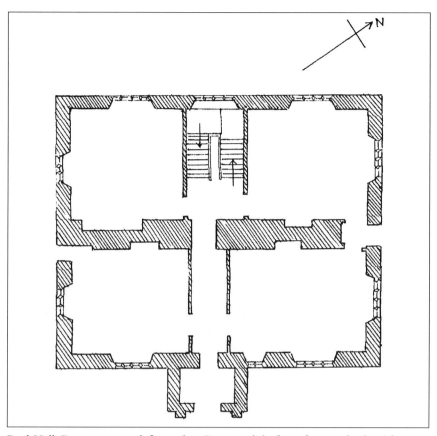

Red Hall, Bourne, ground-floor plan. Passage-glide from front to back with lateral stack wall marking the heirarchic division of the house (*Author*).

John Werden, and like Wharton seems always to have been the centre of a working farm, a source of extra income for Mr Werden and possibly his hobby as well. The entry passage at Burton is abbreviated – no more than a *sous-rampe* beneath the second flight of the main stair, which in this case is at the front of the house: no sooner has one negotiated it than one is at the hub from which all rooms open, such is the miniature scale. There is neither surviving decoration nor greater size to indicate that any room has primacy, only perhaps their position on the entrance front (and away from the farm buildings) to suggest that the two that flank the stair could be thought of as constituting the 'upper' side: there seems never to have been a hall in anything like the traditional sense – only a hallway.

Burton Hall in fact is a siding: the main line goes on to Red Hall at Bourne, Lincolnshire, another suburban house, almost certainly built by a London grocer named Gilbert Fisher in about 1610. Here we are back to the passage leading through to the stair at the far end. To get there, however, it must pass through an arch in a thick masonry wall containing all the stacks – an important development. In all the previous houses the stacks were external: from now on the tendency is to internalise them – sometimes, as here, putting all economically into a single wall which also serves to provide good bearings for principal beams. The overall plan, however, remains: four roughly equal-sized rooms per floor and hence no evident predominance, though on the front that to the right of the entrance is slightly the larger and pushes the porch and passage off-centre: in almost all these houses aesthetics and symmetry give way to convenience, at least in small matters. According to Fisher's probate inventory[2] he had a hall, dining parlour, kitchen and pantry on the ground floor (there is no basement): the kitchen fireplace is clearly in evidence in the south-west room, but otherwise the room names were probably assumptions by the probate appraiser, and my guess is that the stack wall was to some extent a social divide, that the best rooms were all at the handsomely-windowed front (including a great chamber incorporating the porch room on the first floor, and a miniature long gallery at the top). So Fisher probably dined in the hall - not like his medieval betters but simply because it was the biggest room, linked by a small lobby to the one behind, which I suggest was a general-purpose office-cum-pantry-cum-servery. Though Fisher aspired to gentry status, we are dealing with a modest household: two unceiled attic rooms were probably sleeping spaces for servants.

John Thorpe evidently had a keen interest in small villa-like plans, and in his book there are ten for squares with four rooms to a floor.[3] One of his plans (no. T.28) is fairly like that of Red Hall, though it is for a larger house with canted bays front and back and an additional service stair; though I do not find arguments aimed at squeezing Thorpe's quart into Fisher's litre persuasive, it is clear that he was trying out variations on a popular idea, and it is not impossible that Fisher picked up one of these. The interest of this one however lies partly in its having been made for Sir William Rigdon, whose father had married into a long-established Lincolnshire gentry family. Fisher by contrary was only a small step up from the yeomanry; and John Fetherston who built Packwood House in Warwickshire had not yet

Wynford Eagle, Dorset, built by Thomas Sydenham, 1630. The house absorbed two cottages into a square plan with a smart new front of Ham Hill stone (*Author*).

crossed the line. But increasingly there is evidence that these neat small houses were not necessarily signs of inferior lineage. Wynford Eagle in Dorset was built about 1630 by William Sydenham of an ancient and far-flung Somerset family; and he did not even start from scratch, though he ended with a plan close to that of Red Hall. Sydenham was evidently not wealthy, and what he had inherited on the Wynford site was apparently a small two-unit house built of drab local oolite, with a central axial stack and lobby entry. Conceivably this house had already been doubled back to back with two parallel roofs and a slightly smarter north front in alternating strips of limestone and flint – in which case what happened in 1630 was the splitting of the wall between the two halves to allow for a central passage leading from the fine new porch in the middle of what was now to be the entrance front on the west – which alone he could afford to face with Ham Hill ashlar. This had an unfortunate consequence for the design of Sydenham's show front: the inner slopes of the roofs had to be supported on the walls flanking the passage, but the outer slopes were left as they were, the roof trusses being cramped to fit narrower and now asymmetrical gables, with a smaller gable over the passage between: an instructive case of making do.

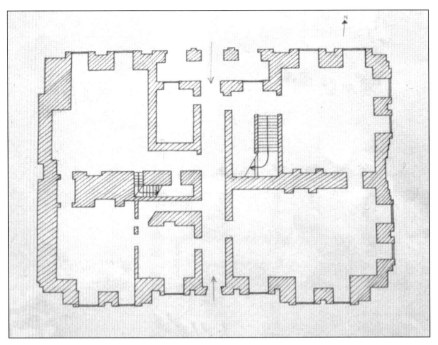

The Dutch House, Kew, Surrey ('Kew Palace'), built by Samuel Fortrey, 1631. Ground-floor plan showing the very narrow passage glide marking a left/right heirarchic division (*Author*).

Typically these quite modest houses divide socially front to back, with the best rooms on the entrance front. But the passage entry may act as the divide, especially in larger houses. This is certainly what eventually happened at Boston Manor at Brentford, Middlesex (see p. 138ff), though if the final state of its plan was due to alterations or even an addition by James Clitherow who bought the estate in 1670, this would explain the contrast between rationality on one side of the entrance vestibule and disorganised muddle on the other. If, however, the overall layout of Boston Manor can be relied on, it was an early example of an upper-class quasi-metropolitan adoption of plans coming up from lesser ranks in the provinces: in this it was shortly to be followed by the more complex Forty Hall at Enfield, Middlesex (see 206ff), and by the Dutch House at Kew, whose royal takeover in the 18th century has disguised the evidence of its earlier history. The Dutch House (see pp. 180ff) had been the house of Samuel Fortrey, a London merchant of Dutch descent who built it in 1631. Here for the first time the passage has become a true example of what Celia

Fiennes later called a glide, running unobstructed from front to back. To allow for this the best stair is tucked sideways into a corner of what was plainly the upper side; the other half had to make do with something much more cramped, though panelling surviving from Fortrey's time suggests that he kept an office and snug for himself away from the grander and more public suites.

The glide at the Dutch House is really narrow – only about five feet wide, an access route and no more. By contrast the vestibule at Boston Manor is a miniature reception hall; and at the much smaller Pendell House, Bletchingley, Surrey, of 1636, the passage which serves on three levels to give access to all four rooms is wide enough to house some furniture and at the far end for a staircase which, in both scale and quality, outclasses the rest of the house. The space is something more than a passage and feels like a hall in the modern sense, a place of introduction, a room to arrive but not stay in, a vestibule in which to take off one's coat and perhaps wait on a chair for the owner to come and greet one. But like all modern halls - and not at all like ancient ones - it also has the essential function of *leading* to the ground-floor rooms and via the staircase to those above. The

Pendell House, Bletchingley, Surrey, built 1636. An artisan version of the square plan built for the Master of the Tallow-Chandlers, doubtless as a family resort from London (*Author*).

apparently formidable symmetry noted by Ian Nairn[4] is imperfect, the passage at all levels being off-centre in order to allow rather larger rooms one side than the other; consequently the porch is also, though

Berdon Hall, Essex. The spectacular staircase, possibly an insertion of 1655 into a timber-framed house later encased in brick (*Author*).

a little fudging could have coped with that. The side elevations make no effort at symmetry and the stacks are any old where. At one time Jones's name was tentatively invoked, but Pendell is much more like a lesser Forty Hall than the spawn of Chevening, Kent. The basic plan was nothing new in the 1630s, the vestibule-hall merely a modest stretching of the passages we have seen from Whitehall on. Only in its relative spaciousness does the entrance vestibule, half of whose function now is to *contain* the stair (rather than just lead to it), ask to be understood as a minor version of what Roger North later called a *sala d'entrata*.[5]

Was Pendell House designed as a villa? Its builder was a London businessman well up in his trade as Master of the Tallow-Chandlers, who could evidently call on the work of a competent, even if somewhat wilful, City bricklayer: a man wealthy enough to afford a miniature estate in the country where his family could spend their time away from the nuisances and distractions of London, doubtless also for his enjoyment and relaxation at weekends. A villa, then. What, however, this type – centred now on its dual-purpose staircase hall – developed into was the characteristic home of the junior gentry, those who farmed the land about their house or became parsons and often squarsons of the parish and its church.

It was in the early 17th century that in England the staircase really came into its own as a show feature of the house which could support any amount of decoration: in all the houses I have mentioned, something has been done to meet Roger North's recommendation that stairs 'should be made as easy, delightfull, and inviting as possible; or in short as deceiving as may be, to perswade there is no such inconvenience as staires, by bribing and enterteining all the sences with better objects'. The staircase can, as at Pendell, be the best individual feature and the one on which most care has been bestowed. At its richest it gains a 'hall' of its own. In its present form Berden Hall, Essex, is a brick encasing of about 1570 of an earlier timber-framed house. It was probably part of a monastic holding and passed through several high-ranking hands after the Dissolution; the rebuilding may have been at the hand of Sir Thomas Sutton, who had other properties nearby. It was evidently in 1655 (the date on a rainwater head) that Berden was given an extensive though largely cosmetic facelift, and this may well be when the spectacular staircase was built. The house has the statutory passage entry and four-room layout of the 'square ideal', but it spreads its wings, the rear rooms are narrower than those at the front, and so leave room for a really spacious stairhall – recessed to allow light into the centre. As the plan shows, it is at the cross-roads of the house: a glimpse of the stair is visible from the front door but it is only revealed when one reaches the middle, and then unmistakably as *the* feature, for the rest of the interiors are quite run-of-the-mill. Berden seems always to have been at the heart of a working farm (what appear to be housing for drying racks survive in the attic), and the unusual disposition of the main rooms, in diagonally opposite corners of the ground floor, suggests that there was no real division between upper and lower sides. Movement from garden to yard is easy, via the lateral passage, and the hall, if it was called such, with the best chamber above, is on the yard side, directly in front of the kitchen.

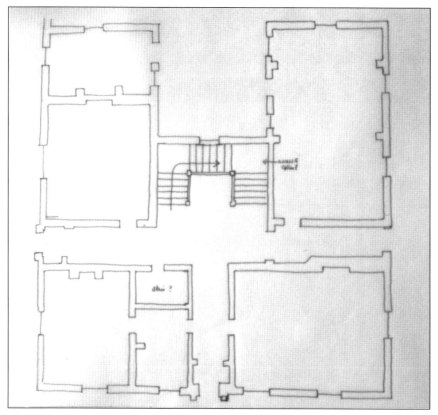

Berdon Hall, ground-floor plan. The entrance passage was opened into a small vestibule in 1655. Note the 'T' of access corridors (*Alison Maguire*).

Who lived at Berden is an interesting question – a gentry house which, according to one's viewpoint was either less or more than that. We are looking for a Jacobethan gentleman farmer. Sutton made over his Essex holdings to the trust which ultimately founded the London Charterhouse as a school and almshouse: if Berden were one of them, the trust would presumably, if they did not sell it, have put it in the hands of a gentleman steward. Toseland Hall, Huntingdonshire, is a house of closely similar character, date and size – a secondary house of Sir Nicholas Lake, again apparently designed for working a farm. Its staircase is a much more workaday affair than Berden's and thrust to one side rather than being treated as a major circulating feature; but there is a similar T-layout of access routes, though in this case the entrance passage has widened lopsidedly into a small waiting hall; and at Toseland there is a clear social division between front and back.

It appears to be a characteristic of a number of these compact and orderly houses that they perform at least a double function for those who live in them: home as well as farm, home perhaps as well as office. Office, that is, not simply in the sense that any country house needed a room in which the squire would discuss the estate with his steward or bailiff, and the latter would deal with tradesmen and tenants, but in a way more directly concerned with the owner's professional work. Prynce's work as feodary of Salop – the sovereign's deputy in the Court of Wards – will undoubtedly have had its own office in the county town; but Prynce, owning country estates, nevertheless chose to live in a house only just outside the town where his official work lay: though he cannot be seen as working from home in the current sense, his busy private life as an unlicensed solicitor would presumably have called for an office for receiving clients. In any event the suburban site of the house is significant.

So also, for different reasons, it was for John Hall, eponymous builder of the hall at Bradford-on-Avon, Wiltshire, one of those buildings which, the more one learns about them, seem the more resistant to attempts to fully understand their history or working: what I do know about it I owe in large measure to discussions with colleagues, among whom I must single out my wife for her sharp eyes and perceptive intelligence. We have looked hard over and again, and still there is a mystery at its heart – indeed more than one. The house,

The Hall, Bradford-on-Avon, Wiltshire, built by John Hall, *c.*1610. The main front drawn by George Moore for C.J. Richardson's *Elizabethan Architecture* (1837).

built probably by Hall in about 1610, is famous now for its spectacular south front, whose concentration of bravura display not even Wollaton or Burghley can equal – all the more amazing in the house of a provincial family without powerful connections in a remote industrial town.

Since the 13th century Bradford had been a clothworking town of some standing, and it has never ceased to be industrial, though clothiery has given way to rubber and later to engineering. The Hall family, who took their name from their house, were apparently not clothiers themselves but had long owned both grist and fulling mills in the town, of which by the 16th century they evidently had a monopoly; they also owned quarries from which some of the stone for the building of Longleat had come in the 1570s, and there is even an unconfirmed story of John Aubrey's that the father of the presumed builder of the present house was Sir John Thynne's son-in-law. The Halls were landowners also, and the Hall, though close to the centre of the town, has its own lands stretching eastwards along the Avon – currently of about 200 acres. So Bradford Hall is a country house too, and efforts have been made to interpret it as that pure and simple. I think it must have been something more, and hence in another sense less, than this. Its family history is not obscure: the last John Hall died in 1711 and via his supposed illegitimate daughter it became the property of the Duke of Kingston, whose bigamous wife, the Countess of Bristol, clung on to it till her death in the 1780s. It was sold in 1802 to a local clothier who allowed it to decay; and by 1848, when it was bought by Stephen Moulton, was in a bad way. One must penetrate Moulton's inevitable repairs and alterations and perhaps some by the Kingstons to discover the house's original form and function.

Moulton was an industrialist who founded the rubber works which became Bradford's staple for a hundred years. He turned the house round, moving the main entrance to the north side, the original back, to provide a more direct approach from the town and his own works, and removed the drive which had swept round from the west and south. The great stair was presumably irreparable and was replaced by a new one, clearly on the site of the original and probably reproducing its form. Further changes in the 19th century included the despatch of the kitchen to the basement, but the

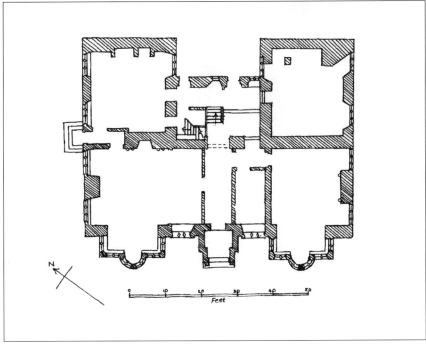

The Hall, Bradford-on-Avon. The original ground-floor plan as reconstructed (*Susan and Andor Gomme*).

essential layout of both main floors seems to be as it was in the time of the Kingstons. And though it has been stated that almost all the facing stonework is Victorian we found little to support this: as one can judge from the drawing which George Moore made for Charles Richardson's *Observations on the Architecture of England* (1837), the external walls seem to have survived well.

Most of the rest that I have to say about Bradford Hall is contentious. Looking at it, one would suppose that it was a brand-new house of the early 17th century on a virgin site. But Leland, visting in 1542, spoke of one 'Halle, or de la Salle, worth £100 annually', who lived in 'an attractive stone house at the end of the town, on the right bank of the Avon';[6] and recently Pamela Slocombe found re-used arched trusses over the west range which are probably 15th-century.[7] They fit the width of the present wing, suggesting, it seems, that the 17th-century house may have been built partly on the footings of its predecessor, one of whose cross-wings was aligned along the present west front. This is quite plausible. Nevertheless it

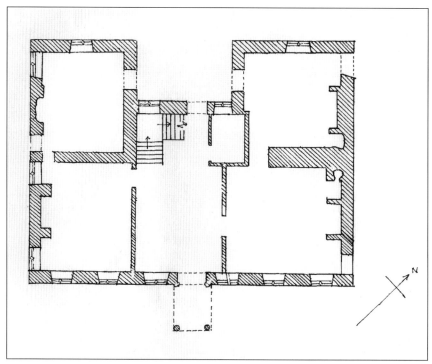

Wick Court, Gloucestershire, built probably *c.*1655. Ground-floor plan (after Linda Hall). The passage widened into a full unheated entrance hall.

seems to me clear beyond question that the overall design of the new house was *sui generis*, fashioned entire as a unity. Apart from its dazzling south front, what is most striking about Bradford Hall is the designer's apparent passion for symmetry: almost as much as Hardwick it strives for symmetry all round. Both the east and west elevations are precisely symmetrical – to the extent of balancing chimneys at the north end by dummies at the south; only on the north front, avowedly for servicing and tradesmen, does the position of the staircase push the entrance door to one side and its windows climb in diagonals with the rising of the stair; and even here the somewhat contorted fluing seems to have been arranged to allow symmetrical pairs of chimneys.

By 1610 it was no longer unusual for the front door to be in the middle of the entrance front. But it was still something of a novelty, though not by that time unique, if, as now at Bradford, it opened into the middle of the hall. At first glance, in the carefully balanced layout, symmetry seems once again to have been a paramount concern, and it is emphatically confirmed on the principal chamber floor. But here we reach major problems and points at issue. The most obvious unusual feature of the present ground floor is that the hall has no hearth. Is it possible that it never had one? I offer two rather distant and different analogues, both of which may turn out red herrings. Geographically close to Bradford, Wick Court was built either by the Wynter family of Dyrham in about 1625 or by their successor Thomas Haynes forty years later. The plan is a half-way stage between Berden and Bradford – the passage now widened to a full but unheated entry hall broad enough to enclose at the back, and without division, a large open-well staircase and a bit more. On another tack, Churche's Mansion at Nantwich, Cheshire, was built on the edge of the town by a local merchant who seems to have had a finger, or more, in most of the town's industrial enterprises, including tannery and saltworks. It gives every appearance of being a standard hall-and-cross-wings house, though since the date is already 1558 it has a single-storey hall and chamber above. As one would expect, these two rooms are the best-appointed in the house; yet there appears to be no way in which either of them could have been heated. Was Churche's 'mansion' principally used in connection with his business, and were these rooms for showing off wares rather than entertaining guests?

Arthur Oswald could not accept an unheated hall and decided that the partition dividing the hall from the present dining room was an 18th-century insertion into what had been a continuous hall.[8] (The present partition is from Stephen Moulton's time, but its predecessor with a Georgian-looking dado was in place in 1837.) To back this up Oswald argued a parallel with the long-lost Claverton Hall, near Bath, which Richardson also illustrated in his book. The parallel is tempting – perhaps too much so to be true; and Richardson's evidence is questionable because he was only eleven when Claverton was demolished, and his drawings were in consequence 'taken from sketches by the accurate and tasteful pencil of W. Twopenny, Esq.'; they are furthermore not self-consistent – disagreeing with one another even over the number of bays. (Twopeny [sic] was in fact an extremely fine and accurate draughtsman, as can be confirmed by his drawings of still existing buildings; Richardson was cavalier in his use of them.) The proposal would however enable the dining-room fireplace to be near the supposed upper end of a traditional hall, yet one which would have been exceptionally long and entered in an untraditional way.

The chimneypiece in the dining room, west of the hall, is a piece of Jacobean gigantism, grotesquely large for the wall in which it stands and awkwardly shoved into one corner of the room. To put it mildly, it does not look right: more frankly, it is a botch. As odd as anything is the disproportion between the chimneypiece and the diminutive doorway next to it, whose height is determined by that of the lobby to which it leads. Yet the two can hardly not be contemporaries: Mark Girouard recently discovered that the pilaster-jambs, and less closely the arch of the doorway are taken from a drawing tipped into Serlio's *Architecture* and reproduced in Peake's English translation published in 1610. This gives a likely *terminus ante quem* consistent with decorative work elsewhere in the house, though Serlio's drawing was also included in the Dutch edition of his book available in England half a century earlier. The flue from the fireplace is raked diagonally to a point just on the hall side of the partition, to rise thence into a stack in the valley between the west and middle transverse roofs. All Bradford's chimneys are either in the valleys or stand on dies at the base of gables; the arrangement of flues throughout the house is in consequence very peculiar, lots of them

The Hall, Bradford-on-Avon, dining-room chimneypiece and adjoining door
(*C.J. Richardson,* Elizabethan Architecture, [*1837*]).

being sharply raked; and it is a fair assumption that the dining-room
flue is original to the early-17th-century build, and hence that there
was always a fireplace in this position. Whether there is a now blocked
flue within the back wall of the hall is unknown: the fluing survey of
1968, probably didn't include this area since there was no visible
hearth. But it is extremely unlikely that a competent builder would
have joined two flues into one, and the only other available in the
relevant stack serves the great chamber immediately above.

This must await a possible excavation of part of the back wall of
the hall. Meanwhile what would be the most likely explanation of the
anomaly? Oswald's requires possibly the least engineering either of
the fabric of the house or of presuppositions trained on traditional
forms. Though the little door would still be unhappily shouldered by
the huge fireplace, the latter would no longer be in a corner, and the
much larger hall – 50 feet long – would be heated. On the other hand
the symmetry, which the external design and upper-floor plan insist
on so forcefully, would be lost, and the splendid porch would lead
into a point in the room which is neither one thing nor another. As

against this, leaving the partition in place would mean either that the hall was always unheated or that it had lost its fireplace, or conceivably that it had been removed to the dining room – a hefty job, and to what purpose? Neither of these explanations is plausible in the context of all that we know of the design and use of Jacobean houses. It is now clear that the central stack has only two flues; yet the hall must have been heated. It cannot have been so big as Oswald proposed; and the porch would be expected to lead into a passage, which at Bradford would go directly to a putative archway to the foot of the great stair. There will have been an end-hall in which the great fireplace was in the centre of its north wall. The narrow space east of the passage was probably an office otherwise missing from a house which would certainly need one. The resulting layout is not symmetrical, but it is in any case plain that there never has been structural symmetry in the front range, which is a continuous rectangular box made rigid by transverse beams; that the courtyard walls of the wings are in line with partitions in the front range is coincidence (and in one case of comparatively recent date), though conceivably, if Pamela Slocombe's provisional conclusion about the form of the earlier house is correct, partly influenced by it.

The working of the rest of the house is fairly easy to follow. It is plainly socially ordered front to back: on the ground floor all the lower rooms are at the back and are literally on a lower level. The large segmental arch of the hearth with a smaller oven opening to one side is unmistakable evidence of the kitchen in the north-east room – linked by a corridor to that to the north-west which once also had two (smaller) hearths and may have been a combined pastry and buttery with a way through the small west lobby into the end of the dining room or hall. The south-east room was certainly the great parlour: here too a towering chimneypiece dominates the room – its Vredemanesque carving being one of the signs suggesting the presence of William Arnold. The stylar wainscot here and in the oak room above appears to be all original, though there are places where the panels have to be adjusted to fit; and this room is unique in the survival of its ceiling plasterwork which elsewhere is entirely pastiche. The rebuilt open-well stair leads past a mezzanine landing to another on the principal upper floor, where the division is precisely as it now is below, and even more emphatically symmetrical. The great chamber, wholly renewed in the 19th or early 20th century, is in the middle over the hall, originally with a door near each end of its north wall. It was not designed *en suite* with the flanking chambers, which, because the landing is on the 'wrong' side of the spine, must be approached via lobbies like internal porches carved out of a corner of the rooms immediately behind. The implication of this device - awkward, now that the rooms are independent of one another – is that at each end of the house the pair of rooms was designed to make a single apartment – anticipating apartments of state later in the 17th century.

The mezzanines (above the former and the present kitchens) pose an interesting question: when were they inserted? That they both have Victorian fireplaces is neither here nor there: originally they may not have been heated at all. That their floors cut across the middle of windows on the east and west fronts (hidden by transoms) is also inconclusive. Such shifts, as Roger North would call them, occur elsewhere. But for the north-west mezzanine one piece of evidence is telling. Between the buttery (the present kitchen) and the dining room is the lobby which opens on to the garden through what is plainly an early Jacobean doorway. The door is necessarily as low as the lobby, whose ceiling level determines also the height of the petite-looking Serlian doorcase in the dining room. The lobby has a plaster cornice of late- 17th- or early-18th-century date: exactly the same mouldings are on the ceiling of the main stair and of the back 'inner' hall. The lobby in its present dimensions must therefore be original; its ceiling level is fixed by the floor of the north-west mezzanine, which can therefore be also taken to be an original feature. The balancing mezzanine is above the old kitchen and makes the latter rather low: our original assumption was that the kitchen had once risen from its lower floor level through the whole of the ground floor and that the mezzanine had been inserted in the late 19th century when the kitchen was moved into the basement. But builders and their clients were not always so considerate of their cooks; and with only two apartments on the main chamber floor bedroom accommodation at Bradford is in short supply. So, since there is good reason to accept one mezzanine as original, I believe that we should take both on board: they are, after all, linked by their own landing; and mezzanines were not then quite a novelty.

Who designed this remarkable house will probably never be known for sure. Following a suggestion by Arthur Oswald, Mark Girouard at one time was inclined to think that Robert Smythson might have provided a plan for the exterior.[9] He has subsequently rejected the idea on the ground that Smythson was at the very end of his life when Bradford is believed to have been built and unlikely to move from his Nottinghamshire base. Oswald however further identified what he called the 'very close resemblance' between the main entrance doorcases at Bradford and Wollaton, observing in both 'the semi-circular arch with classic enrichments, the block-like imposts, and strapwork in the spandrels'. The Bradford doorcase is also in other respects like that of Doddington Hall, Lincolnshire, begun in 1593 and attributed by Girouard to Smythson - though not necessarily so like that both might not be simply examples of a widespread form. What of the much-discussed compass windows, so striking a feature of the Bradford façade? Compass windows are not so rare at this period as has sometimes been suggested – think of Wootton Lodge (Staffordshire) or Burton Agnes (Yorkshire) – though their particular form at Bradford, in which the semi-cylindrical bow is the three-dimensional centrepiece of a tripartite composition, can perhaps be matched only in the celebrated façade of Sir Paul Pindar's house in Bishopsgate, London, in Thorpe's design for Campden House, Kensington, and, perhaps most significantly for Bradford, in Walter Ralegh's abortive attempt to reinstate the old castle at Sherborne (Dorset) in 1592. In the south-west, compass windows are also known to have been built in the north range at Berry Pomeroy (Devon), now securely dated to c.1600. Most importantly in the present context, four of them appear on a plan of Cranborne Manor (Dorset) which is almost certainly the 'plott' that Arnold is known to have made in 1609. Cranborne was badly damaged in the Civil War, and if the wings containing these windows were ever built, they have not survived.

A case for Arnold has been strongly argued by Anthony Wells-Cole.[10] It is once again essentially stylistic (as well as in this case geographically plausible): the shell-headed niches in the White Room are exactly like those in the north loggia at Cranborne and on the front of Montacute, Somerset; there are rams' heads on the study chimneypiece copied, like those on the hall screen at Montacute, from Vredeman de Vries's *Das Erst Büch*'. Wells-Cole goes on to claim that this proves that the interior of Bradford was indeed designed by Arnold. It does not quite do that: it only proves that the same print was used in both cases, and in addition, despite the unqualified assertion that Arnold designed and built Montacute for Sir Edward Phelips, all we know for sure is that Montacute has details that replicate some at Cranborne, and that Phelips commended Arnold to Dorothy Wadham, who in 1610 brought him from Somerset to Oxford to build her new college, where he proved himself thoroughly competent in an intriguing mixture of styles: the frontispiece of the east range might suggest a blown-up version of the parlour chimneypiece at Bradford, though it is in fact a more consistently classical imitation of that in the Fellows' Quad at Merton College, built two years previously by John Akroyd. It is however widely agreed that Arnold is very likely to have been the designer and builder of Montacute, that he was an architect and mason of more than average ability and that the multiple use of specific identifiable prints in carved overmantels and other decorative features at a string of west-country houses, gives Arnold a good claim to have been the craftsman responsible for detailed interior work at Bradford. It does not take us much further with Bradford's most famous and startling feature – its south front. Yet the more I think about Bradford Hall the more I feel its design is a unity; and finally I have to admit that after all, despite its position and the business activities of its builder, it might seem – if we could ever sort out the problem of its hall – to behave really quite like other medium-sized country houses put up by wealthy professionals of one kind or another.

4

Some later Jacobean Villas in Scotland

Charles McKean

In 1727, inspired by an admiration for Lord Burlington and Chiswick House, the architectural patron Sir John Clerk of Penicuik set out rules for the design of a 'country seat' in a private poem of that name. It was written for the edification of his family and progeny rather than for publication.[1] One might have expected from Clerk a panegyric for a 'British' architecture, but he suggested instead, and at considerable length, that the new architecture for the northern part of the new Britain should be created from a fusion of indigenous Scottish architectural traditions with a rediscovery of the classics. When he wrote,

> Each region of this great terrestrial Orb
> A various Dress and Culture will require

he was indicating that national identity had to be maintained within the greater Britain: for, aware of Scotland's shortcomings, he was nonetheless a fierce Scots patriot.[2]

His poem had much to say about the concept, role and characteristics of a villa as perceived in the early 18th century. However, his prescription could have applied equally well to an earlier generation of villas constructed in Scotland – the U-plan villas erected between 1600 and the later 1630s, initially under the influence of Queen Anna's court. Given that Clerk spent much time excoriating Scotland under the Stewarts, his poem underscores just how modern these earlier villas had been in all aspects save in their refusal to adopt classicism or a pure form. They are the subject of this chapter.

The power of Palladio's clients lay in mercantile activity in a city like Venice. Their villas, by contrast, were elegant houses where they might enjoy blissful ease, and a command over nature. So the builder of the *suburban* villa (defined as one within an easy day's journey from the town) was likely to be a merchant, a banker or politician – like Hadrian or Pliny – whose income derived from and whose power lay within the city, but who retired, as Clerk put it, to

> … a little villa where one may
> Taste every minute's Blessing sweet and gay
> And in a soft Retirement spend the Day.

Clerk's villa had to be architecturally distinctive:

> Mark how the Plinian Villa was disposed
> And how the Ancients form'd their rural Seats
> To various Purposes, in various Shapes.
> The different Architecture spoke the Use …[3]

It was neither a great house nor intended to be so; rather – in Scotland at least – it was a smart house for a person of lesser rank, lying within a day's ride or less around the greater towns and cities. Since the owner's primary source of income was not from the land but from urban activity, these villa properties were rarely large in extent – an estate extending to perhaps twelve acres or less.[4] However, contrary to Clerk's view that the villa should have a distinctive architecture, that was only achieved in the early 17th century in the group inspired by Queen Anna's court – which, curiously, were mostly built for courtiers and government officials rather than for urban entrepreneurs. The latter's suburban villas were usually identified less by form than by scale.

No research has yet been undertaken into the Renaissance suburban villa in Scotland. Glasgow, for example, which was moving from the third to the second largest town of Scotland in the 17th century, offers no coherent picture. Only a few of the houses mentioned in Crawfurd's 1720 *General Description of the Shire of Renfrew*[5] can easily be identified as villas of the Glasgow élite, and

Crawfurd's interest lay in their planting rather than in architecture. Of Ranfield, built possibly in 1568 for a canon of Glasgow Cathedral, Crawfurd notes only that it was 'adorned with pleasant orchards and gardens, beautified with very much planting and regular avenues.'[6] The villa nature of this property was confirmed in its later sale in 1654 to Glasgow's Lord Provost Colin Campbell, whose descendants changed its name to Blythswood after their town property.[7]

Availability of relatively small plots close to the city was essential, and former ecclesiastical land sometimes provided that opportunity. In 1590, James VI granted lands in Govan to those who had previously rented them from the archbishopric of Glasgow, on the undertaking that they would improve them, providing a further impulse toward the development of the smaller suburban house or villa.[8] As the 17th century progressed, Glasgow's mercantile élite appear more likely to purchase such villas; yet in 1631, one of the ministers of Glasgow Cathedral, John Maxwell, rebuilt his villa of Auldhouse in the then fashionable U-plan, possibly in emulation of the Court style (see later).[9] Simultaneously, that same fashion was also adopted for the seats of minor estates closer to the city, such as the 100-acre Stobcross.[10]

One of the essences of a villa, as Clerk observed, was that it should be compact:

> Now would you choose a Villa where retir'd
> From busy crowds, and from domestick noise.
> You may possess the Sweets of Leisure Hours;
> Then raise a structure so confin'd in size,
> As may secure this valuable prize. [11]

Compactness was a feature that could apply equally well to the suburban villa as to the seat of a fourth-rank landowner, to a dower house, the house of the heir, or even to the seaside or fishing villas of the great families. These small houses could sometimes be indistinguishable from each other. The seat of a third-rank landowner, Earlshall in Fife **(Plate 2)** for example, might well approximate the form of a villa of someone of grander degree. It was, for example, considerably smaller than Chancellor Seton's villa of Pinkie, Musselburgh. For all its compactness, there can never have been any intent that Earlshall be perceived as a unitary composition, *à la*

Palladio. There was no question of it being viewed in the round. Albeit that its lodging and service wing are held together in tension by the entrance screen, only from its gardens to the east, could the real form of the house – a U-plan – be perceived.

In the Glasgow hinterland, the tendency was for merchants to build a miniature replica of the greater country seat. That was the form of one of the few identified indisputable merchant's villas, built by the successful Glaswegian merchant and philanthropist George Hutcheson at Partick, on the river Kelvin, a couple of miles west of Glasgow.[12] Constructed in 1611 by the Kilwinning master-mason William Millar, the unit of measurement for the new house was determined as 'ye said George's awin fute,' and it was designed to a 16-foot module.[13] Save the mason's contract, all we know of this 'very handsome house' is a late-18th-century sketch,[14] and an early-18th-century description: it was 'well finished and [suitably for a villa] adorned with curious orchyards and gardens, stately avenues and large enclosures, sheltered with a great deal of planting so that it has become one of the sweetest seats upon the River Clyde in this shire.'[15] This pretty, compact, four-storeyed house, which lacked the yards required to keep a larger estate in business, otherwise

Blackness, by Dundee. A Baltic merchant's Renaissance villa in 1894 (demolished) (*RCAHMS, C/12752*).

exemplified the extent to which villas like this were not yet defined by notions of a distinctive form.

Judging from the maps of Timothy Pont of Angus and the Carse of Gowrie, *c*.1587,[16] Dundee, a more prosperous port – and a larger town – than Glasgow during the 16th century (as a consequence of its trade with the Baltic), seems to have enjoyed a denser scattering of villas for the town's elite throughout its hinterland. Moreover, although precious few survive, they appear to have taken a distinctive form that sets them apart from being considered as the smaller country houses of the lesser gentry. Built by the elite of Dundee – wealthy merchants – they eschewed the significant vertical emphasis of the typical Scottish country seat in favour of something much more horizontal. These houses, of which Invergowrie, Blackness or Pitkerro would be good examples, were horizontal in proportion, comprising a long principal storey above a ground floor of cellars and kitchens, sometimes with a dormer-windowed attic above. Invergowrie, for example, which took this form, was the house of the Dundee merchant family Clayhills: one brother ran the business from Dundee, another from Königsburg, and the third from Stockholm. There were variations, but the form of this house greatly resembles houses in Baltic countries, of which the Arnot House in Kedainai, Lithuania (built for a Scottish merchant) is a good example. The principal difference is that the Kedainai house was built of brick, and the Dundee one of stone. Research is still in its infancy, but the combination of the availability of relatively small plots of land, and substantial mercantile wealth (merchants formed the port's élite to a far greater degree than in comparable European towns), suggests that there might have been a substantial number of such houses. These horizontally-planned houses rather resembled the new free-standing residential wings added to some earlier country seats, as, for example, at Sauchie, and at Wester Powrie. The latter, dated 1604, was probably built in response to the king's confirmation of the lands, six years earlier, to Thomas Fotheringham 'upon which the predecessors of the said Thomas made great policy, especially on the tower, mansion and manor, … which place the said Thomas now wishes to repair'.[17]

Miniature versions of larger country seats was the expression adopted for the myriad villas that surrounded the capital, Edinburgh. Craigcrook, for example, built in the lee of Corstorphine Hill in the

'Marian' style of the 1550s by the merchant William Adamson, was a *petite* replica of country seats that could then be seen throughout the country. When visiting the capital in 1600, the Duc de Rohan observed 'more than a hundred country-seats are to be found within a radius of two leagues of the town.'[18] Such a quantity in such a small compass clearly implied that the majority would have to have been villas rather than the seats of even lesser country landowners. They were relatively low-slung houses in good locations, adorned with beautiful gardens, with sometimes astoundingly elaborate fountains,[19] and courtyards – everything comfortable rather than heraldic. Predominantly, they were the suburban villas of the new men –wealthy merchants and town councillors, wealthy craftsmen, State office holders (particularly the Keepers of the Royal Mint – naturally) and – above all – lawyers and law lords.[20] Of twenty-seven such surviving houses in the immediate neighbourhood of Edinburgh identified by Joyce Wallace, a quarter were built for city merchants, another quarter for lawyers or judges, several each for court officials and city council officials, only two for a landed family and one for a craftsman – the goldsmith Gilbert Kirkwood who built Pilrig in 1638.[21] A similar number survives in various conditions of alteration in the Lothians (the Scottish Home Counties), and there were once clearly many more. They differ slightly in rank and wealth, and quite considerably in their expression. It would naturally be to such new men that one generally, might look for new ideas in architecture, since they would normally be free of the predisposition to celebrate ancestry and rank in their architectural expression. In Scotland, for the most part, that is not the case. In the burst of building in the earlier 17th century – particularly from 1616 to 1636 – that heralded the new architectural ideas for the villa as a building type, adventurousness was as apparent in the higher ranks.

The real power in Scotland, however, lay not in the towns and their merchants, lawyers and craftsmen but with the greater magnates in the countryside. Motivated primarily by rank, lineage and kinship, Scottish aristocrats used the architecture of their country seat as the principal mode of expressing this. The minute building elevations on Pont's maps of Scotland imply at least four distinct ranks of landowners.[22] At the apex, aristocratic dignity was focused upon what they called the 'ancient paternal seat'[23] – the house that expressed all their rank, and retained the mediaeval tower house that symbolised their lineage; but since it was often anachronistic and old fashioned, they frequently chose to construct or purchase a more contemporary house, relegating the paternal seat to periodic visits and the most symbolic of ceremonial occasions. Their new house, however, was usually much grander than a villa: it was their seat of power and display. In addition, they might also have a villa – in other words a summer house, a seaside villa, a hunting lodge or a fishing pavilion. The latter two can usually be identified from their unusual accommodation: large kitchen but few cellars (since the food was being caught), and a large hall but few chambers (since most guests stayed under canvas). In other words, they were small and unencumbered with the customary estate paraphernalia.

Scottish architecture appears to have received a new impetus with

Queen Anna's Belvedere, Dunfermline.

the arrival in Scotland in 1590 of Queen Anna,[24] sister of Christian IV of Denmark. As her chamberlain and sacrist, she appointed the much travelled Catholic William Schaw, Master of the King' Works, and royal architect.[25] Alexander Seton, Lord Fyvie and president of the Court of Session, was appointed keeper of her palace of Dunfermline. Seton, likewise Catholic, had spent much time being educated in Rome, including in the arts of architecture, and he was appointed chancellor from 1605 to 1622.[26] He was regarded as Scotland's primary cultural patron. The three were close friends – so close that when Schaw died in 1602, Seton inscribed a memorial to his 'most intimate loving friend'[27] and Anna (inter alia) that 'he was most skilled in architecture.' In 1600, Schaw designed a new Queen's Jointure House adjacent to Seton's own lofty new lodging.[28] It was a self-contained royal lodging later known as Queen Anna's Belvedere, perched above the gateway into Dunfermline Palace. Since she elected to have most of her children born there, we may assume it was Anna's favourite house, as is also implied by its description as 'the ordinar residence of the Queen'.[29] Approximately cruciform in plan, it communicated with the royal apartments by a long, sloping 'Gallery of Communication' along the western perimeter,[30] and in Germanic fashion, an oriel – presumably from the principal chamber – appears to have faced up the street.[31] The concept of having a self-contained villa constructed athwart and over a road provides an intriguing ancestor of Queen Anna's house in Greenwich some seventeen years later.[32]

A further ancestor of the Greenwich Queen's House might have been another villa – or rather extension – constructed in Culross, Fife, about the same time by Edward Bruce, Lord Kinloss, Master of the Rolls in London where he had made his home. To the Commendator's House at Culross Abbey overlooking the Forth, which he owned, he added a *jeu d'esprit* built of beautifully cut ashlar. Clerk would have approved:

> Those walls are still the best, where massy stones
> Are cut in Squares, and so together joined,
> As scarce the Eye can the Division find.[33]

Judging by the cornice at second-storey level, this long, nine-bay

Culross Abbey House (*RCAHMS*).

pavilion of square-cut stone was probably capped by a continuous flat roof or belvedere. Accommodation within was scanty, the space behind a cross wall being sufficient only for circulation. To the river, the principal floor comprised a long gallery faced internally with ashlar – as though you were looking through an open screen down onto the Forth. The only other accommodation was on the ground floor or the chambers in the corner towers. Aonghus MacKechnie has suggested that its principal function was to give Lord Kinloss the opportunity to offer King James VI a pleasant break as he made a watery progress from Stirling to Dunfermline.[34] A hypothetical reconstruction, with its flat roof, balustrade, and massy chimney-stacks likewise appear to presage the Queen's House in Greenwich. Curiously, Preston House, in East Lothian, built for the son of Edinburgh's Lord Provost in the early 17th century, might have been comparable, since its eight-bay front was flanked by two-storeyed, ogee-roofed towers, save for the fact that the towers stepped forward in a different manner.[35]

Perhaps the most vivid expression of the villa as the seat of invisible power at this stage in its architectural development is the suburban villa of Pinkie, reformatted not long after Schaw's death by Alexander Seton. On two great stone tablets in what remains of one

Conjectural reconstruction of Culross Abbey House based upon John Slezer's *c.*1678 drawing (*Author*).

73

Pinkie House, Musselburgh. Chancellor Seton's suburban villa viewed *c*.1895 from the privy garden. The house was still harled (*RCAHMS, C34334*).

of the privy gardens, Seton, describing himself as a man 'who above all loves every kind of culture and urbanity,' proclaimed how he had transformed this former property of the abbey of Dunfermline:

> For his own pleasure, and that of his noble descendants and all men of cultivation and urbanity, Alexander Seton, who above all loves every kind of culture and urbanity, has planted, raised and decorated a country house, gardens and suburban buildings. There is nothing here to do with warfare; not even a ditch or rampart to expel enemies, but in order to welcome guests with kindness, and treat them with benevolence, a fountain of pure water, a grove, pools, and other things that may add to the pleasures of the place. He has brought together everything that might afford decent pleasures of the heart and mind. But he declares that whoever shall destroy this, by theft, sword or fire, or behaves in a hostile manner, is a man devoid of generosity and urbanity, indeed of all culture, and is an enemy to the human race.[36]

Barely a summer house survives of this mythical Attic landscape with its groves and ponds – save the 'splendidly monumental'[37] Doric fountain or well in the inner court of the house, sitting by the principal entrance. The powerful sophistication of this *jeu d'esprit* with its 'imperial' crown and Horatian mottoes, demonstrates that had the

Pinkie, entrance court and Doric fountain drawn by R.W. Billings, *c.*1846 (*Author*).

Scots wished to design a building according to the rules of Italian classicism, they could have done so with great style: but had opted to do otherwise. It is equally obvious that the face that Pinkie presented to its inner court was an entirely different one to the garden. The garden façade was harled and monolithic, its austerity broken only by

Painted ceiling in the Gallery at Pinkie (*RCAHMS, MLD 69/35*).

a string-course and its rhythmic skyline. Any martial symbolism was relegated to tall chimney stacks (some of which appear to be ornamental only), probably originally with ornate caps,[38] that once alternated with an array of dormer windows and finials.[39] Two tiny square studies look north over the sea, and the belvedere at the head of the public staircase is elaborately decorated with slender tourelles. To this cultivated humanist and patron, his villa at Pinkie expressed the architectural equivalent of the concept of beating swords into ploughshares.

Since at least half of the inner court, and the entire outer court are now missing, the extent of Seton's alterations is not clear. It is difficult to establish the axis of entry, the location of the state apartment, or of the guest chambers; and it is evident from the stonework that, when Seton added the celebrated long gallery with its magnificent painted ceiling as the third storey of the eastern wing, he was adding to an existing structure.[40] The paintings in the gallery are appropriately Stoic, derived from scenes by Vaenius, Vredeman de Vries, and de Batilly.[41] In most cases, the original is subtly changed, in one case to include a portrait of the patron himself. It was from this house that Seton exercised almost two decades of invisible power as the Chancellor of Scotland, whereas he kept his private family life to another house at Dalgety in Fife (now vanished).

Although all the attributes – save the form – of the Italianate villa were present at Pinkie, it is only obvious from the inscription that Seton left us. It is otherwise largely indistinguishable from a smaller Scottish courtyard house with gardens. Much the same might be said of the house of Castlestead, the villa built in 1606 by David Murray, 1st Viscount Stormont, in the northern grounds of Falkland Palace, and – judging by the details of its windows – almost certainly designed by the royal architect, David Cuninghame of Robertland – although Murray himself had something of a reputation as a designer.[42] Castlestead was a flamboyant courtyard villa with a tower – perhaps capped by a belvedere, loggia and gallery, evincing, like its contemporary Pinkie, that a formal single unity was not yet being sought after.[43]

That had to wait for James Murray of Kilbaberton, who became royal architect in 1609, and with him, the later Jacobean villa in Scotland began to emerge with a distinctive form and particular

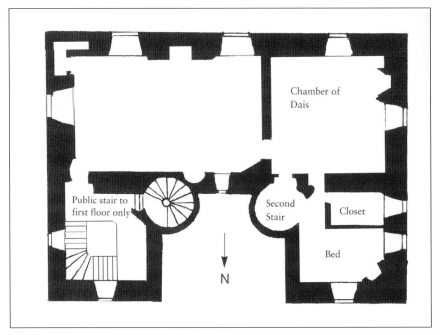

Plan of Baberton after MacGibbon & Ross (*Author*).

insignia.[44] The paraphernalia of belvederes, gables, high chimneys, dormer windows, and studies in the form of turrets was not rejected: it was refined and reorganised, along with the introduction of two new motifs. The first was the 'buckle' quoin – a corner stone expensively carved in the form of a strapwork buckle or stirrup;[45] and the other was a chimney-stack evolved into a square ashlar column capped by an elaborate cornice, placed on angle.

In place of the heterogeneous shapes of Pinkie and Castlestead, the new villa offered visual control, achieved by re-ordering the evolving requirements for privacy that had emerged over the previous half century. A family tower or wing had been developing at the opposite end of the 'main house' or *corps de logis* from a guest wing. Since the guest wing generally contained the public staircase, it projected to the front whereas the family wing faced the rear. In the new villa, however, as exemplified in Murray's own country villa of Kilbaberton (Plate 3), built 1616-22, the family wing moved from the rear of the house to balance the entrance or guest wing on the façade. There would be a staircase either within, or in the angle, of each wing so that each chamber could be reached directly without having to pass

78

from one chamber through another in enfilade. The design of Baberton was carefully controlled, and gained more power thereby, but it was still a heraldic house with its chimney-stacks, finials, aedicules and buckle quoins. Moreover, whereas the design was in balance, it was also distinctly asymmetrical, and entered through the west wing rather than on central axis.

Central to Murray's client-base were the technocrats assisting Chancellor Seton to run Scotland in the king's absence – the 'New Octavians' – a leader of whom was Henry Wardlaw, chief receiver of taxes and William Schaw's successor as Anna's chamberlain at the palace of Dunfermline, whom Murray accompanied on inspections of royal palaces.[46] It was probably Murray who designed his U-plan villa at Pitreavie, near Dunfermline. More lavish and more imposing than Baberton, Pitreavie's plan has a comparable compactness, but there is greater rigour (and wealth) in its ashlar exterior and sophistication of its planning, with its extraordinarily symmetrical fenestration, and string course separating the *piano nobile* from the

The villa of Sir Henry Wardlaw at Pitreavie, near Dunfermline, Fife (*RCAHMS, E/01278*).

79

cellar floor. What is striking is just how sedate, if not sober, Pitreavie was when compared to other U-plan villas or town houses that followed a similar model – the Argyll Lodging in Stirling, for example.

A century later, Clerk was to approve of enfolding wings, albeit his exemplar at Mavisbank was to be very different from his predecessors. Nonetheless, the notion of a villa welcoming guests in 'kind embrace' appears just as appropriate to the early 17th century:

> See the noble scene which is disclosed,
> When with expanded wings and kind Embrace
> Th'inviting Fabrick seems to lure its Guests;
> These usefull wings supply her daily wants,
> And ease the burden of Domestick Cares;
> They fence her peace full hours from irksome noise
> And many ways new Comforts give to Life
> Such are the tender mother's clasping Arms…

Visitors appear to have entered between the wings of most of these villas, turning right or left into one of them for the entrance staircase.[47] Mostly, the wings extended to the north, leaving the villa and its privy garden to face south, but occasionally – where the view warranted – that was reversed. Having made a fortune in butter in London, Tam Dalyell, Kinloss' son-in-law, returned to Edinburgh and began to retrofit the older courtyard house of The Binns, near Linlithgow, in 1616. (Since the house was much damaged by a mock-historic makeover by Robert Burn in the early 19th century, we cannot be entirely certain what Dalyell constructed, for its original stair, gallery and belvedere are all lacking.)

It seems probable, however, that The Binns was intended to be entered from the south (leaving a superb view over the Forth to the north), directly into a new laigh (low) entrance hall carved from former cellars, from which a stair led to the state apartment above. How The Binns' two wings were arranged might be inferred from how Sir Thomas Hamilton, a successful lawyer, remodelled the old tower of Tyninghame as his country villa in 1628. An inventory explains how the villa worked. The eastern (right hand) wing was intended for guests who had their own hall and chambers; whereas the west wing contained the family state apartment.[48] This very

The Wrichtishousis, Edinburgh. Drawing by Francis Grose, late 18th century (*National Galleries of Scotland, D.24*).

modern division of family from guests appears to characterise the later Jacobean villa in Scotland.

The adoption of the U-plan villa appears to have led to another significant change. One originally approached the older Scottish country seat normally through a court of service buildings, and an inner court. These courts were cleared away in the U-plan villa, so that visitors enjoyed a vista of an embracing form like a miniature version of the Château Maisons-Laffitte, near Paris – albeit with a Scottish rather than a classical expression. In that context, therefore, by virtue of the similarity of treatment of chimneys in the gables, falls the now vanished villa of Wrichtishousis[49] – probably the most flamboyant of all of them, built for the Napiers, a family doing well in Edinburgh. One entered from the north between enfolding wings, into a porch at the centre and then up into a seven-bay gallery from which one could have moved to the east (guest's and public) wing or the west (family and private) wing.[50] One senses that the right (west) wing was that of the guests from its more elaborate decoration, its public stair tower containing chambers and its highly ornate belvedere above. The porch was capped by miniature tourelles similar to those on the barbican at Lübeck.

These low and horizontally proportioned houses were all within easy reach of Edinburgh, and had no need of height to emphasise rank, antiquity, kinship or lineage. Nonetheless, it was inevitable that

81

a strong fashion from the court would percolate elsewhere – particularly where the planning was found to be so adaptable. Thus the U-plan villa became the characteristic form for the aristocratic town house or urban *hôtel* in the 1630s, and was also adopted by grand and small in the shires, – particularly by those with court associations. The Earl of Orkney's new wing in the palace of Kirkwall and the Burnett of Leys' seaside villa at Muchalls, Aberdeenshire, both took the form of a free-standing U-plan villa: not the larger U-plan of equally grand parallel wings as in Wrichtishousis and Tyninghame, but the smaller version of Kilbaberton where the private wing was balanced against the staircase wing with guest chambers, public rooms between. Modified, this plan was then adapted for country seats of higher rank – or, as in the case of Cowdenknowes, Borders, where a new wing was added to an older inner court near the ancestral tower. When the Earl of Winton came to devise a villa at Winton, to which he could retreat from his most magnificent ancient paternal seat of Seton Palace barely ten miles away, he selected the fashionable U-plan villa – and, almost certainly Murray or his executant architect William Wallace – albeit with a striking elaboration of belvedere, wrythen chimneys and an entrance loggia. When Lord Southesk reformatted

Muchalls, Aberdeenshire, drawn by R.W. Billings *c.*1846 (*Author*).

Winton, drawn by R.W. Billings *c.*1846. The house is depicted before the disas-
trous alterations by John Paterson who raised up the entrance level, and disposed
of the loggia (*Author*).

his seat of Kinnaird, Angus, the house he built bore a striking
similarity of plan to Winton.[51]

Merchants and lawyers of Edinburgh had been observing these
shifts of fashion, and there was a distinct move toward plainness and
further compactness. John Shairp, an Edinburgh lawyer, reformatted
Houston House, West Lothian, in a compressed U-plan, with virtually
no space between the wings, and a south facade of a plainness
comparable to Pitreavie's. When the lawyer Sir Alexander Hamilton,
amended the house of Priestfield, Edinburgh into Prestonfield, the
result was a similarly compact U-plan suburban villa decorated with
the characteristic ashlar 'buckle' quoins of the court style; and a
circulation similar to Houston's, and very much more compact than
his brother's at Tyninghame.

In Angus, Queen Anna's master of household, Sir Harry Lindsay
abandoned his huge seat of Finaven for an altogether more
fashionable villa at Careston, internally decorated top to bottom with

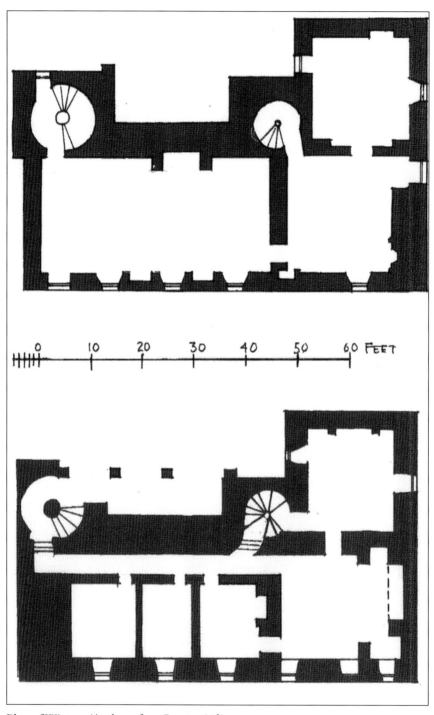

Plan of Winton (Author after *Country Life*).

carvings based upon Vredeman de Vries. Careston became his principal residence rather than a villa, and the 'court plan' was modified accordingly:[52] probably U-plan, belvedere capping the western wing and, perhaps, like Winton, entered through a loggia.[53] It was a much taller house and was probably adorned with greater aristocratic display. It was very similar indeed to the Earl of Moray's seaside villa of Pettie, Nairn, which he reformatted into a tall U-plan house and renamed Castle Stewart. A distinctive feature is the rectangular study cut into each corner on the diagonal (as in Pittullie,

Craigston, Buchan (*RCAHMS, AB/520*).

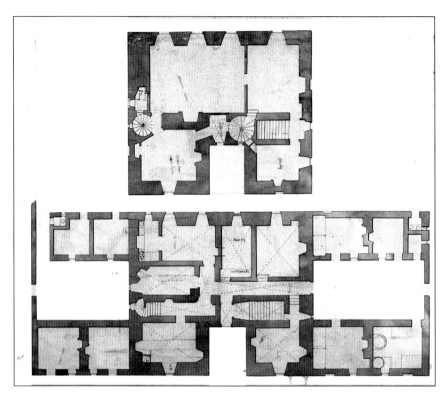

Plan of Craigston (*Courtesy of William Urquhart*).

Banffshire and as customary in Bavaria).

A principal characteristic of the court-style villa had been its low horizontality, in contrast to the tall flamboyant expressionism of north-eastern houses like Craigievar or Crathes; but even this distinction was becoming blurred. Craigston, by Turriff, was the seat of the scholar and translator of Rabelais, Sir Thomas Urquhart. Reformatted between 1604 and 1607 into the fashionable U-plan, Craigston remained a very 'tall house.'[54] When Clerk wrote:

> Above the Attick Floor a Platform Roof
> May be extended like a spacious Field
> From when the many Landskips round
> May be with ease and with Delight survey'd
> Then to complete the whole, a Balustrade[55]

adding later:

Then on its Summit by the Plummers' Art
Collected Waters may in copious stores
Gainst all misfortunes guard or sometimes flow ...[56]

He could have been referring to Craigston. Its balustraded belvedere is seven storeys up, its ornamental balcony lining the gallery six storeys up, and a cistern collects water from its platform roof. Craigston's plan is comparable to the court villa, albeit the plan was modified according to the exigencies – the original stairs, walls and dimensions – of the original tower. In essence, Craigston achieved a splendid blend of the Court villa and the north-eastern tall house with its requirement for a belvedere, skied gallery and public stair rising to its apex.

At least thirty U-plan villas were built in Scotland during the 17th century, some modified or extended into an H-plan, such as Sir Harry Paterson's House of Bannockburn, or Sir David Murray's remodelling of Scone Abbey. Most were compact, compressing the principal features of the larger country seat into an efficient plan that replaced the old double-courtyard entry with a vision of control. As the century waned, echoes of the villa's framing wings persisted in the flanking service wings of James Smith's masterly Melville House or Traquair. In most respects, the Scottish lineage of these houses remained constant and visible: the state apartment remained on the *piano nobile* (although one or two adopted an entrance level 'laigh hall') and relative rank was expressed through scale and decoration. That these houses were far from either antiquarian or anachronistic is emphasised by the fact that a description penned by Sir John Clerk of Penicuik, over 130 years after Queen Anna and her friends William Schaw and Alexander Seton first began building, remained so relevant to them. It is surely an indication of just how modern these later Jacobean villas had been.

Acknowledgements:

I am particularly grateful to Charles Wemyss, Matthew Davis, Kate Newland, Michael Pearce, and James Simpson for their help and advice in the preparation of this chapter. I am indebted to Sir Robert Clerk for his permission to quote from 'The Country Seat'.

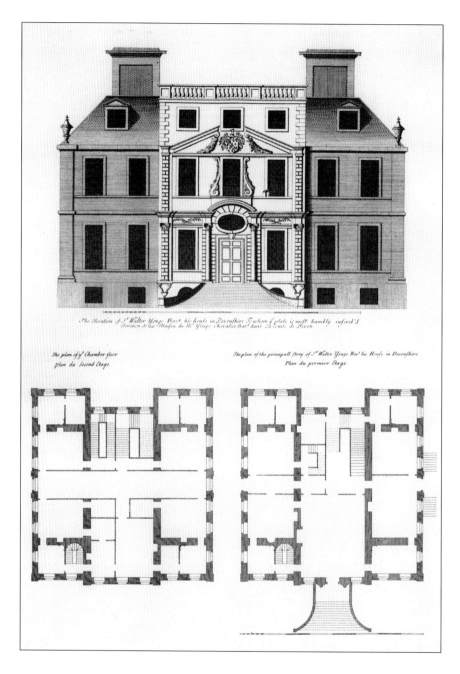

Plate 1: 'Sir Walter Tonge, Bart. his house in Devonshire' (Escot): elevation and plan of principal (right) and chamber storey from *Vitruvius Britannicus* I (London, 1715), pls 78-9: see page 97.

5

Plain English or Anglo–Palladian?
Seventeenth–Century Country Villa Plans

Patricia Smith

The following abbreviations for principal rooms are used throughout the plans in this chapter:
   CP – common parlour (also known as little parlour; family living/dining room)
   K – kitchen
   P – parlour (principal ground floor entertaining room)
   W – withdrawing room to parlour

This chapter considers the evolution of interior planning in smaller country houses of the 17th century.[1] The word 'villa' in the early part of that century could refer to any 'country mansion or residence, together with a farm, farm-buildings or other buildings attached, built or occupied by a person of some position and wealth; a country seat or estate'.[2] Although the term did not, at that time, carry a qualification of size, today it does; and the houses discussed here all accord with the fundamental idea of the villa as a compact house, neat and regular in plan, polite in architectural form. Such buildings are clearly distinguished both from the great country mansions, and from vernacular manor houses.[3] They were typically either the main homes of modest landowners, or secondary seats of the aristocracy; and, like Palladio's *case di villa*, served the dual roles of functioning country house and retreat from the court or city.

The transformation of the traditional great house into a compact modern form dominates the chronicle of 17th-century English domestic architecture. The century began in the great age of what John Summerson so aptly named the 'prodigy houses', when the scale of a courtier's mansion, its grandeur and its capacity to entertain and lodge large retinues all more or less directly reflected his power and wealth.[4] Within thirty years, the great aristocratic palaces were looking more like liabilities than assets, as royal progresses and other stately visits dwindled and ceased, to be followed by the long lacuna of the civil war and interregnum, when building big was potentially foolish.

History dictated that conspicuous spending should be replaced by more subtle means of conveying superiority. The art of economy, that is to say the way a man planned and utilised his resources to best advantage, could prove more admirable than extravagance, even for those of substantial means. At the same time, men of the professional and merchant classes and smaller landowners were pushing up from below the ranks of the courtiers, acquiring the confidence and cash to build themselves pocket versions of the great country houses. Here, therefore, was a climate in which small could be beautiful. By experimenting with compact forms, English patrons, their architects and builders were able to make a virtue of necessity, and their creative efforts in effect gave birth to what we recognise today as the English villa.

In a period when classicism was infiltrating native English architectural styles, one might expect that classical planning – and since, we are speaking of villas, Palladian planning – would similarly influence established approaches to interior layout. In practice, there proved a sturdy resistance to such novelties. While a great man's house might look outwards to impress his peers and neighbours, the interior was his home. Architectural styles could change fast and frivolously, but domestic behaviours were ingrained; few owners would willingly exchange their comfortable ancestral habits in order to adopt outlandish ideas from 16th-century Italy.

The plan of a house was the vehicle for household life; well understood zones effectively segregated or integrated different classes of occupant – the family, visitors and servants – in a manner required by propriety and function. This functional zoning in Elizabethan and Jacobean houses is very familiar, embodied in the hall, parlour and

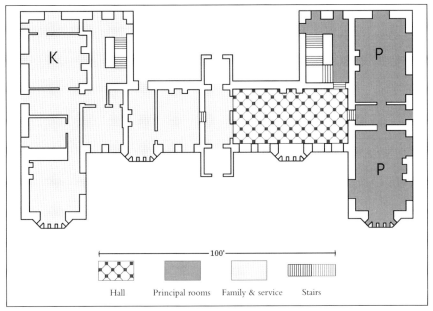

Fig. 1: Montacute House, Somerset, *c.*1590-9, for Edward Phelips.
Architect: attrib. William Arnold.

service ranges; Montacute House **Fig. 1** is a typical example from the
end of the 16th century. The hall or entrance range was universal
territory, used as a grand and common entrance, waiting room and
circulation space; a public place where occupants of every status
might cross paths. Although anyone might enter through the screens
passage at the low end, only the family, guests and those providing
them with service could proceed beyond the dais at the high end. The
parlour range beyond this point was essentially for private domestic
use and for entertainment of visitors. In all but the most stately of
homes, by the beginning of the 17th century, only the more formal
occasions would be hosted in a great chamber or dining room on the
floor above; by the end of the century, all major reception rooms had
been progressively repositioned onto the same storey as the hall.

The hall and parlour ranges presented the two formal or show
fronts of the house, and almost always had an orthogonal relationship.
This typically English practice had many advantages, notably in
orientation. Assuming the general topography allowed it, a builder
could set one of his two important façades to the favoured south and
the other to the east or west, both also good choices in the English
climate. The great stair was almost always placed at the pivot of these

two ranges, either occupying a compartment between hall and parlour, or placed in a stair tower at the front or rear (as at Montacute) re-entrant angles. To the low side of the screens passage, past the refreshment areas of buttery and pantry, was the service range, usually including the kitchen and often nearby the winter parlour, where the family could retreat in the colder months. Thus formed the familiar U, H, and half-H plans, as well as the full quadrangle created when a fourth range (usually comprising lodgings or other minor apartments, or the gatehouse to a large complex) enclosed the court.

These arrangements were embedded in the English way of life. The challenges of creating a compact house were to draw in the tentacles of the spread structure, retain all the features and spaces a gentleman or aristocrat would require in his home, and above all maintain distinct and recognisable zones of use and occupancy. This paper outlines three of the more important routes by which this was achieved during the course of the 17th century. There were others, but none so widespread or successful in producing prototypes for what would eventually become the fully developed villa forms and plans of the 18th century.

Route 1: from single range to nominal double pile

The distinguishing characteristic of a compact or villa plan was the doubling (or tripling) of room ranges, in order to compress the habitable spaces into a smaller overall footprint. The most primitive form of doubling comprised no more than the thickening of the hall range; the parlour and service ranges, or wings, remained single span, usually limited by cost and availability of structural timbers to about 20 feet. **Fig. 2** shows this evolution in three H-plan houses: **(a)** an unidentified plan from John Thorpe's Book of Drawings; **(b)** Yotes Court, Kent; and **(c)** Denham Place, Buckinghamshire.[5]

In the John Thorpe plan the great and back stairs are sited at the junctures of the long hall range and the shorter side wings. At Yotes, the back stair occupies a similar position, but the great stair now moves to a compartment behind the hall, where the range has been doubled. This thickening is scarcely part of the main house: the rear range of Yotes is covered, not with the modish hipped roof visible on the other three sides, but with three old-fashioned gables.[6] Denham Place is a larger house of similar proportions to Yotes Court, and here

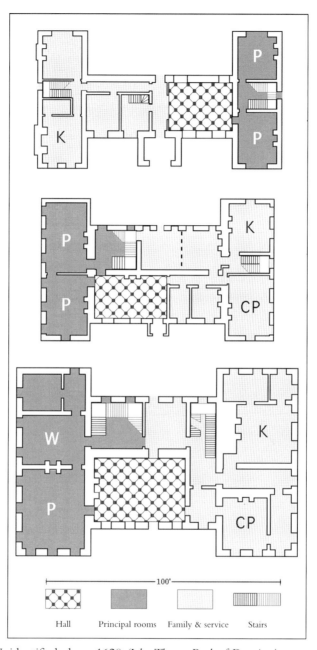

Fig. 2(a): Unidentified plan, *c*.1620 *(John Thorpe Book of Drawings)*.

Fig. 2(b): Yotes Court, Kent, 1656-8, for James Master. Architect: attrib. 'Mr Vezy'.

Fig. 2(c): Denham Place, Buckinghamshire, 1688-91, for Sir Roger Hill. Architect unknown; mason-contractor, William Stanton.

93

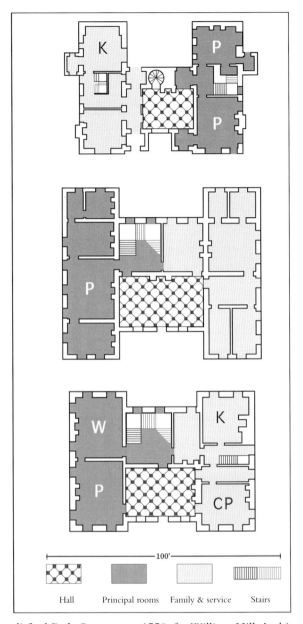

Fig. 3(a): Poundisford Park, Somerset, c.1550, for William Hill. Architect unknown.

Fig. 3(b): West Woodhay, Berkshire, 1634-6, for Sir Benjamin Rudyard. Architect unknown.

Fig. 3(c): Honington Hall, Warwickshire, c.1675-82, for Henry Parker. Architect unknown.

both great and back stairs are placed in the rear thickening of the hall range. Very similar arrangements exist, for example, at Tyttenhanger, Hertfordshire, (*c*.1655) (see pp. 216-22) and Highnam Court, Gloucestershire, probably built a few years later.

The very wide, shallow ground plans of this group resulted from retaining an offset hall, with the central entrance leading into one end of it (pragmatically modified in the case of Denham, where the hall is edging towards a central position). Such houses inherited the essentially spread form of the earlier buildings from which they were derived. A truly compact house required a centralised hall, so that the wings could be brought as close as possible together. **Fig. 3(a)** shows Poundisford Park, Somerset, typical of a smaller 16th-century house where a central hall required an offset front door, to comply with the English habit of entering through the screens passage at the low end. This undesirable asymmetry was routinely disguised by architectural devices such as matching the porch to the hall bay, and placing the front door on its inner flank. John Thorpe and John Smythson even produced plans with double entries and screens in the early 17th century; executed examples of this bizarre idea included Raynham Hall, Norfolk (1622-35).

By the mid 17th century, however, the requirement for classical regularity would not permit such architectural fudging; the entrance and hall would both need to be centralised. West Woodhay, Berkshire **Fig. 3(b)** and Honington Hall, Warwickshire **Fig. 3(c)**, the 17th-century counterparts of Poundisford, show this development.[7] A central door into a central hall would not have been an easy innovation to adopt. The arrangement exposed the whole of the hall directly to the exterior and did away with the entrenched idea of a high and low end.[8] There is just one sign that the old processional route from front door to great stair had not been entirely forgotten: at both West Woodhay and Honington, as at Yotes and Denham, the great stair still occupied the parlour end of the doubled hall range. Despite the formal symmetry of entrance and hall, the wings still observed their distinct and segregated functions, including, at this stage, the kitchen still being positioned in the service wing.

It is a moot point as to whether we would choose to describe these little H-plan houses as country villas (although there is no reason why not), but no-one can deny Chevening, Kent, that

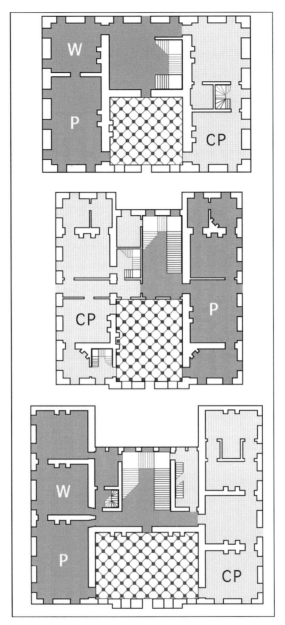

Fig. 4(a): Chevening, Kent, before1630, for Lord Dacre. Architect unknown; attrib. Inigo Jones.

Fig. 4(b): Escot, Devon, 1680-8, for Sir Walter Yonge. Architect unknown; attrib. Robert Hooke.

Fig. 4(c): Uppark, West Sussex, 1690-5, for Ford Grey, 3rd Lord Grey of Warke, later Earl of Tankerville. Architect unknown.

appellation. The original plan **Fig. 4(a)** has long been misunderstood because its only known representation, in an estate plan of 1679, is shown in inverse relationship to the accompanying elevation.[9] Inverting that plan to its proper orientation gives a conventional room arrangement with the hall at the centre front, the staircase hall behind, the great dining room to one side, with its withdrawing room beyond, and the little parlour to the other side, with a chamber behind it, over the kitchen in the basement. The originality of the plan lies mainly in the extreme compaction of the footprint to a rectangular block, with no trace of projecting wings. Chevening shows how it was possible for an essentially conservative plan to exist within an apparently new overall form. Escot, Devon **Fig. 4(b)/Pl. 1**, if indeed it was built as *Vitruvius Britannicus* shows it, is another example.[10] The footprint is deep to a fault, the elevation self-consciously fashionable; yet here is the usual arrangement of great hall with stair behind, parlour wing to one side, family wing to the other.

By the end of the 17th century, houses of this plan were commonplace. Most were modest in scale with three-bay halls being typical; but Uppark, Sussex **Fig. 4(c)** had a most extravagant five-bay, double-height hall, almost a throwback to the glory days of courtier houses; its builder, Lord Grey of Warke and later the turncoat Earl of Tankerville, had been a prominent supporter of the Duke of Monmouth. Its parlour enfilade stretched backwards in an old-fashioned single-pile range to include a state bedchamber beyond the great parlour and withdrawing room. Stanford Hall, Leicestershire, built by William Smith in 1697 for Sir Roger Cave, is almost identical in plan.

Chevening, Escot and Uppark all show a radical change in storey planning which was more or less complete by the end of the century. Whereas Elizabethan and Jacobean houses sat on the ground, perhaps with some cellars, in the post-Restoration period almost all were being built with raised ground floors above a half-sunk basement. Many service rooms could now be banished to this basement, and the kitchen usually went into a separate building: it was only rarely located in the basement, as the typical ten-foot height was scarcely enough. The 'high' side of the house now housed the important entertaining rooms and the 'low' side was for family rather than public use.

The examples discussed so far demonstrate how English owners and architects contrived to develop a compact house plan by little more than a gradual compression and rationalisation of layouts that had been in place for centuries. A template for the villa form had been created by stealth, through evolution rather than revolution, adhering loyally to entrenched lifestyles and preferences. Technically, all these houses were of double-pile construction, but only in name, not in function; all retained the orthogonal relationship between the two principal fronts; and no significant room occupied the rear range, or had its major outlook to the rear: all characteristics which are decisive for this type.

Route 2: from small courtyard to true triple and double pile

A second type of compact plan evolved from the 16th- and early-17th-century small courtyard house. Unlike the large spread quadrangles of a Burghley House or Kirby Hall, where the court was a major open space overlooked by many important rooms, in these smaller houses the courtyard was often little more than a large light well or inner yard.

An unidentified plan by John Thorpe **Fig. 5(a)** shows that, although the footprint of these houses looked very different from their H- and half-H-plan equivalents, the distribution of internal space was very similar.[11] However, the compaction process already under way forced some of the rooms associated with the parlour wing around onto the rear range of the courtyard. It was thus but a short step to losing the courtyard altogether, leaving a compact block of triple-pile form, in which the central range was allocated to the stairs, and the habitable rooms lined up to the front and rear. Thorpe Hall, Northamptonshire **Fig. 5(b)**, illustrates the effect. Where there would once have been a small open court was now no more than the extension of the screens passage to a rear door. The entry at Thorpe was through a screens passage into the offset hall, and thence to the great stair and great parlour. To the other side of the screens passage were service rooms, perhaps even the old buttery and pantry. Above, there was a great chamber and its suite. So far, so traditional: but with no long wing to accommodate them, the great parlour and its attendant rooms had nowhere to stretch out except across the rear elevation. The outside of the house (see p. 119) told a different story,

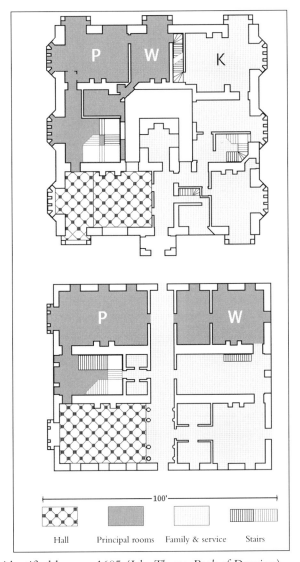

Fig. 5(a): Unidentified house *c*.1605 (*John Thorpe, Book of Drawings*).

Fig. 5(b): Thorpe Hall, Peterborough, 1653-6, for Chief Justice St John. Builder: Peter Mills.

of course: its great bay windows, lighting only the ends of the hall and parlour, implied that the parlour front was to be read, in the old style, as being at right angles to the entrance front.

Melton Constable, Norfolk **Fig. 6(a)**, made no such claim to a right-angled relationship between hall and parlour wings; it was a chunky sandwich of two opposite-facing room ranges with the stairs

99

and chapel as the filling. As at Thorpe Hall, the screens passage extended through the building to a central rear door; but the great stair here opened out from that passage. One simply bypassed the offset great hall to reach it; the central axis now took precedence over the orthogonal relationship. Despite this show of centrality, Melton was as polarised as Thorpe, with the great hall, great stair and great parlour all lying to one side of that axis.

Finally in this sequence of examples is a slimmer and more elegant sandwich, Eltham Lodge, Kent **Fig. 6(b)**. Again, the main axis passed through an internal lobby containing the great and back stairs. The

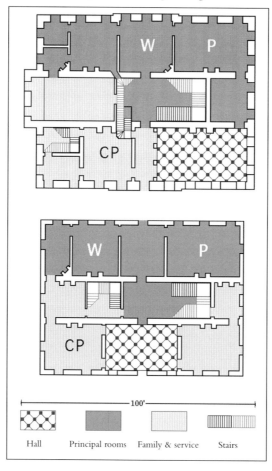

Fig. 6(a): Melton Constable, Norfolk, 1664-70, for Sir Jacob Ashley. Architect unknown.

Fig. 6(b): Eltham Lodge, Kent, 1664, for Sir John Shaw. Architect: Hugh May.

significant change here was that the hall itself had been drawn, by the dictates of symmetry, to the centre of the front range, although the great parlour remained resolutely to the 'high' end of the rear one; and Eltham, perhaps unsurprisingly given that its architect Hugh May was responsible for the state rooms at Windsor Castle, had an old-fashioned great chamber on the first floor.

This particular line of development led towards a true house of two or three ranges, as Roger North described it, and was still largely an evolution of a native English form; but it did cross an important barrier.[12] Placing the great parlour and its suite of rooms along the rear, rather than the side of the building, undermined the long held tenet of polarised interior planning. It also presented new problems. If the preferred south was chosen for the garden-facing parlour range, the entrance front would inevitably face north, or vice versa. Alternatively, if east and west were chosen for the main fronts, south would be allocated to an unimportant side elevation. Whereas the orthogonal principle of two adjacent show fronts had allowed for untidy or unsightly offices to be hidden away behind the 'low' sides, parallel ranges did not; such buildings would be visible and would have to be incorporated into the overall composition, at considerable extra expense: leading, in due course, to the 18th-century norm of main block with office wings. The apparent willingness of owners to overcome such significant difficulties perhaps indicates how far the demands of form had begun to overtake considerations of function.

The deep triple-pile plans from the middle of the 17th century had another major drawback: the siting of the great stair in a constrained, poorly-lit central range. It might be argued that, at a period when the principal rooms were gravitating to the hall storey, this was a bearable loss. However, there was no arguing with an Englishman's love affair with his great stair, which remained, like the hall, a status symbol, to be built broad and easy, and decorated lavishly. Two glorious attempts to create a truly great stair in a central range were made by Wren at Tring Manor, Hertfordshire (see p. 227), and Hawksmoor at Easton Neston, Northamptonshire, but they were both exceptions to the rule.

An alternative solution was to assign the great stair its own compartment on the front range, next to the hall; the central range then became dispensable, and could disappear as the small courtyard had done before it. The first Cliveden, Buckinghamshire, occupying a spectacular site above the Thames **Fig. 7(a)**, was a true double pile with a significant enfilade of rear rooms overlooking the river below; but the Duke of Buckingham's great stair next to the offset hall

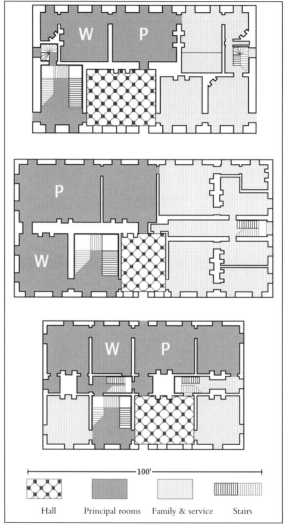

Fig. 7(a): Cliveden, Bucks, *c.*1676–8, for George Villiers, 2nd Duke of Buckingham. Architect: William Winde.

Fig. 7(b): Unidentified house, possibly related to Cliveden, 1660s. Architect: Christopher Wren.

Fig. 7(c): Longnor Hall, Salop, *c.*1665–70, for Sir Richard Corbett. Architect unknown.

retained its traditional grandeur as an introduction to what must have been a magnificent suite above. We can perhaps guess at the upper storeys by taking as a reference an annotated Wren plan **Fig. 7(b)** which is tantalisingly similar to the executed Cliveden, although Wren proposed a vestibule and large anteroom rather than a great hall.[13] The double-pile formula with stairs on the front range also appeared in much simpler houses, such as Longnor Hall, Shropshire **Fig. 7(c)**;[12] it was also employed in much larger houses, such as Belton House, Lincolnshire, and Burley-on-the-Hill, Rutland.

Route 3: from Palladio to the English cruciform

The third main type of compact plan evolved from the villa designs of Palladio, or more specifically the idealised versions published in the second of his *Four Books of Architecture* in 1570. Although there was no English translation of the text until 1715, the plates were self-explanatory, even for those with no Italian. Palladio's villas usually comprised a relatively small central block with the spreading wings and outbuildings of a working farm. This main block offered a promising new model for the English house-builder seeking inspiration for the compact house. Palladio's formula was geometric, almost always based on a large hall or *sala*, often rising into the attics, occupying the centre of the block, with a recessed portico or loggia in the front, rear or both.[15] The main reception rooms were distributed on either side of this *sala*/loggia core, and rigorous mirror symmetry dictated that any asymmetrical features, such as service stairs, should be hidden away in enclosed compartments.

The earliest attempts at English Palladian planning focused on the idea of the single room or *sala* running from front to rear of the building, re-interpreting it as a through hall, with or without a loggia to front or rear. Robert Smythson did it at Hardwick, started in 1590; his unexecuted plan, rigidly Palladian in its symmetry, gave way in execution to a much more conventional layout, most notably creating space for a monumental great stair.[16] A fundamental flaw in most Palladian villa plans, from the English point of view, was the lack of provision for a prominent great stair. Even arch-Palladian Inigo Jones had to sacrifice purism for common sense when he designed just one great spiral stair for the Queen's House (see plan p. 158).

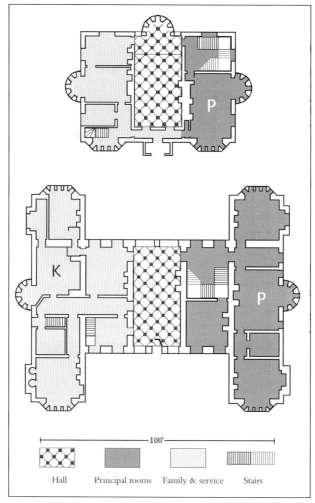

Fig. 8(a): Nottingham House, Kensington, after 1605, for Sir George Coppin. Architect: John Thorpe.

Fig. 8(b): Somerhill, Kent, 1610-13, for Lord Clanricarde. Architect: John Thorpe.

John Thorpe produced several through–hall plans, at least two of which were executed. Nottingham House, Middlesex **Fig. 8(a)** was a compact suburban villa, and the ghost of its plan still remains at the core of Kensington Palace.[17] Somerhill, Kent **Fig. 8(b)**, was an enlarged version of Nottingham House, with additional side ranges.[18] Another very similar design was Charlton House, Kent, 1607 (see pl. 4). Apart from the transverse hall, these Jacobean houses were conventionally planned, with the familiar polarised distribution of space and

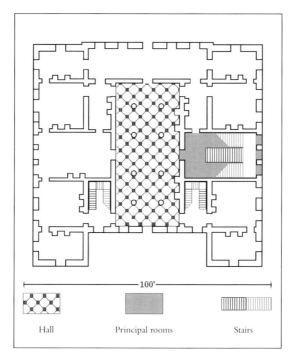

Fig. 9: Gunnersbury House, Middlesex, *c*.1658-63, for Sir John Maynard.
Architect: John Webb.

little attempt at mirror symmetry. It was just a nod to Palladianism. In a practical sense, the long transverse hall entered on axis was too uncomfortable, the dais end too exposed, the route through to the stairs and principal rooms too obscure, for English habits and taste. The idea was doomed from the start, the last serious attempt being made at the end of the 1650s by John Webb at Gunnersbury House, Middlesex **Fig. 9**. Webb strictly observed the Palladian form of *sala* and loggia on the *piano nobile*, with the hall and garden hall in the rustic below. He dealt with the great stair by placing it at the centre of one side, at right angles to the central axis; opposite was a corresponding great space, with no stair.[19] It is impossible to guess at room uses, or to identify specific functional zones. This very academic planning exercise was for a suburban rather than a country villa, and would not have passed muster in a permanent home.

Meanwhile, other avenues were being pursued towards the holy grail of rational, symmetrical plans in the spirit, if not to the letter, of Palladianism. One of these was to reinterpret the Palladian idea of

105

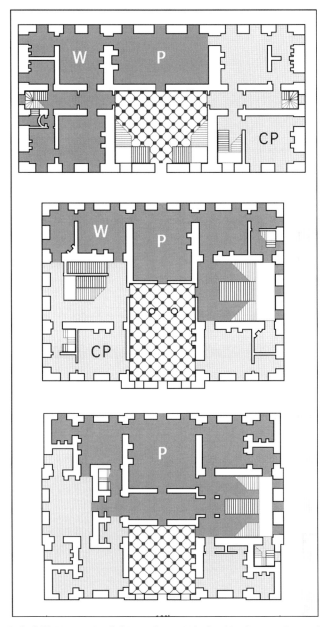

Fig. 10(a): Coleshill House, Berkshire, after 1649, for Sir George Pratt. Architect: Roger Pratt.

Fig. 10(b): Kingston House (Kingston Lacy), Dorset, 1663-5, for Sir Ralph Bankes. Architect: Roger Pratt.

Fig. 10(c): The Grange (Grange Park), Hampshire, c.1670, for Sir Robert Henley. Architect: William Samwell.

loggia and *sala* as two internal rooms, hall and great parlour, back to back. This was the kind of classical planning the French adopted in their *chateaux* and *hotels*, with the *vestibule* to the front and *salle* or *salon* behind, and it seemed to work very well on the continent.

It was this interpretation that Roger Pratt seized on in designing Coleshill, Berkshire **Fig. 10(a)**, started in 1649.[20] The precedent set by Coleshill in English house planning lay principally in setting the great parlour immediately behind the hall, and on axis with it. This arrangement became so routine in the 18th century that it is difficult for us today to understand how outrageous it might have appeared in the middle of the 17th century. The customary progression through the hall to the great parlour in the adjacent range had required at least one change of direction, and it was never possible to see the whole of each space from the other. The senses of privacy, anticipation and reserve were all lost when the great parlour was placed on direct axis with the hall. Once the great central doors between the two spaces were thrown open, all was revealed; everything that went on in one room could be seen from the other. This was not at all the English way, and must have come as quite a shock to received practice.

The traditional polarity of the English house now became less clear. The original uses of the Coleshill rooms are not known, but the back stair and common parlour are easily identifiable, and in the late 17th century the room opposite the common parlour, above the kitchen, was used as a nursery, so it is possible that the house was always occupied in a more polarised way than its plan would suggest. The great double stair filling the hall was a magnificent interpretation of the Palladian external stair, but it cannot have been successful; flights starting at the front door were much too exposed to visitor traffic.

In the 1660s, Pratt tried again to design English country villas according to Palladian principles, and it is possible that he had seen in Webb's Gunnersbury a solution to his own problems with the great stair. His Kingston Hall, Dorset **Fig. 10(b)**, now known as Kingston Lacy and much altered, involved a deep plan with the hall and great parlour running the depth of the house and the great stairs to the side, as at Gunnersbury. Pratt, determined to pursue his ideal of mirror symmetry, placed the great back stair in a matching and wasteful compartment on the opposite side. William Samwell did better at The Grange, Hampshire **Fig. 10(c)**, now Grange Park, ruinous and almost completely obliterated with overbuilding: coming ten years after Pratt's Kingston, it was almost its spatial twin, although Samwell, by far the more ingenious and pragmatic architect, did not attempt a literal reflection of great and back stairs as Pratt had done

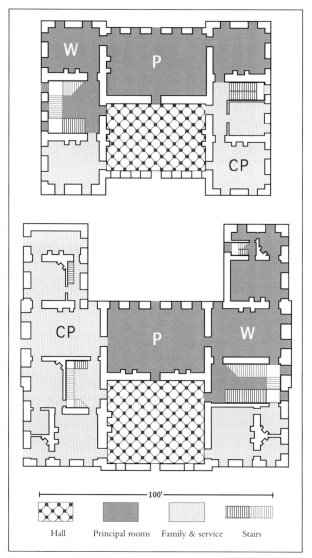

Fig. 11(a): Umberslade Hall, Warwickshire, c. 1695-1700, for Andrew Archer. Builder: Francis Smith.

Fig. 11(b): Stoke Edith Park, Herefordshire, from 1697, for Paul Foley. Architect: attrib. Paul Foley.

at Kingston. He made an even more curious and economical plan at Eaton Hall, Cheshire, with two offset stairs of only modest size, and no fewer than six ground-floor apartments.[21]

None of these early 'English Palladian' plans was entirely successful, but their authors must be credited with establishing a planning principle which was to become an extremely important, indeed a predominant form for the next century: the cruciform plan, where the great hall and great parlour formed a continuous block from front to rear, flanked by stairs on either side. The remainder of the house resolved itself more or less simply into four groups of smaller rooms, or apartments occupying the corners of the building, where natural light was maximised. Crossed axes appear in many of Palladio's villa plans: for example, Villas Pisani, Foscari and Barbaro each had a cruciform *sala*, and at Villa Ragona the four principal rooms formed a cross centred on the stairs.[22] There are many other examples. It is this distinctive cross-axial feature, as well as the overall symmetry of the villas, that seemed to intrigue the English.

Once established, this cruciform idea went from strength to strength. It did not long sustain the very deep and difficult footprint of Pratt's and Samwell's work, and proved adaptable to more familiar forms, including the stubby H-plan at Umberslade Hall, Warwickshire **Fig. 11(a)**), and the half-H plan at Stoke Edith, Herefordshire **Fig. 11(b)**). It turns up in the most unexpected places – for example, at the original villa-like house of 1697 that remains today at the core of Shugborough, Staffordshire, or even in the central core of Vanbrugh's great baroque Castle Howard, Yorkshire, designed in 1699.

Conclusion

The three types of historical planning developments described in this chapter, which ran chronologically in parallel, not in sequence, were a direct outcome of the varied social and cultural choices made by owners, who represented every class of landowner, from gentlemen, knights and baronets up through the peerage to dukes. These men expressed their preferences and prejudices by the way they and their families chose to live. Many continued building to traditional plans, but simply wrapped them in modern elevations, or incorporated up-to-date interior features and décor to impress their peers. Others were bold enough to embrace the new and the foreign in architectural form and function, and adopt the different ways of living this implied.

It was suggested at the beginning of this paper that these developments were the forerunners of compact, villa-type plans which would become commonplace in the 18th century, and indeed these patterns can be traced. The traditional orthogonal approach, with the staircase in a thickened hall range but no important rooms facing to the rear, survived as a popular compact plan into the early decades of the new century. It can be found at houses of every architectural style, both new and remodelled, including Kings Weston, Gloucestershire (1710-19); Chettle House, Dorset (*c*.1715); Hilton Hall, Staffordshire (1717); Chicheley Hall, Buckinghamshire (1720-1); Crowcombe Court, Somerset (1723-39); Swynnerton Hall, Staffordshire (1725-9); Mawley Hall, Shropshire (1730); and, perhaps surprisingly, even Colen Campbell's Palladian villa design at Stourhead, Wiltshire (1720-4).

The triple-pile plan with stairs in the central range was less frequently adopted, but it can be seen at Cottesbrooke Hall, Northamptonshire (1702-11); Trewithen House, Cornwall (*c*.1715); and Compton Place, Sussex (1726-9), another Campbell house; while the double pile with stairs in a compartment on the front range was chosen for Antony House, Cornwall (*c*. 1720), and Hursley Park, Hampshire (1721-4).

A group of interesting and sophisticated hybrids evolved around the turn of the century, combining elements of both orthogonal and cross-axial planning: houses such as Swallowfield Park, Berkshire (1689-90); Newby Hall, Yorkshire (1690); the pre-Adam Kedleston Hall, Derbyshire (*c*.1700); Norton House, Gloucestershire, known as Burnt Norton (*c*.1716); Buntingsdale Hall, Shropshire (1719-21); Ditchley Park, Oxfordshire (1720-4); and Clandon Park, Surrey (1730-3).

All these plan types, were eventually lost to the sovereignty of the cruciform and related axial forms, which gained rapidly in popularity with the neo-Palladian movement from about 1715 and remained enduringly popular – if, by then, somewhat aesthetically and practically exhausted – right into the middle of the 18th century.

6

Gardens and Courtyards of the Seventeenth-Century Villa and Smaller House

Sally Jeffery

In 1669 John Aubrey sat down with his watercolours and a small book of paper, and made some sketches of his house and garden at Easton Piercy in Wiltshire, as he would have liked them to be. His title page was decorated with a cartouche which featured the word villa prominently, surrounded by quotes from Ovid and Virgil.[1] It was really a very modest house, symmetrical and well-proportioned perhaps, but not appearing especially Italian. However, the garden he proposed did have features often associated with Italy. It was terraced into four principal sections, with pools, statues, fountains, cypress trees, regular planting and enclosing walls. It is not known whether Aubrey's house and garden were ever created in the form he showed, but the sketches illustrate the powerful appeal of Italy and the classical world, and the idea of the villa.

It also illustrates the fact that while Italy was often in the mind of those designing gardens, 'Italian' could mean a variety of things. Places as different as Easton Piercy and the garden of Wilton House in the same county were both considered by Aubrey to be 'of the Italian mode'.[2] Few people, however, attempted to create anything like the most famous Italian gardens since they required not only detailed knowledge and resources, but also if possible a large hillside site. John Evelyn, who had spent a number of years in Italy, designed some of the most notable examples. At Albury Park in Surrey in 1667-70 there were extensive terraces and ramps echoing those of the Villa d'Este at Tivoli, and a tunnel through a hill was intended to evoke the Posillipo near Naples, reputed to have been cut by Virgil's own magic.

The settings for villas in the Veneto were usually different from the large and elaborate layouts near Rome and Florence. Palladio recommended rising ground for a site if this were possible,[3] but the Venetian *terra firma* was predominantly flat, or only gently undulating. Views out were emphasised by spacious platforms or terraces with porticoes and large flights of steps, as well as the fact that the most important rooms were on the *piano nobile*.[4] The houses were usually at the centre of a productive estate, so the gardens were small and were contained within the wings or courtyards immediately surrounding the house. Simple grass plats and paths were arranged in strict geometric patterns, and would have been set with terracotta pots of citrus trees, and other prized specimens. Avenues of trees were used to announce the grand approach road to the centre of the villa, or to extend the axis beyond it.

When Inigo Jones visited Italy, we know that he looked in detail at the work of Andrea Palladio in the Veneto. When he returned he was one of the most knowledgeable designers of his generation. Stoke Park, at Stoke Bruerne in Northamptonshire, built for Sir Francis Crane *c.*1630, apparently had a garden inspired by Palladian models. Bridges, in his *History of Northamptonshire*, discussing the building, stated that Crane 'brought the design from Italy and in the execution of it received the assistance of Inigo Jones. It consists of a body and two wings'.[5] It was set on rising ground and faced south-east towards the garden. There were two terraces, both of which survive. On the upper level, within the colonnaded area in front of the main house and pavilions, the terrace was simply grassed and divided symmetrically by paths.[6] From this vantage point the views out were evidently very important, for both pavilions have balustraded porches revealing a broad sweep of landscape. The lower terrace was larger. Almost nothing is known about its original arrangement, except that there were steps down to it from the centre of the upper terrace. Early-18th-century views by Peter Tillemans show espaliered trees or climbing plants growing against the retaining wall, ornamented with niches, and walls on the other three sides.[7] In the rusticated basement of each pavilion, giving onto the lower terrace, was a doorway, which led (at least in the one which survives) into a vaulted semi-basement

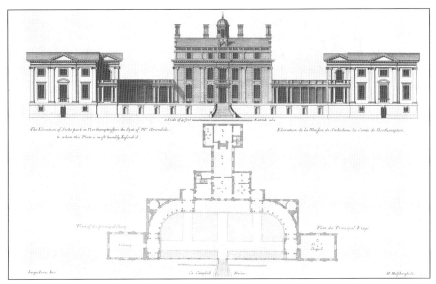

Plan and elevation of Stoke Park, Stoke Bruerne, Northamptonshire, with grassed upper terrace crossed by paths, and retaining wall to the lower terrace. From Colen Campbell, *Vitruvius Britannicus*, vol. 3, (1725) (*British Library, 649.b.5 vol. 3*).

chamber with three wide niches. This might well have been arranged as a summer house, a bath-house or a kind of grotto, although there is no visible water supply now. There is still a straight avenue of trees leading to what was the back of the house, but there was also an avenue on the garden side leading up to the centre of the lower terrace, and thus to the main door.[8] It is unclear whether this was for use or purely for show, but it was an essential part of this rigidly axial design.

This was an exceptional design. If Jones was responsible for the house, in part at least, as seems very possible, it is likely that the setting can also be attributed to him in its main lines. It may also be that Crane, who had particular business contacts with Genoa, brought ideas for the garden design from Italy as well as that of the house.[9]

John Webb made reference to the villa form at Gunnersbury House, Middlesex (*c.*1656-63) and at Amesbury House, Wiltshire (*c.*1660), but apparently referred only fleetingly to any sort of Palladian setting. It is difficult in both cases to gain any accurate idea of what the gardens were like because the surviving evidence dates from the 18th century. For Gunnersbury, Daniel Defoe, writing in 1742, mentioned the 'noble Terrace, the whole Width of the Garden, from whence you have a fine Prospect of the neighbouring Country, and on which you may walk dry after the greatest Rains', but thought the gardens were 'laid out too plain, having the Walls in View on every side',[10] while John Rocque's plan of the cities of London and Westminster of 1744-6 shows some simple square plats, surrounded by orchards and vegetable gardens, a pair of short canals, and an avenue leading towards Gunnersbury Lane. An engraving of 1761[11] (which may be a composite view and not entirely accurate)[12] shows a scalloped wall of the kind used by Palladio at the Villa Badoer, Fratta Polesine.

Amesbury's original setting is also difficult to reconstruct, but it too certainly had an enclosed entrance courtyard and a range of walled gardens behind, with one arranged on the central axis. The arrangement shown on Henry Flitcroft's survey plan of 1726[13] gives some idea of the scheme designed by Webb, but may include some subsequent changes. Almost nothing of this remains, except the impressive pair of gate piers, niched on both sides, which once pre-sumably guarded the entrance courtyard. They are a particularly grand example of a type which was becoming fashionable in England in the mid 1650s, and which Webb also used on a reduced scale at Gunnersbury.

Gardens on smaller sites continued to draw on the tradition of a series of walled enclosures, often somewhat irregular, and created partly for pleasure, but more for production. These were particularly in favour during the Commonwealth when the concepts of good husbandry and productive gardens were much admired and discussed. However, the influence of Europe continued to be felt. Gardens were often arranged axially, and divided into regular sections by walls and hedges. The planning of the most accomplished gardens, especially those designed by architects as part of an overall scheme, increasing-ly exhibited a high degree of regularity and symmetry.

Such regularity in smaller gardens was already being demonstrat-ed early in the century. A particularly good example appeared in William Lawson's book, *A New Orchard and Garden*, of 1618.[14] He shows a sequence of six regular square areas divided by paths, arranged in pairs to form a rectangle. Nearest the house are what could be two grassed gardens, with espaliered trees and topiary fig-ures. Below them are an orchard and knot garden, and below them two kitchen gardens. The whole is fenced, with fruit trees against the boundaries, and a river separating the house from the garden and also

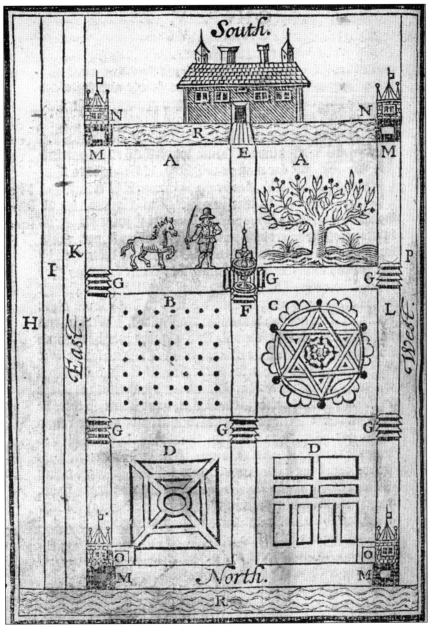

Plan of a garden as recommended by William Lawson, with six squares containing topiary, espaliers, fruit trees, knots and kitchen gardens, separated by walks, with a mount at each corner overlooking running water. From William Lawson, *A New Orchard and Garden* (1618) (*British Library, B620[5]*).

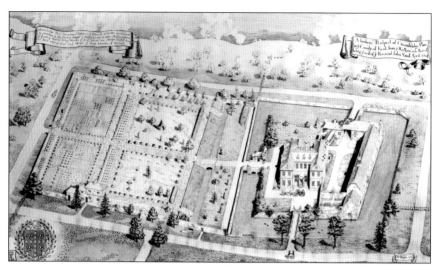

A Birdseye Prospect of Groombridge Place in ye County of Kent. A drawing by Charles Eamer Kempe of 1884 showing the house in its moat, and the garden rising to the north (Country Life *Picture Library*).

running along at its foot. Overlooking it there are four mounts, one at each corner. They are planted with fruit trees, and provide shelter for fishing, or for making music. Lawson says 'you might sit in your Mount, and angle a peckled Trout, sleighty Eel, or some other dainty Fish'. This is an excellent example of a garden of modest size and careful arrangement. Many gardens of the early part of the century were nowhere near as regular and well organised as this, but the idea took hold and was regarded as something of an ideal.

A wonderful survival of such an arrangement is Groombridge Place, Kent, which retains its form although the planting has been much altered. A new house was built between 1652 and 1674, within an old moat in the same position as the former house. Perhaps a garden already existed, but the present layout must be contemporary with the house. The owner's name was Philip Packer, a good friend of John Evelyn since his student days. In 1674, when Evelyn visited, he saw the new house 'built within a moate & in a woody valy'. He was critical of what Packer had done, commenting that 'a far better situation had been on the south of the wood, on a graceful ascent'.[15] In fact, the garden faces north.

A plan drawn by Charles Eamer Kempe in 1884 shows a series of gardens lying to the north side of the moated house, rising up the hill, creating a gently terraced effect with a central path aligned on the centre of the side of the house. There is a spacious entrance courtyard at the front, with substantial gates and piers. A short canal lies parallel to the north side of house. A garden house or pavilion (now enlarged) was built on the west wall, aligned to a narrow bowling alley running east-west, but the rectangular divisions arranged in pairs recall Lawson's plan. The whole is walled, with access from the house or from gates at the top. An estate plan of the mid 18th century[16] shows much the same arrangement, with orchards to the north and west beyond the walls, and an avenue leading from the chapel towards the house.

Thus, if a house was rebuilt on an old site, as at Groombridge, efforts would be made to relate the garden to it. The resulting designs varied, according to the site and also to the importance attached by the owner and his designer (if he had one) to regularity. A garden designed at the same time as a new house would generally be

Balls Park, Hertfordshire as shown by Sir Henry Chauncy in *The Historical Antiquities of Hertfordshire* (1700), dominating its sloping site, with entrance court to the north and gardens on the east and south. A double avenue of trees leads to the main gate, with further avenues in the park (*British Library, L50.8*).

117

arranged axially to complement it and provide a regular setting, with walled enclosures front and back, and often to the sides as well. Thought would also be given to selecting a site on raised ground to give a prospect, and building with the main gardens to the south to benefit from the sun. A south-east aspect was considered particularly beneficial.[17] Balls Park in Hertfordshire, built *c.*1638-40 for Sir John Harrison, a wealthy tax farmer and supporter of the royalist cause, provides an example of a house and garden designed together in a symmetrical arrangement, surrounded by walls with a central entrance and corner pavilions. The house was approached from the north through a grassed walled courtyard separated from the stable and service area on one side and the pleasure garden on the other, which were walled and were entered through their own subsidiary gates. Behind were regularly planted orchards, also in their own walled enclosure. The productive areas were therefore incorporated into the overall layout as in Lawson's plan, but kept separate according to use.

Another example of a house and garden designed as one, a little later in date than Balls Park, is Thorpe Hall, near Peterborough, this time for a parliamentarian, Oliver St John, Chief Justice to Oliver Cromwell. It was built in 1654-6, to the designs of the London surveyor, Peter Mills, and is one of the most useful illustrations to survive. The main lines of the original arrangement survive.[18] There are heavy stone walls round the perimeter of the rectangular site. The house sits exactly in the centre, with entrance court to the north, gardens to east and south, and stables to the west, and the main axes marked out by paths and gates. The main north-south axis is marked by two sets of imposing gate piers in the walls. The entrance court, perhaps grassed originally as at Balls Park, is approached by the most elaborate of these, with seated niches on the outside, and niches occupied by elaborately decorated half-columns on the inside. They are topped by eagles, and decorated with lions' heads, and a pair of crouching lions. In the centre of the south wall, the piers reflect those of the entrance but without the crouching lions. The piers on the east and west walls are simpler, without niches or lions' heads and are echoed in design by the corner posts of the walls. The main garden lies to the east of the house, divided by a path down its centre, and with a terrace overlooking it. At the back on the south and west are

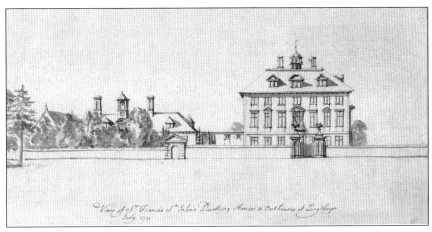

A sketch of Thorpe Hall from the south in 1721 by Peter Tillemans, with the cupola, great gate piers and gate to garden (*British Library, Add. MS 32467 f.154*).

further gardens, perhaps orchards originally, separated by hedges. 17th-century houses often had cupolas for viewing, but in any case, it was possible to look out from the upper windows and enjoy the view. Thorpe Hall, though not on rising ground, originally had a cupola[19] (now gone) but the gardens could be viewed from any of the windows of the house, and the landscape beyond the walls could be seen from the upper storeys. In addition, the house was built on a raised basement which extended to a viewing terrace on the east, overlooking the main garden. Many gate piers of this period were built with outward-facing niched seats so that the traveller could pause by the entrance and view the way he had come. The idea of viewing the surrounding scenery was taken a step further at Thorpe Hall, with not only outward-facing niches in the front and back gate piers, but also regularly placed pairs of niches along the outside of the walls.

The houses of Sir Roger Pratt and Hugh May provide good examples of the continuation of these ideas into the post-Restoration period. Pratt's most famous house is Coleshill, Oxfordshire (formerly Berkshire), completed *c*.1662 with earlier advice from Inigo Jones. The evolution of its design is complex, and there is space here for only the briefest summary. What is of particular interest, however, is that apparently Sir George Pratt had already started to build his new house when his cousin Roger went down from London, accompanied by Inigo Jones, and decided that the building should be abandoned and started again on a better site. Thus we have two London architects, one very distinguished and one at the beginning of his career, advising on the drastic and expensive step of abandoning a building already begun and starting all over again.

The story is told in the Commonplace Book written in the 1740s by Sir Mark Pleydell, based principally on the account of an old joiner, John Buffin, who had worked on the house and had died many years before.[20] The detail may not be completely reliable, but his vivid image of the individuals involved and their advice to change the site is probably correct. He said that the old house stood 'in ye orchard fronting ye street'. There was a fire, after which a new house was started, perhaps *c.*1650. We do not know where Sir George initially began to build his new house, but it is likely to have been close by, and probably also fronting the village street. It is described as being 'in ye present cucumber garden, and raised one storey, when Pratt and Jones arriving caused it to be pulled down and rebuilt where it now stands'. The new house was finally built a little way away from the village street, facing north-east and dominating a south-west-facing hillside with good views. It survived until a fire in 1952.

In his writings on 'Scituation', Pratt, following Palladio, recommended ground gently rising towards a house, in order to achieve 'a most pleasant prospect of the country round about'. He recommended an avenue (of limes, for preference) leading to the house and equal to its width.[21] When he and Jones were thinking about the site of the new house at Coleshill, we know that they had an old productive garden to consider, although we know very little about its form. A house facing onto the village street would have had more restricted views. They chose a situation on higher ground with a good prospect from both terrace and cupola, and to which an impressive approach avenue of trees could be planted. They must also have been concerned to make the courtyards and gardens as regular as possible to provide a suitable setting for the new house. Pratt had spent a considerable time in Italy and was well aware of the importance of regularity and symmetry. The same applied to Jones, and they would doubtless easily have agreed on the new site.

What was achieved can be seen in a detailed survey of the Coleshill estate by William Brudenell in 1666, which luckily sur-

A Platt of the Mannor of Coulsill, drawn in 1666 by William Brudenell (*Berkshire Record Office*).

vives.[22] There were many changes in the gardens during the 18th century, followed by the almost complete removal of the walls from *c.*1780. This is well documented, so an attempt at reconstructing the original mid-17th-century setting of the house in further detail is possible.

It is important to note that the main road which now runs through Coleshill and borders the present gardens was not in existence when Brudenell made his survey, but was constructed later to by-pass the old village street and allow the gardens to be much enlarged. By overlaying Brudenell's plan on a modern map we can see that his broad lines may be relied upon, and the position of the old road, which still exists, becomes clear.

In about 1687 Celia Fiennes visited Coleshill and wrote:

> By Farington is a fine house of Sir George Pratts called Coalsell; all the avenues to the house are fine walkes of rows of trees, the garden lyes in a great descent below the house, of many steps and tarresses and gravel walkes with all sorts of dwarfe trees, fruit trees with standing apricock and flower trees, abundance of garden roome and filled with all sorts of things improved for pleasure and use; the house

is new built with stone …. The Cupilow … gives you a great prospect of gardens, grounds, woods that appertaine to the Seate, as well as a sight of the Country at a distance.[23]

From Brudenell's plan, as well as from the description above, we know that the gardens at Coleshill were walled all round, and also divided internally, apparently by walls. There were three main gardens set out formally down the hillside, terraced, and with gravelled walks, and planted as was usual both 'for pleasure and use', as Celia says. They were roughly aligned to the house. On the plan, however, three further gardens can also be seen to the side of the main gardens, nearer to the village street, and they may be an indication of the site of the old house. The new house was approached, again according to Brudenell's plan, along an avenue of trees and through a series of rather irregular walled courts, which nevertheless must have contrived to give a sense of symmetry. Sets of gates are discernible which gave access to the house and its entrance courts, and more or less line up on its central axis. There are gates into a side court, and what appears to be a pavilion at one corner, perhaps with a niche looking outwards. At the foot of the gardens stood a summer house, on the wall, and also a pigeon house.

This arrangement survived until the end of the 18th century, although the gardens within the walls were much changed. By 1801, the old walls and courts had mostly been removed, and the ground was newly landscaped.[24] In addition, the new turnpike road had been built to by-pass the old village street. The owners of Coleshill extended their grounds into the space vacated by the villagers' houses, which were demolished, and so changed the layout of the entire area. A few stretches of original wall survive giving an idea of its height and appearance.

The late-18th-century changes to the garden involved not only taking down most of the courtyard walls at the front but also moving the gate piers and niches. This is confirmed by the bills of the masons who did the work. The great gate piers were taken down from the 'Green Court' in 1780–1 by Robert Strong, and rebuilt where they now stand 'against the new road' with a new pair of oak gates.[25] Interestingly, they must have been viewed as too important to destroy, probably because of the possible association of Inigo Jones with their

The great gate piers at Coleshill in their present position next to the turnpike road, behind a ha-ha (*Author*).

design. They were set up again purely for show, since a new ha-ha was dug directly in front of them, but they framed the view of the house from the new road. The old piers are very impressive examples of a kind which are still to be seen *in situ* at Thorpe Hall, with niched seats.[26] A new main entrance to the house was constructed from another point on the turnpike road. Robert Strong also took down a pair of large shell-headed niches in 1780. His bill records this as 'Taking down the Neeches in the Green Court and Rebuilding Do.'[27] They now stand opposite the Clock House in what became the service entrance.

Thus we know that there were both 'Great' gate piers and 'Neeches' in the Green Court. This, presumably, was the square area closest to the front of the house on Brudenell's plan. The position of the Great Piers is marked, but where were the niches? Perhaps they stood beside the main piers like those at Groombridge Place, facing outwards to greet the traveller, or perhaps one is shown by Brudenell to the left of the house, looking out over the countryside as the seats at Thorpe Hall do. Grassed entrance courts (or green courts) such as

123

the one at Balls Park became usual at this time. Francis Bacon referred to 'A Greene in the Entrance'. He continues: 'The Greene hath two pleasures; The one, because nothing is more Pleasant to the Eye, then Greene Grasse kept finely shorne; The other, because it will give you a fair Alley in the midst …'.[28] England was celebrated for its fine grass.

At Coleshill, the house was originally approached via at least two more sets of gates – apparently leading from the village street, and giving access into the first and second courtyards. It is unclear exactly what they looked like, but we would expect them to be less grand than those in the main entrance court. In fact, another pair of gate piers, smaller and rusticated, does survive, possibly in their original position, and definitely of less importance, and there is an engraving of another set, similar but without rustication.[29] It is interesting to observe the hierarchy of design according to position and importance, as at Balls Park and Thorpe Hall.

Pratt's own house, Ryston Hall, Norfolk, was built 1669-72, just after Coleshill. An early painting shows how the house, courtyards and gardens worked, and helps to give an idea of what Coleshill's setting might have been like.[30] The house had a flight of steps up to the front door, and a walled front courtyard with four simple grassed plats, each containing a tree – a green court. There were three sets of gates and piers providing entrances on three sides. The walled gardens behind seem to contain flowers, with four further divisions and large gates and piers in the centre of the end wall. Another garden to the side was for fruit and vegetables, overlooked by the stables and service buildings. Ryston gardens and courtyards were less elaborate and smaller than those at Coleshill, and as at Coleshill, complete regularity was not achieved. However, both gave an illusion of much-desired axiality.

Fashions changed after 1660, with a number of very extensive gardens and parks inspired by the examples in France. In the smaller garden, fashions changed too. The concept of a separate pleasure garden became more popular. This would still be walled, but planted with plain grass, clipped evergreens, shrubs and perhaps flowers. Increasingly, plants from other countries were being mixed with the natives, and exotics were much prized. Citrus trees and other tender plants were overwintered in green houses and set out in the summer.

Productive gardens were still present, but were more likely to be relegated to the further reaches of the walled areas. Sir Stephen Fox's at Chiswick is a good illustration of such a garden.[31]

Fox, a very wealthy courtier, who held posts as Paymaster of the Forces and Lord of the Treasury, retired to Chiswick fairly late in life and had a house built there by Hugh May in 1682-4. May no doubt also designed the entrance courts and gate piers, one set of which survive in the garden. It was what John Macky called 'a regular Palace a-la-modern, with very extensive Gardens'.[32] However, although the house itself was perfectly symmetrical and modern in the plain brick fashion of the moment, it stood near a road and close to Lord Burlington's house and stable next door. The garden, which was probably inherited from the previous house, was long and narrow, with several irregularities which had to be incorporated into a geometric layout. John Evelyn, a friend of the family, discussed the garden with Lady Elizabeth Fox, and noted some of these defects. 'I wonder at the expense', he wrote, 'but women will have their will'.[33]

May is on record in praise of the fashion for plain gardens, with good gravel walks, excellent turf and plants set out in pots. This was what he called the 'walking garden'. Flowers were better seen by themselves, and fruit should be grown in a special walled area.[34] These ideas are reflected in Fox's garden. A little of its appearance can be glimpsed at the side of an engraving showing Chiswick House next door, and later estate plans and other records add to this. There was a terrace behind the house from which King William is said to have viewed the garden and declared: 'This place is perfectly fine, I could live here for five Days'.[35] There was also a series of walled enclosures on the central axis. The first had a central gravel walk between two clipped yew hedges, with grass each side and further walks beside the walls, lined with yews clipped as round-topped standards. Beyond were two more gardens, one where fruit, in particular, was cultivated, and another known as the wilderness or grove. To the side of these were more walled areas, one of which was specifically arranged with diagonal walls for fruit, but both of which were probably used as kitchen gardens as well.

However, the most prominent architectural feature of the garden was a grand new greenhouse in the classical style, probably also by May, which stood slightly to one side behind the stables, and very near the boundary with Chiswick House. Here Fox and his wife grew a collection of exotic plants. They purchased orange trees, bay trees and tuberoses, and no doubt a number of other desirable plants which required protection in the winter. These were the most fashionable components of the late-17th-century garden, and were displayed in pots in front of the greenhouse during the summer.

When architects such as Inigo Jones, John Webb, Peter Mills, Roger Pratt and Hugh May were involved in the design of villas and small houses, their influence extended to the setting. Patrons too were becoming more conscious of how to place their houses. Courtyards, garden walls, gates and gate piers, terraces and garden buildings were seen as part of the overall scheme, and ideally were created by a single mind. Occasionally, when the patron and/or designer had spent time in Italy, the influence of Italian examples was very strongly felt, as at Stoke Park, but more often a sequence of walled enclosures which sprang from an earlier tradition was the main theme. Sometimes it was a struggle to apply the principles of regularity and symmetry, although they were increasingly held to be important by architect and client. Plans could be partially frustrated by a previous layout, as at Coleshill, and by clients and their wives, but it is interesting to observe how difficulties could be overcome, so that the regular formal garden inspired initially by Renaissance ideas had become the norm for the smaller house by the end of the century.

7

The Environs of London: the Suburban Villa as Rural Retreat

Caroline Knight

There has been much, often fruitless, discussion as to the definition of a villa. For my purposes here I regard it not as a building type, but as a place of occasional escape from a city, in this case London. The rapid increase in the population of London, from about 200,000 in 1600 to 575,000 in 1700 was not matched by an expansion of the boundaries of the city, so over-crowding was rife. Diseases such as the plague, sweating sickness and smallpox spread easily, and the pollution from coal fires made the air filthy. It was only after the Fire of London in 1666 that expansion westwards became accepted, and the better-off moved from the City or Holborn area to the newly built West End. So for most of the 16th and 17th centuries rich and poor were living close together in a densely built environment, and the attractions of a house in a nearby village were obvious.

London's prosperity meant that families from widely differing backgrounds could enjoy these suburban houses. Lawyers were in London for the legal terms, members of Parliament during Parliamentary sittings, peers and bishops attended the House of Lords, courtiers were in attendance at the various royal palaces in and around London, and merchants had to keep a close eye on their businesses. All these families would need to live in London; and even if they owned country estates, they would barely have time to visit them apart from the summer break. So a house conveniently close would be somewhere to bring up the children in a healthier environment, while allowing the head of the household to keep in touch with his London interests. It could also be fun, with an informal but active social life. Gardens were not just for pleasure, but provided fruit and vegetables which could be sent to the London house as well as consumed on the spot; and some additional land was required as grazing for horses and perhaps one or two cows.

Travel by water allowed easy access to the Thames-side villages such as Greenwich to the east or Richmond to the west, and many of the royal palaces were approached by boat; but travel by coach was very slow, especially in winter. The best routes out of London were still the old Roman roads, such as Ermine Street to the north and Watling Street to the south-east, and it was the villages on or near these roads which were particularly favoured. As London spread, the villages closest to London were built up, and the wealthy bought their suburban houses a little further out – a process that began in the 16th century and which still goes on today.

Unlike country houses, it is rare for these suburban houses to have continuity of ownership through several generations. Often they were left to a widow, allowing the new head of the family to keep possession of the London house and the country estate; the upheavals of the Reformation and the Civil War also led to frequent sales. Changes of ownership do not help the survival of these houses; and the continual expansion of London and the improvements in transport in the 19th century made distant country houses more accessible, just when the land around suburban houses was being built up, making them less desirable. Those that still exist often do so because the local council bought the land as public open space, and found itself burdened with an old house, expensive to maintain and of more or less historic interest.

In this period there was no standard type of house. Instead there was an experimental approach to design which made these houses talked about and influential; and because of their proximity to London they were easily seen. In 1593 John Norden wrote that Middlesex was 'plentifully stored, and as it seemeth beautified, with many faire and comely buildings, especially of the merchants of London, who have planted their houses of recreation not in the meanest places.'[1] And in 1663 Count Magalotti described the journey of Cosimo III, Grand Duke of Tuscany, into London from the south-west, noting that the seven miles from Brentford into London 'is truly delicious from the abundance of 'well-built villas and country houses, which are seen in every direction.'[2] Architects were rarely employed until the post-Restoration period, and most houses seem to have been designed by the usual combination of owner and builder, sometimes with the help of architectural books. Early houses had a similar courtyard plan to those in town or country, but throughout the 16th and 17th centuries there were experiments with compact plans, until a double-pile plan became established as the most common type, and spread from London to the country. That shrewd amateur architect Roger North notes this, writing *c*.1698 that 'not onley in the cittys and townes, a compact model is used, but in all country seats of late built.'[3] The following examples give some idea of the variety of plans which were used, of the people who built them, and of the varied subsequent history of the houses.

Canonbury Place, Islington

The pre-Reformation Church owned large amounts of land round London, and some ecclesiastics had substantial suburban houses: surviving examples are the Bishop of London's palace at Fulham, and Cardinal Wolsey's Hampton Court. Less well known than either of these is Canonbury, built by William Bolton, who from 1509 until his death in 1532 was Prior of St Bartholomew's in Smithfield. The high ground on which the house was built, only two miles from Smithfield, provided fresh air and fine views over the City of London. It was a large brick courtyard house with a substantial walled garden, providing fruit and vegetables for Prior Bolton's table and that of his household, as well as being a pleasant and private place to walk. Although parts of the house survive, there has not been a full archaeological investigation of this most interesting building, and it is not entirely clear how much of the surviving building dates from Prior Bolton's time. It seems to have come into Thomas Cromwell's hands even before the suppression of St Bartholomew's in 1539, as he was paying for work there in 1533; it changed hands several times in the mid 16th century, until in 1570 it was bought by Sir John Spencer, one of the richest City merchants; it has not been on the market since then.

Canonbury Tower, *c*.1598-9 (*Author*).

Spencer may have bought Canonbury as an investment, as he let it until the 1590s, when he carried out substantial work, probably turning it into a double courtyard house. These improvements may be linked to his time as Lord Mayor in 1594/5, when he bought Crosby Hall in the City to use for his mayoralty. The decoration has a florid quality which seems entirely appropriate to a very rich man: the five-storey tower leads to two rooms still with their original panelling and chimneypieces, where the woodwork has Serlian panels and strapwork mixed with classical motifs. The first floor great

130

chamber, now disguised outwardly by 18th-century sash windows, has a fine plasterwork ceiling with the royal arms and the date 1599. He also made garden improvements, adding two octagonal pavilions to the far corners of the walled garden. Both of these are now attached to early-19th-century houses, and one has Prior Bolton's rebus re-set over a doorway.

This is a splendid example of the house of an extremely wealthy City merchant; but in the next generation it belonged to the aristocratic Comptons, Earls of Northampton. Spencer's only child, Elizabeth eloped with William, Lord Compton, who thus inherited Spencer's fortune in 1610, estimated between £500,000 and £750,000. The young couple let Canonbury House, but carried out lavish improvements at Castle Ashby; a chimneypiece and overmantel from Canonbury were later moved there.[4] By the 18th century these large, old-fashioned houses were not easy to let; parts of the house were demolished, other ranges divided into separate houses, and in the early 19th century the surrounding land was developed by the Comptons as the Canonbury estate. Without the continuous ownership of one family, it is most unlikely that this house would still exist.

More important for the development of the suburban house are the various experiments with compact plans, and the following examples will demonstrate variations on this, first the H-plan, then the double-pile plan.

Sutton House, Hackney

This medium-sized house was built c.1535 by Sir Ralph Sadleir, an ambitious man who served Henry VIII as Gentleman of the Bedchamber, civil servant and diplomat; he is a good example of the new men coming to power under the Tudors, not because of their ancestry but because of their intelligence and administrative skills. He had a London house, but by the mid-1530s was rich enough to build a modest but comfortable house not far north of the City. Hackney was already a favoured village for City people, and the site near the church which Sadleir acquired was not large enough to allow for a completely symmetrical building. It was known as The Bryk Place, presumably to distinguish it from timber-framed buildings nearby, and the façade still has some of the original diaper brickwork. The original gables, some of which probably had carved barge-boards, were replaced by a parapet in the 18th century. Instead of the usual courtyard plan, he built an H-plan house, an early example of a type which was much used later in the 16th century for both suburban and country houses. The hall is in the centre, flanked by a service and a guest wing, each approached by its own staircase. The hall is modest in scale (about 9.25 metres or 30 feet long) and of only one storey, allowing the great chamber to be directly above it – a neat bit of planning which was used widely later on. Both hall and great chamber have simple panelled walls, undecorated ceilings and wide stone chimneypieces, with more elaborate linenfold panelling and another stone chimneypiece in one of the parlours, and there is some early 17th century wall painting on the west staircase.

However, Sadleir only kept his new house for fifteen years. Successful and upwardly mobile, the king rewarded him with the 8,000-acre estate of Standon in Hertfordshire; this was only about fifteen miles north of the City, so easily accessible from London. By 1550 he had rebuilt the house there and acquired the freehold, so he sold his Hackney house. In 1670 it became a school, and changed little until 1750 when it was split into two dwellings; but since Hackney was by then a fairly poor and unfashionable suburb of London, the minimum was spent on the conversion and much of the interior was left intact. Bought by the rector of St John's, Hackney in 1890, it was used for parish activities until in 1936 an appeal raised enough money for the National Trust to buy it and save it from developers. This was a decade or so before their Country Houses Scheme, and the Trust simply let it as offices for fifty years. Its historic interest was not properly recognised until the 1980s when locals, shocked at the vandalism which was taking place when tenants had left, put pressure on the Trust to restore the house and open it to the public.

Charlton House, Charlton

This is one of the finest Jacobean houses in the London area, standing on high ground about two miles east of Greenwich and with extensive views over the Thames valley.[5] It was built 1606–12 by Sir Adam Newton, a Scot who had come south with the Stuart court as tutor to Prince Henry, the heir to the throne. Its sophisticated plan points to a professional architect, and it has recently been suggested that perhaps John Thorpe or Robert Smythson may have been involved in its design.[6] There are striking similarities to the plan of Hardwick Hall in Derbyshire, built about ten years earlier. If so, this would be an unusual case of a provincial building influencing a suburban house.[7]

Built of brick with stone details, it is another version of an H-plan house, but it is much larger and more imposing than Sutton House, having three storeys and a double-pile central range. Like Hardwick, the double-height hall runs through the house from front to back, and has a gallery at first floor level to ease access across the house; like Hardwick, the state rooms are on the second floor; and like Hardwick, the flat roofline is broken by towers, here ogee-capped. On the ground floor the service rooms are to the south and the chapel, a parlour and perhaps an open loggia to the north. In this north range is a vigorously carved stone chimneypiece, probably removed from the Queen's House during changes in the early 1660s, and installed here by Sir William Ducie, the then owner.[8] The state rooms on the upper floor include a long gallery with views northwards towards the Thames, a withdrawing room and a splendid great chamber above the hall, as well as a state apartment on the south side. Unusually, many of these rooms still have their original fine plasterwork, that in the great chamber having the royal arms of James I and Prince Henry.

The house stayed in the family till 1659, then passed through various hands until bought in 1798 by the widowed Lady Wilson. Her descendants, the Maryon-Wilsons, commissioned some sensitive alterations by Norman Shaw in 1877-8. Since 1925 it has been owned by the London Borough of Greenwich and is partly used as a nursery school. Considering the quality of the architecture, it is a little-visited house which deserves greater recognition.

Boston Manor, Brentford

Driving along the elevated section of the Great West Road into London one can see mellow brick gables among clumps of cedar trees, an oasis of greenery amid inter-war housing and offices. This is Boston Manor, an early-17th-century house of compact and perhaps innovative plan, and – unusually – built by a woman.

133

Boston Manor, chimneypiece in the great chamber c.1623 (*Author*).

The property was part of Sir Thomas Gresham's Osterley estate, and at his death went to his stepson, Sir William Reade, who was already living at Boston Manor. When he died in 1621 his much younger second wife, born Anne Goldsmith, at once set about

134

rebuilding the house as a double-pile brick house of three storeys; a lead downpipe is dated 1622. The house is gabled, and not completely symmetrical, but it may be one of the first houses to have been built without a hall and screens passage: the evidence for this is the plasterwork ceiling of the entrance hall, which appears to be complete, suggesting that it was an entrance corridor.[9] Like many of these houses, the gardens were clearly important, and the entrance hall leads straight through the house into the gardens beyond.

The great chamber on the first floor still has an impressive plaster ceiling dated 1623, decorated with panels of the Five Senses and the Elements and with Mary Reade's initials, so it must predate her second marriage to Sir Edward Spencer. The overmantel, also in plasterwork, has a scene of the Sacrifice of Isaac, a most unusual choice for a decorative feature, and based on a print by Abraham de Bruyn.[10] The state bedchamber leading off this room also has fine plasterwork, with a deep frieze discovered during restoration work in the 1960s behind later panelling. The family rooms were probably over the service end of the house, and it is possible that this was part of a slightly later phase of building.[11]

The survival of this house is mainly due to the Clitherow family, who owned the house for over 250 years. James Clitherow, a City merchant, bought it and fifty acres of land in 1670 for £5,336.[12] He added the service wing to the north, put in sash windows, and probably added the window surrounds and cornice. A descendant remodelled the gardens in the 1750s, changing the axial approach to a longer winding drive, opening up the earlier walled gardens, and turning some ponds into a picturesque lake. A lost portrait by Devis shows Mr and Mrs James Clitherow in their fashionable new gardens.[13] General John Clitherow inherited the house in 1847, a time when the Jacobethan style was much appreciated. He used the London firm of Hawkesley to restore the plasterwork ceilings and embellished the staircase with carved newels, as well as adding an over-scaled screen across the hall.[14]

With the westward expansion of London the house was not rural enough for the Clitherows, who lived mainly on their Yorkshire estates. In 1922 they sold the contents of Boston Manor and offered the house for sale, but no buyers came forward. A large but old-fashioned house in a built up area was no longer a desirable place for a well-off family to live, and it was sold to Brentford Urban District Council for £23,000 in 1924. As so often, the council was after the 20 acres of land to use as public open space, and ignored the historic aspects of the house. After some bomb damage in World War Two the house was restored for use as a school, and is now in the care of the London Borough of Hounslow, partly flats and partly open to the public.

Ranelagh House, Chelsea

Sir Christopher Wren designed very few private houses, but Ranelagh House is a likely candidate, although Lord Ranelagh, noted for his knowledge of architecture and gardens, may have played a role as well.[15] Until its demolition in the early 19th century it was a fine example of the type of compact double-pile house which Roger North described as 'the model … for a suburbian house, neer a square …'[16]

Richard Jones, made Earl of Ranelagh in 1677, was an Irishman who saw public office as a way of lining his own pockets. In the 1670s the Duke of Ormonde made him Chancellor of the Irish Exchequer, then Vice-Treasurer of Ireland. In both posts he was so incompetent and corrupt that he left Ireland in disgrace, and in 1681 had to sell his suburban house in Chiswick in order to pay his fines.[17] In spite of this setback to his career, James II made him Paymaster-General, a post which automatically made him Treasurer of the Royal Hospital, Chelsea, which was then being completed by Wren. It was this latter appointment which allowed him in 1688 to start building himself a fine suburban house at little cost to himself.

Ranelagh already had lodgings in Whitehall Palace, and at the Royal Hospital had the Steward's lodgings for his own use; but this was not good enough, and he persuaded Wren to order the building of a house for him just to the east of the hospital buildings, with its own approach road; the eastern end of this drive is now Ranelagh Grove, but Chelsea Barracks occupies the western part of the drive. Bowack writes: 'The house of brick, cornered with stone, is not large but convenient, and may well be called a Cabinet … In furnishing his Lordship spared neither labour nor cost. The very greenhouses and stables, adorned with festoons, urns etc, have an air of grandeur not

Ranelagh House, entrance front. Watercolour by Elizabeth Gulston, *c*.1800
(*Royal Borough of Kensington and Chelsea*).

to be seen in many prince's palaces.'[18] It was of two storeys with basement and attics, double-pile in plan, with six rooms per floor; and was set in seven acres of grounds which Ranelagh had, typically, persuaded the king to grant him. With Wren completing the building of the Royal Hospital and large sums going through the accounts, it was easy for the Treasurer to fudge them; C.G.T. Dean's researches into the building accounts of the Royal Hospital show that about £10,000 is unaccounted for, making it probable that Ranelagh's new house cost that sum, and slipped through the accounts disguised as 'diverse other works' and 'other small buildings.'[19] The overmantel carvings by William Emmett, who was also working on the main building, seem to have been absorbed into the general accounts, and the only item which Ranelagh paid for himself was the wall painting on the stairs by Henry Cooke. In plan the house had one unusual feature: instead of the usual division between the hall and other rooms, here the entrance hall had a screen of columns dividing it from the principal staircase and the corner room on the garden front, giving a sense of flowing space untypical of its date.[20]

137

Ranelagh's effrontery can be seen in the petition to William III in which he asked for a new and longer lease on his seven acres (which he later enlarged to 23), stating as he did so that he had 'diligently overseen the building and finishing of ye Royal Hospital near Chelsea without any advantages to himself …'[21] This is a stark contrast to Sir Stephen Fox, the previous Paymaster-General and Treasurer, who employed Hugh May to design him a rather similar house at Chiswick, but paid for it entirely from his own pocket.

The later history of the house is brief. Ranelagh was more or less bankrupt at his death in 1712, but his daughter Lady Catherine Jones was allowed to stay on in the house for her lifetime. In 1730 her trustees divided it into several lots for sale. On one of these the Rotunda was built, dwarfing the house nearby, and in 1742 the Ranelagh Pleasure Gardens opened. The house was demolished in 1805, as was the Rotunda, and in 1826 the Royal Hospital at last managed to repurchase the land which had originally been theirs, on which Soane built an infirmary.

Conclusion

These examples demonstrate the changing taste in houses from the rambling courtyard house for a large household, through the more compact H-plan house, to the double-pile house, introduced in the early 17th century and still popular over a century later. These suburban houses differed from the country seats of great families and did not require the staff of stewards and bailiffs who administered great estates; they could be run with fewer servants, and extra staff could come from the London household as required. They were places where the owner could relax away from the pressures of work and city life, enjoying the fresh air and gardens, yet able to ride up to London in an hour or two if necessary.

These houses were highly desirable, so that finding one with attractive gardens and good views was hard, and high prices were paid. We have seen how Sadleir could only acquire a small plot in Hackney. But they were a luxury, and if times were hard they would be sold, as Ranelagh had to sell his house at Chiswick. This meant that houses changed hands frequently, and it is often difficult to track the alterations made by various owners. It is also hard to see if there was one style which appealed to the City merchant, another to the aristocrat, as the constant changes of ownership blur these distinctions.

In 1844 C.J. Richardson wrote in *The Builder*: 'Very little is known of the very beautiful and interesting specimens of old architecture still remaining in the neighbourhood of London …'[22] But many more such houses have gone since then. In the villages closest to London hardly any still exist. Sutton House in Hackney is an exception, in a village much favoured by Londoners in the 16th century, but going downmarket with the increasingly industrialised East End nearby. More typical is the loss of Ranelagh House in Chelsea, another popular village but with only two early houses still there.[23] Canonbury, close to the City, survives in a much altered and reduced form, due to its long history of ownership by the Compton family; while Boston Manor and Charlton, both much further from central London than Islington, Chelsea and Hackney, were saved in the 20th century through their purchase by the local council, although the historic houses were considered less important than the gardens and park. It is only today, with more research being carried out into these houses and the context in which they were built, that the houses themselves are being investigated and restored.

8

Inigo Jones's Designs for the Queen's House in 1616

Gordon Higgott

Inigo Jones's Queen's House at Greenwich is justly celebrated as Britain's first truly classical villa. As a detached lodge in a semi-rural setting, symmetrical in plan and elevation and classical in all its details,

The Queen's House, Greenwich, from the south-east. Begun by Inigo Jones for Queen Anne of Denmark in 1616 and completed for Queen Henrietta Maria in the late 1630s. The three-window bridge rooms on the flank elevations were added in 1661, and the colonnades beneath in 1809-11 (*Author*).

the Queen's House is in the tradition of the Italian Renaissance villa. It has affinities with the grandest of the early Florentine villas, Giuliano da Sangallo's Medici villa at Poggio a Caiano of about 1485 onwards,[1] and with the smaller suburban or rural villas that Andrea Palladio and his follower Vincenzo Scamozzi built in the Veneto region in the later sixteenth century: for example, the Villa Rotunda on the outskirts of Vicenza (see p. 148) and the Villa Molin near Padua (below), both of which Jones examined carefully during the first few months of his tour of Italy with Lord Arundel between July 1613 and October 1614.[2]

But although the Queen's House owes much to the work of Palladio and Scamozzi, the building itself is distinct in character from the typical Palladian *casa di villa* ('house in a rural estate'), or *casa suburbana* ('suburban house'). Such buildings are usually compact in plan and cubic in form, with a hipped or pyramidal roof and a portico

Vincenzo Scamozzi's Villa Molin on the Battaglia Canal, near Padua, built in 1597 and typifying the Palladian villa form. Jones saw this building in 1613 and later recalled the design of its portico (*Václav Sedy*).

on at least one principal front. They often have just one principal floor, or *piano nobile*, raised above a half-height basement storey. At the Queen's House the ground and first floors are of equal height, the

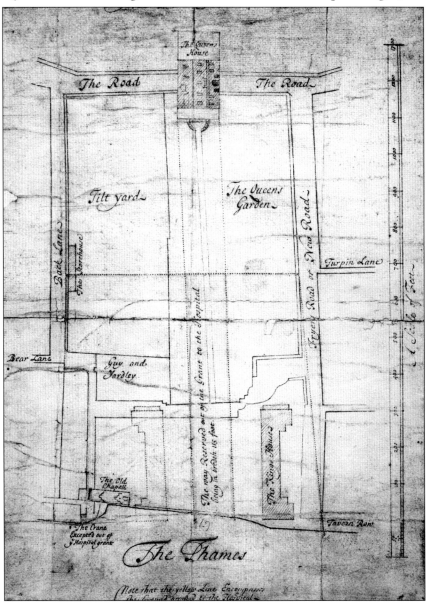

Site plan of Greenwich Palace in *c*.1694, showing the Queen's House as a combined side elevation and plan, straddling the walled road between the park and the Queen's Garden, and set close to the tilt yard of the palace. North is at the bottom (*National Archives, MR/1329 (2): English Heritage/NMR: Queen's House archive*).

elevations are long and broadly proportioned, and the roofline is flat and balustraded, without pediments. It could be described as a hybrid building type, partly a villa, partly a palazzo, and partly a bridge over a public road; but it is clearly more than this, for no Palladian villa or town house has a roof platform above its principal apartments, accessible from a staircase adjoining its main hall. In this chapter I would like to shed more light on the character and purpose of the Queen's House by considering, first, the functions that the building was designed to fulfil on its site at the southern boundary of the palace precinct, then the initial design that Jones prepared in 1616, and finally the nature of the design on which work began in the same year, as this appears to have remained essentially unchanged when work restarted on the building in 1632, after an interruption of fourteen years.

History and purpose

The Queen's House was begun for Anne of Denmark in October 1616 at the southern end of the Queen's garden in Greenwich Palace,

Wenceslaus Hollar. Panorama of Greenwich, 1637. Most of left half of the etchings, showing the view as far as St Paul's Cathedral. The door in the wall to the left of the Queen's House is on the site of the former Tudor gatehouse. Hollar depicts a single large octagonal roof pavilion above the round stairs on the north side of the building *(John Charlton,* The Queen's House *(London, 1976), end paper)*.

143

west of the tilt yard.[3] Described in the following year as the queen's 'curious devise',[4] it was intended as both a garden lodge and a bridge to connect the garden and the royal park on the south side of the Deptford to Woolwich road. In the latter function it replaced the 'olde house over the parke gate', which was demolished as work began, and which is prominent in Anthonis van den Wyngaerde view of Greenwich in 1558.[5] The site of the gatehouse is probably marked by the door shown in the wall immediately left of the Queen's House in Hollar's panorama of Greenwich in 1637, the earliest and most dependable view of Jones's building (see p. 143). Work stopped on the new building in April 1618, probably as a result of Anne's declining health. By then only the brick carcases of the ground floor ranges had been finished; little had been spent on stonework, and a well known view of the incomplete structure in the background of a painting datable to the summer of 1632 shows small ground-floor windows with arched heads, suggesting openings like those in Hollar's view, but with their brick relieving arches exposed.[6]

Work resumed under Charles I's Queen Henrietta Maria in the summer of 1632, and by 1635 – the date on a plaque on the north front – the architectural shell was complete. The terrace and steps on

The Queen's House from the north in about 1937. Until the ground was cut back to form the lower flight of steps in 1935-6, little of the basement of the main building was exposed to view (*English Heritage/NMR: Queen's House archive*).

the north side were built between 1635, when Jones sketched a design for the central door to the basement vaults, and 1637, when the paving was finished.[7] Most of the decoration of the principal rooms in the north range was finished in 1637-8. However, up to the cessation of work in 1641 no decorative work appears to have been carried out in the rooms in the southern range in the royal park. Evidence for an increased emphasis on the more private northern range is in a remarkable scheme for painting its façade with figurative and decorative motifs and a *trompe l'oeil* ornamental frame around its central arched window, known only from a photograph of a lost pen-and-ink drawing of the north elevation (see p. 146).[8] This decorative scheme was sketched in pencil on the pen drawing by an unidentified draughtsman, who added notes in Italian. The pen drawing itself records the design in about 1635, as it shows the date plaque above the central window, but does not show the terrace, and it depicts two roof pavilions rather than the one that appears in Hollar's view of 1637. Too fine in its drawing style for Jones, it may be the work of Nicholas Stone, who was capable of very neat ruled and freehand pen drawing, and who oversaw the stonemasons' work.[9]

The bridge function of the building meant that its first floor needed to be a full storey height above the ground for the bridge-room to stand clear of the road. The two parallel ranges were long to accommodate rooms either side of a large central hall, and the loggia on the south side was recessed to afford privacy to those viewing the hunt in the park. In terms of plan, the northern of the two ranges could not easily extend much more than about 50 feet (15.25 metres) beyond the road because of a fall in the ground level beyond the line of the present north façade. In 1616 the ground on this side of the road appears to have been a raised plateau as far as the present façade; but when Daniel Alexander built colonnades on the old road line to link the Queen's House with the new buildings of the Royal Naval Asylum in 1809-11, he cut back the ground on the north sides of the colonnades, adding steps and making the ground slope down evenly to reveal the top part of the basement of Jones's building.[10] A further line of steps was formed during restoration works in 1935-6, exposing more of the basement. That the building was meant to sit on level ground is apparent from the steeply raked internal sills of the basement windows - designed to take light from above - and from

Unidentified draughtsman, possibly Nicholas Stone. Pen and ink drawing recording the design of the north elevation of the Queen's House in about 1635, before the addition of the terrace in 1636-7, and when Jones was considering two octagonal roof pavilions. The drawing bears pencilled sketches for trompe l'oeil decoration in another hand, added probably in about 1640. The drawing was at Newby Hall, West Yorkshire, before its loss in 1973 (*Unattributed photograph in author's collection*).

the stepped stone plinth at the top of the basement.[11] Had Jones intended his basement to be below this plinth he would have clad its walls in matching stone. In fact, as his early side elevation design shows (see p. 150), he regarded the whole site as level from north to south.

Perhaps the most significant factor determining the external appearance of Jones's building was the use of the roof of the northern range as a viewing platform. This is the reason for the flat balustraded roofline on both ranges (on grounds of symmetry), and it explains the absence of a temple-front portico on the south side, since in the Palladian villa or palazzo type a pediment can only be used in conjunction with pitched roofs.

The Queen's House was built at the extreme southern end of the palace precinct, some 1,100 feet back from the river, on raised ground that commanded views northwards over the Queen's Garden and tilt yard, and east and west along the Thames (see p. 142). The view eastwards was especially important in the light of Greenwich Palace's role as the welcoming point for foreign dignitaries arriving by ship.[12]

In the earliest known design, side arches in the porticoes would have allowed the queen to take advantage of these lateral views (see p. 150). In the completed building this 'look-out' function was transferred to the northern range. On the elevation of *c.*1635 the two principal first-floor rooms – the Withdrawing Room (or Cabinet Room) and the Bedchamber – have long iron balconies. Above are two large octagonal pavilions, providing access to the roofs (see p. 146). These roof pavilions would have been a full storey in height (18 feet), and half the widths of the roof areas either side of the hall. They are in the tradition of the roof turrets and banqueting houses of Tudor and Jacobean country houses and garden lodges, whose lead flats were places of social recreation – Longleat, Wollaton, Hardwick Hall, Charlton House and the Holdenby Banqueting House being amongst the best known examples.[13] As Hollar's panorama shows, only the roof turret on the east side, above the round 'tulip' staircase, was actually built. Its octagonal base survives, incorporating a skylight and a modern door, but its disappearance below the balustrade since the 19th century has obscured its original significance. The other turret, on the west side, would have served the smaller backstairs, next to the Queen's Closet, adjoining the Bedchamber. It would have given the queen completely private access to the roof, and as its staircase was small, it could also have been an enclosed viewing turret.

The viewing platform on the east side of the north range of the Queen's House. The base of the original octagonal roof pavilion is on the left. It occupies half the width of this section of the roof (*Author*).

That the east side of the roof was meant for royal use is shown by the continuation of the enrichments of the staircase balustrade all the way to the top (see colour pl. 6).

The other unusual feature of the completed building that demands a fuller explanation is the great hall in the centre of the north range (see p. 161). Proportioned as a cube and covered by a flat ceiling in nine compartments framed by hollow, beam-like soffits, this great room had an enduring influence on English domestic architecture. It inspired the staircase entry hall at Coleshill House in the 1650s, the Stone Hall at Houghton Hall in the 1720s, and its compartmented ceiling was widely adopted by Palladian revival architects.[14] Notwithstanding its importance, however, the genesis and purpose of this room at the heart of the building remains obscure. There is no precedent in the villas or urban houses of Palladio or Scamozzi for a two-storeyed, galleried hall with a flat ceiling in beamed compartments. Such ceilings are found in porticoes and single-storey halls, as at Palladio's Villa Badoer and Villa Cornaro, and over principal

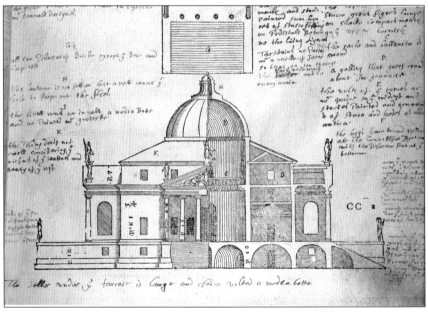

Andrea Palladio, the Villa Rotunda, Vicenza, completed *c*.1569, in Inigo Jones's annotated copy of Palladio's *I Quattro Libri dell'Architettura* (Venice, 1601), II, p. 19, bearing many notes from his visit on 24 September 1613, including comments on the design of galleried hall and the four arched porticoes (*Worcester College, Oxford: Author*).

Plate 1: Sketch by John Aubrey of Sir Francis Bacon's Verulam House, built in a corner of his estate at Gorhambury, Hertfordshire (*Bodleian Library, Oxford*).

Plate 2: Earlshall, Fife, viewed from the garden (*Charles McKean after R.W. Billings*).

Plate 3: Baberton House, Edinburgh, Sir James Murray of Kilbaberton's own villa. The centre was filled in during the 18th century (*RCAHMS, ML. 3708*).

Plate 4: Charlton House, Greenwich, entrance front (*Geoff Brandwood*).

Plate 5: Boston Manor, Middlesex (*Malcolm Airs*).

Plate 6: Queen's House, Greenwich. The upper flight of Inigo Jones's round staircase in the north range. The elaborate wrought-iron decoration of the balustrade continues up to roof level. The threshold to the first-floor gallery is in the centre (*Gordon Higgott*).

Plate 7: Front of Kew Palace, Surrey (*Historic Royal Palaces*).

Plate 8: Reconstruction drawing showing the Georgian Royal Complex at Kew. Kew Palace is to the upper right of the drawing, the White House to the lower left (*Drawing: Jonathan Foyle © Historic Royal Palaces*).

Plate 9: Watercolour of the entrance front at Forty Hall, Enfield, Middlesex, in the 1790s, when the building was newly rendered, from Daniel Lysons, *Environs of London*, vol. II (1795) (*Additional plate in copy held at the Guildhall Library, Corporation of London*).

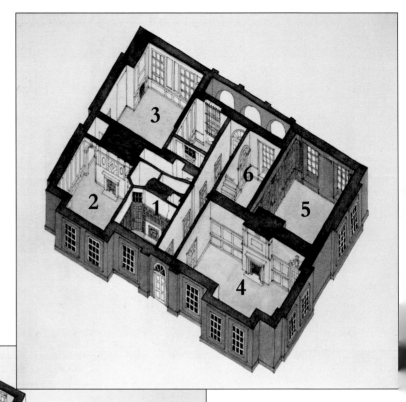

Plate 10 (a) & (b): Kew Palace: the use of rooms in the Georgian period (*Drawings by Robin Wyatt © Historic Royal Palaces*).

(a) Top: Ground floor: 1 library ante-room, 2 the King's library, 3 pages' waiting room, 4 King's dining room, 5 King's breakfast room, 6 staircase.

(b) Bottom: First floor: 8 Queen's boudoir, 9 Queen's drawing room, 10 ante-room, 11 Princess Elizabeth's bedroom, 12 Queen's bedroom, 13 Queen's ante-room.

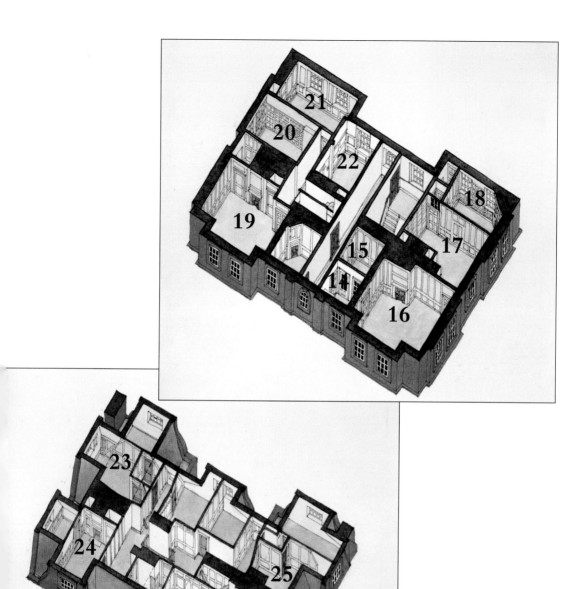

Plate 10 (c) & (d): Kew Palace: the use of rooms in the Georgian period
Drawings by Robin Wyatt © Historic Royal Palaces).

c) Top: Second floor: 14 ante-room, 15 inner closset, 'powder room', 16 Princess Augusta's
bedroom, 17 Princess Amelia's bedroom, 18 dressing room, 19 housekeeper's room, 20, 21 &
22 use unknown.

d) Bottom: Attic floor: 23, 24 & 25 servants' bedrooms. Many attic rooms were used for
storage or as bedrooms.

Plate 11: Tyttenhanger, Hertfordshire, showing what was originally the entrance (south) elevation, but which is now the garden front (*Elain Harwood*).

Plate 12: The staircase and first-floor lobby at Tyttenhanger (*Elain Harwood*).

Plate 13: Winslow Hall, Buckinghamshire. First-floor room with painted panels (*Pete Smith*).

rooms at *piano nobile* level, but where a hall rises through two full storeys, as in the circular hall at the Villa Rotunda on the outskirts of Vicenza, or the square hall at Scamozzi's Villa Molin, it is domed or vaulted.[15]

The unusual form of the cube hall prompts the question whether, when work began in 1616, Jones intended only a single-storey entrance-hall, which, when work resumed in 1632, he modified to a galleried two-storey hall – along the lines of his Banqueting House interior of 1619-22. Had this been the case, he would have needed footings for columns to support the upper floor within the central space, positioned like those in the central vaulted hall of a long plan in the RIBA Drawings Collection which in recent years has been associated with the Queen's House.[16] However, nothing of this kind was found in a radar scan of substructure of the floor of the hall carried out for the National Maritime Museum in 2004.[17] Hearths would have been essential for low-ceilinged halls in a north-facing range, even for summer use, but the scan found no trace of these; nor are there any footings for chimney breasts in the central part of the northern basement.[18] Thus we can safely conclude that the design on which work began in 1616 was for a building with a two-storey, unheated, galleried hall at the centre of the north side.

The design for a bridge-villa and look-out

The declared accounts for expenditure on building works for Queen Anne of Denmark at Greenwich Palace and Oatlands Palace between 8 October 1616 to 30 April 1618 include the sum of £10 for 'making the first module [i.e. design] of the newe building at Grenewich, and £16 for 'makeing and p[er]fecting the second module of the same buildinges at Grenewich in the form the same was to be builded and finished by the late Quene Ma[jesties] commaundement'.[19] This statement indicates just two designs for the building: an initial, rejected scheme, and a final scheme that was 'perfected' before being put in hand.

Two drawings that certainly belong to the earliest phase of the design are a side elevation at Worcester College, Oxford, for a small villa in two matching halves linked by a bridge-room set on a road arch, and an unfinished front elevation of a villa with a temple-front portico in the RIBA Drawings Collection (see pp. 150, 151).[20] The

Jones's preliminary design for the side elevation of the Queen's House in 1616.
Pen and brown ink with shading in black chalk (*Worcester College, Oxford: Author*).

front elevation corresponds closely enough to the side elevation in
proportion and detail for there to be little doubt that it is for the same
building. Moreover, it is a design for the principal front of a royal
building, as its shield and supporters are identical to those in the
pediment of Jones's 'penultimate' design for the Banqueting House in
Whitehall in 1619.[21]

The Worcester College drawing is smaller in size and cruder in
detail than the RIBA elevation and can be shown to belong to a
slightly earlier stage in the design process in which villa forms were
Jones's main preoccupation. Its arched porticoes are like those of the
Villa Rotunda and Scamozzi's Villa Molin, and their paired end
columns can be traced to Palladio's Villa Pisani at Bagnolo and to the
small Roman temple of Clitumnus, near Trevi, which Jones visited in
June 1614 and whose similarity with the portico of the Villa Pisani
he noted in his copy of the *Quattro Libri*.[22]

Neither drawing is scaled but it is possible to deduce scales for
each of them and reconstruct a common first-floor plan with
reference to another design that must also belong to this phase: a
sketch by John Webb of the first-floor plan of a villa bridging a
'highway', on a sheet of his sketch-studies of villa and house plans (see
p. 152).[23] Webb's plan is near enough to that implied by both

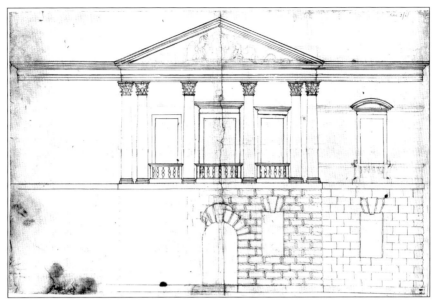

Jones's preliminary design for the front elevation of the Queen's House in 1616, in this case the south or park elevation, corresponding both to the side elevation in the previous illustration and to the plan in the next. Pen and brown ink over incised lines, with additions in graphite and black chalk (*RIBA Library Drawings Collection*).

elevations for it to be accepted as a study of a lost plan by Jones for the Queen's House, even though Webb, contrary to his usual practice, did not identify his drawing as 'Mr Surveyor's' design.[24] It shows the central bridge-room equal in width to the porticoes, and square rooms flanking the porticoes, an arrangement that conforms with the pencil shading on the side elevation and the implied square plan of the roof of its bridge room. On the front elevation, Jones sets the doors and windows of the loggia behind the columns, but offers no suggestion in his pen or pencil drawing that this portico projects from the façade at any depth. It appears to be a design for a front with a recessed loggia and as such corresponds to the bottom half of Webb's plan. This range would have been on the south side of the 'highway' in the park, for a deep recess of this kind would not have been appropriate on the north-facing front.

We can arrive at a scale for the Worcester College drawing from the spacing of the incised lines that mark the widths of the windows and the heights of their sills. On Jones's designs for domestic buildings, typical sill heights range from 3 feet 2 inches on his

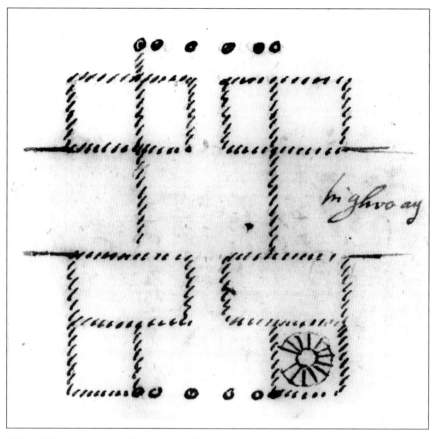

highway

John Webb. Record of a lost design for the first-floor plan of the Queen's House on a sheet of house and villa plans. It appears to record a second stage in the design, in which one range – probably that facing the park – is increased in depth (*RIBA Library Drawings Collection*).

elevation for the Prince's Lodging, Newmarket, of *c.*1618 to 3 feet 6 inches on his house elevation for Lord Maltravers at Lothbury in the City of London in 1638.[25] At the Queen's House itself the rail of the timber balustrade of the great hall is 3 feet 2 inches above the floor, while that of the window and loggia balustrades is about 3 feet 6 inches.[26] If we assume a sill height around 3 feet 4 inches for the Worcester College elevation, the width of the windows between the vertical incised lines scales at 4 feet, a dimension favoured by Jones for windows in smaller domestic buildings. This is 7/32 inches on the drawing, making 1 foot the equivalent of 7/128 inch. On the more carefully drawn but unfinished front elevation, a window width of 4 feet produces a scale of 2 feet to 1 inch. This fits the elevation as a whole, for it produces window sills 3 feet 4 inches high, an entry door 6 feet wide by 12 feet high, and an overall height of 40 feet from the ground to the top of the entablature, only 1 foot more than the equivalent dimension in the fabric itself.

The plan that can be derived from the Worcester College drawing is of a bridge-like villa, much longer than wide, and with just one principal room over the road.[27] This bridge room was probably not meant to be heated as Jones does not show chimney-stacks on his side elevation. In length, from north to south (109 feet), the plan is not far short of the executed scheme (121 1/2 feet), but it is much narrower (70 1/2 feet compared to 115 feet) (p.159). Its layout was determined by the 36-feet wide porticoes at each end, which are a third of the overall length of the plan and create a principal room 30 feet wide. Apart from bridging the road, its only real purpose would have been

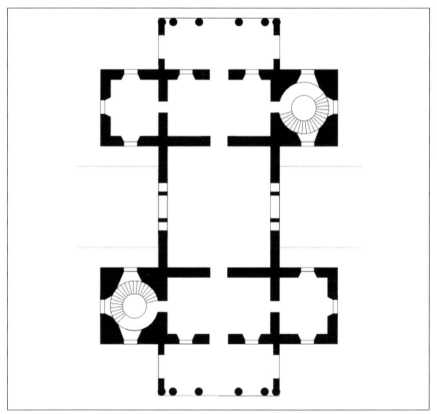

Reconstruction of the first-floor plan of the first design for the Queen's House, based on Jones's side elevation design of 1616 and Webb's plan in the previous illustration (*Line drawing: Alan Fagan*).

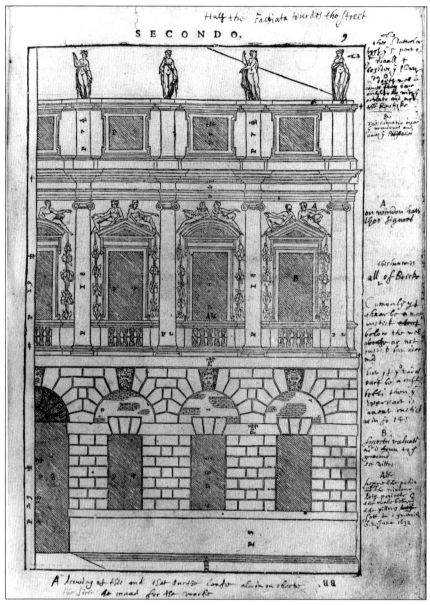

Andrea Palladio. Half elevation of the Palazzo Porto in Vicenza (c.1546-9) in Inigo Jones's annotated copy of Palladio's *Quattro Libri*, II, p. 9. Jones's note in the bottom right-hand margin is dated 2 June 1632 and refers to the design of the window balconies (*Worcester College, Oxford: Conway Library: Courtauld Institute of Art*).

as a small place of private repose and a look-out for views over the palace and royal park, and along the river, east and west. Jones has recast the smaller type of Palladian rural or suburban villa as a miniature lodge and look-out; but it was not a building for formal use, as there were no bedchambers, withdrawing rooms, or imposing entrance-hall.

More of the character of this first design emerges from close study of the RIBA elevation. In the under-scoring and the initial pen-work for this drawing Jones marked a taller central entrance, its arch two rusticated courses down from the floor band. This higher arch, measuring just over 15 feet high by 6 feet wide, would have resembled the entrance arch of Palladio's Palazzo Porto, a building that Jones studied in Vicenza with the aid of Palladio's *Quattro Libri* (see p. 154). For the upper storey of his villa elevation Jones adapted Palladio's window balconies for use as freestanding panels of balustrading set between the columns of his portico (a detail he had particularly admired at the Villa Molin); he borrowed Palladio's window surround and curved pediment, and even his reclining pediment figures (sketched lightly in pencil), to create a façade that strikes a balance between the palazzo and villa forms.

There is, however, a hidden, earlier stage to Jones's front elevation design. Marked with incised lines on each side of his central arch are two identical arched openings, forming a triad of arches, one beneath each bay of the loggia, the scored arc of the right one faintly visible around the top of the ground-floor window. This initial three-arch

The three-arched loggia at the Villa Thiene (*c*.1546), sketch by Jones in 1614 in the margin of his copy of Palladio's *Quattro Libri*, II, p. 64. (*Worcester College, Oxford: Author*).

scheme appears to correspond to the Worcester College elevation, for this has similar high arches in the flank walls, and it is unlikely that Jones would have made the fronts of these porticoes less open than their sides. The idea may have come from the three-arched loggia that Jones sketched at Palladio's Villa Thiene, near Vicenza, on 13 August 1614 (see p. 155), a feature he likened to Sansovino's three-arched Loggetta in Venice (1537-45) and which may have influenced the design of the two-storeyed, three-arched loggia at Houghton Conquest in 1615, a portico that could only have been designed by Jones at this date.[28] However, an open loggia of this type on a small villa plan would have limited the amount of private space available to the queen. Jones's abandonment of the idea is consistent with the development seen in John Webb's study plan, where more private space is shown at first-floor level, in the form of rectangular and square rooms next to the loggia.

It is significant that when work resumed on the building in the summer of 1632 after a break of fourteen years, Jones returned to Palladio's plate of the elevation of the Palazzo Porto for the detailing of his first-floor window balconies, noting near the bottom of the margin ('grenwich ye. 2. June 1632') how the 'podio', or balcony (marked 'A&'), projects from the wall between the columns. However, Jones now simplified his architectural ornaments, reducing

The Queen's House. Detail of the upper-floor window cornices, main entablature and Ionic capitals. Jones modelled these details on Roman examples (*Author*).

the window entablatures to architrave-cornices and eliminating the running mouldings on the walls. There is a distinct Roman-revival character to the finished elevations, not just in the plainness of the walls but in specific motifs. The window cornices, of just three mouldings, are modelled on those of the Temple of Vesta at Tivoli and the Ionic capitals of the loggia, with their unusual necking and abundant leaf carving, on those the Temple of Concord in Rome, both illustrated in Book IV of the *Quattro Libri*. The main Ionic cornice, with its prominent dentil course, derives from Vitruvius's Ionic entablature in Barbaro's 1567 edition of the Roman author's treatise, a book that Jones had annotated from early in his career.[29] The obvious differences between the completed elevations and Jones's initial designs in 1616 have led some commentators to suggest that the building could have been partly or wholly reconstructed from ground level in 1632.[30] Recent investigations of the fabric of the building have demonstrated that this cannot be the case, and we can now be sure that although Jones may have refined his details in 1632 he did not alter the essentials of the design on which work began. There remains the question of the origin of Jones's unique solution for the northern range of the building, in which a two-storey galleried hall is linked by a spiral staircase to a balustraded roof platform.

The two-part summer lodge with hall, loggia and roof terrace

In the executed plan Jones transferred the square bridge-room of his first design to the centre of an enlarged northern range, where it became a two-storey space, linked to the bridge by galleries that continue the bridge platform to the rooms on each side. These are rectangular and square rooms in L-shaped groups, like the group next to the recessed loggia on Webb's plan. They are heated private spaces, closed off by doors, and distinct from the unheated semi-public spaces of the hall, the bridge-room, the open-well south staircase, and the south loggia. The enlargement of the plan to include groups of rooms in the outer parts of the long ranges on each side of the road marked a decisive shift from the simple bridge-villa and look-out of the first design, to a two–part summer lodge with an imposing central hall in the north range. In this revised design the principal entrance and staircase are on the south side, at the beginning of a formal

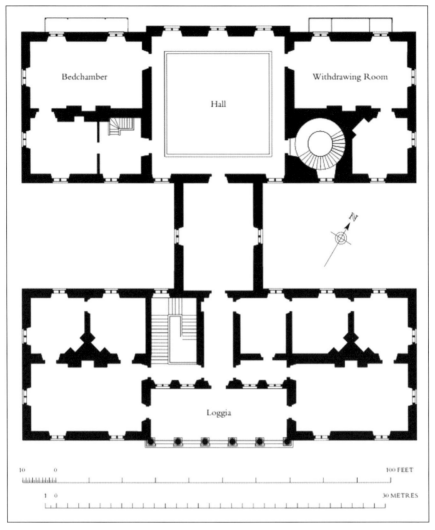

Plan of the Queen's House at first-floor level in about 1640, based on Survey of London monograph, 1937, pl. 14 (*Line drawing: Alan Fagan*).

approach to the hall via the first-floor corridor and bridge-room, an approach that would have been used when the building was entered from the park after a hunt; but the hall was also a point of entry on the more private northern side, where the plain treatment denotes a back elevation, not meant for public view.

The character of the executed scheme, and the distinction that existed in the building in Queen Henrietta Maria's time between semi-public and private spaces, and between indoor and outdoor

158

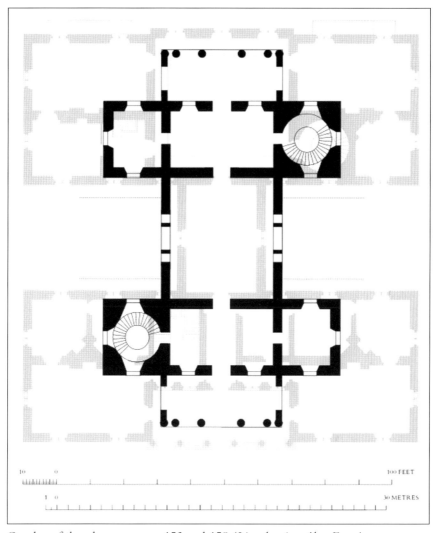

Overlay of the plans on pages 153 and 158 (*Line drawing: Alan Fagan*).

functions, can be discerned both from the earliest surviving drawings and from the fabric itself. The earliest known ground plan of the completed building is a design of 1662 or early 1663 for the aborted corner pavilions, begun in May 1663 (see p. 160). This reveals that the hall had three matching doors on the north side, rather than the door and two windows at present.[31] These three doors are shown on the elevation of *c*.1635 (see p. 146). The outer ones have iron balustrades but no sign of internal sills, suggesting full-height openings closed internally by shutters. When all three doors on the north side were

159

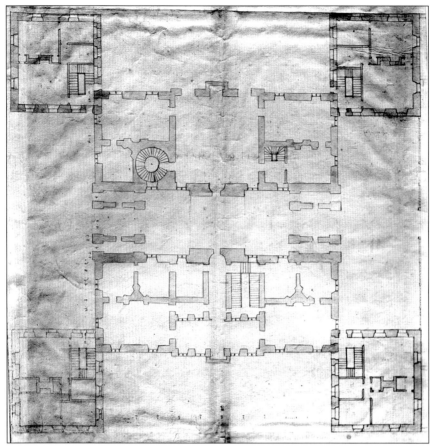

Unidentified draughtsman, possibly Willem de Keyser. Ground plan of the
Queen's House (north at top), prepared in 1662-3 in connection with a scheme
to add corner pavilions to the building in 1663 (*RIBA Library Drawings Collection:
English Heritage/NMR: the Queen's House archive*).

open, the ground floor of the hall would have resembled a loggia as
much as an enclosed hall. It was an unheated, semi-public space,
suitable only for summer use, and it corresponded to the single-storey
entrance-hall at the centre of the south range, which on the plan of
1662-3 is shown with casement windows on both sides. Like the
central part of the north range, none of this part of the plan was
heated. It connected to the hall at ground level through doors in
deep, niche-like recesses that were restored in 1935.[32] That this was a
formal route through the building at ground level is suggested by
Hollar, who shows the large central door on the south side
approached by three converging paths (see p. 143).

The Queen's House. Interior of the great hall in 1967 (*A.F. Kersting*).

What, then, was Jones's inspiration for the cube hall? When he was in Vicenza in August 1614 he was particularly struck by the columned and vaulted entrance-halls that he saw at the Palazzo Thiene, the Palazzo Porto and the Palazzo Barbaran. Such halls, he thought, would 'becom a kings Pallas well', and he wrote a few months later

161

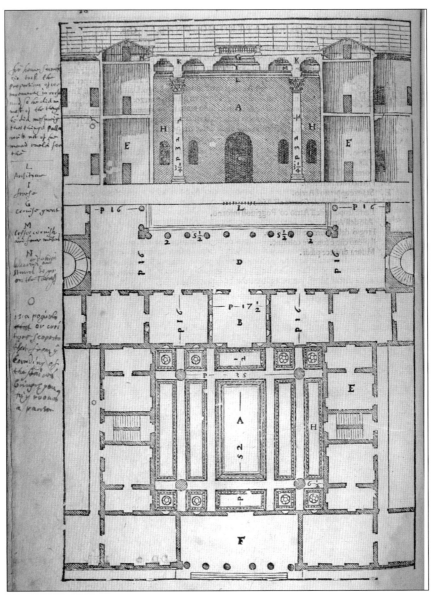

Section and plan of the Four Column Atrium in Jones's annotated copy of Palladio's *Quattro Libri*, II, p. 28. Jones's notes include comments on the relative sizes of the outer and inner cornices of the atrium and the connection between the circular staircase and on the roof platform around the atrium (*Worcester College, Oxford: Author*).

that they 'are varried according to the greatnes of the houses as I obsearved at Vicenza whear ar the best that ever I saaue'.[33] Jones was referring to the *entrata*, or entrance-hall, rather than the *sala*, or

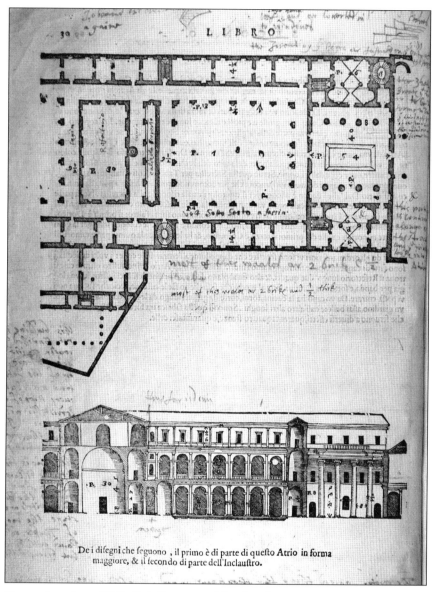

Plan and section of Palladio's Convent of the Carità in Venice in Jones's annotated copy of Palladio's *Quattro Libri,* II, p. 30. On 10 August 1614 Jones sketched details of the oval, open-well staircase at the convent that gave access to the balustraded roof platform of the atrium (*Worcester College, Oxford: Conway Library: Courtauld Institute of Art*).

interior hall, a large, enclosed space for banquets and entertainments, usually on the *piano nobile*, of which the galleried central halls at the Villa Molin and the Villa Rotunda are examples. Palladio describes

163

entrance-halls as public spaces 'where those waiting for the master to come out of his lodgings can stand to greet him and do business with him, and they are the first part (beyond the loggias) which anyone entering the house is presented with'.[34] The cube hall at the Queen's House is as much an entrance-hall as a *sala* and its design is based, in part, on an alternative form of *entrata* illustrated in the *Quattro Libri*, in which timber beams rather than stone vaults carry the upper floor, and which Palladio derived from his reconstructions of the atrium of the Roman house.[35]

Palladio drew the plans and sections of the five types of atrium for Barbaro's Vitruvius and he published more detailed versions of these in Book II of the *Quattro Libri* in 1570.[36] In his reconstruction of the Four Column Atrium the beams are full entablatures, forming square and rectangular compartments on plan, enriched by cornice mouldings, the deepest cornice being that around the central opening of the atrium, or *compluvium* (see p. 162). Palladio followed Vitruvius in treating the atrium as the central space between the columns, rather than the whole space including the side aisles, and he proportioned his atrium spaces accordingly.[37] In the Four Column Atrium, and in the simpler Tuscan Atrium (which omits the columns and side aisles), the space is square in section, with a large arched opening opposite the entrance, and its ceiling is divided by transverse beams into nine compartments. Jones's observations on the Four Column Atrium in his *Quattro Libri* supplement Palladio's captions on the previous page (marked A to L on the plate) and are datable by their handwriting to the early 1620s.[38] They reveal his full grasp of the design of the Roman atrium in the middle years of his career, at about the time he was completing his ceiling at the Banqueting House in Whitehall (1619-22), which is also of the 'atrium' type and, like the ceiling at the Queen's House, has a rounded panel within the central one.[39] He identifies the larger cornice around the *compluvium* as 'G cornice great', and the lower cornices of the adjoining ceiling compartments as 'M lesser cornish and fewer members'. He notices that small gabled openings give access to the roof terrace from the stairs, 'N lucarnes or Lovres [louvres] and staires to go on the Terras', and he comments on the cantilevered gallery ('O') that links the first-floor rooms to these stairs.[40]

The cube hall at the Queen's House is clearly influenced by the atrium form. It is square in section with an arch-like opening opposite the entrance, its nine-part ceiling has a full cornice around the central compartment and half cornices around the outer ones, and the hall is connected to a roof terrace by a staircase (see p. 161). However, it is also a reception hall or *sala*: a room with a double function, on two levels, that was both an indoor and a semi-outdoor space, a main hall as well as a point of entry. With its painted timber balcony, its ceiling for the display of paintings in circular and rectangular panels, and its classical door surrounds at *piano nobile* level, it shares some of the characteristics of the Palladian *sala*. But there is none of the decorative abundance of the halls of the Villa Rotunda or the Villa Molin. This is because from the outset Jones directed his attention to the Roman sources. Beginning in Italy, he studied the Roman equivalent of the modern *sala*, Palladio's Four Column Hall and Corinthian Hall in Book II of the *Quattro Libri*. Against the illustration of the Four Column Hall he noted that the plan was square and that the ceilings have 'Pictures sett in frames'; then, a few years later, he returned to the plate to make the critical observation, 'In this designe the cornice of ye sfondati [compartments] in the midell and on ye sides is all of one hight which shuld nott be'.[41]

The open-well round staircase next to the cube hall is like the one that Palladio shows next to the peristyle in his plan of the Four Column Atrium, but is in fact modelled on the oval staircase that Jones saw at the Convent of the Carità in Venice in August 1614, a building that Palladio had planned and partly executed as his most elaborate reconstruction of the Roman house, and which he published within his account of the atrium hall in Book II of the *Quattro Libri*.[42] This building (now the Venice Accademia) has a cloister designed as a peristyle, a sacristy based on the *tablinum*, or Roman family room, and it had, before its destruction by fire in 1630, an open-roofed Corinthian Atrium with giant-order columns.[43] The staircase is of cantilevered construction with a central void, and it provided access to a terrace around the *compluvium* of the atrium. Jones sketched the staircase, noting the tapering profiles of the stone treads, the positions of the windows ('Lume'), and how the iron balusters were 'fastned on ye outside of The stepps', all details which he was later to follow in the construction of his staircase at the Queen's House.[44] He described the terrace above the atrium, where a roof had been built to keep out the rain, forming a covered terrace 'about the opening of the atrio aboufe [above]', and he concluded, 'the Ovall staire vacuo is exellent and ther goeth an apogio [railing] of iron up to the tope'.[45]

Here is the origin of Jones's design for a flat-roofed summer lodge with an imposing central hall. When he was required to enlarge his first design for the Queen's House to provide longer ranges on both sides of the road, with a hall, a loggia, and heated rooms on both sides of the two central areas, he turned to Palladio's reconstructions of the Roman house, since only this building type offered the classical equivalent of a timber-roofed great hall linked by a staircase to an outdoor viewing platform. This is not to say that Jones's design in 1616 was predominantly Roman revival. It was rather that Jones was reaching back to the Roman sources for the architectural forms that Palladio and Scamozzi had employed, and beginning a process of critical re-evaluation of the modern classical tradition that was only to bear full fruit when he came to complete the Queen's House in the 1630s.

Seen in this light, the brick shell that he abandoned after Queen Anne's death in 1619 marked a decisive advance in Jones's quest for an authentic Roman classicism in the first few years of his career as Surveyor of the Royal Works. That he was able to finish the building for Queen Henrietta two decades later with scarcely any sign of a change in purpose – save for the addition of the terrace and steps on the north side – is ample testimony to the strength and integrity of that early vision.

9

Tart Hall: the Countess of Arundel's 'Casino at Whitehall'

Dianne Duggan

Aletheia Howard, Countess of Arundel, arrived home from Italy late in 1623 with three Italian servants, a gondola, and seventy bales of Venetian furnishings to an exciting climate of Italianate architectural experimentation. She had been spending time with the Arundels' two eldest sons who attended Padua University between 1620 and 1622. The Countess mainly resided in Venice in apartments in the Palazzo Mocenigo-Nero on the Grand Canal, but also stayed close-by to the Brenta canal *en route* to the university. The Arundels had previously visited Italy with Inigo Jones in 1613 for an extended tour that included the Veneto, and their love of Italy is well documented.[1]

From 1614 to around 1620 Lady Arundel had been 'Mistress of Works' for her husband's building projects, including alterations to the Arundel villa at Highgate, mainly a substantial laying out of the grounds, amenities, pergolas and walks in 'the Italian style'.[2] They sold the Highgate house in 1633, and purchased from an Alexander Bennett a relatively isolated 'villa' called Tart Hall on the edge of St James's Park (near the present site of the Royal Mews).[3] Walpole's incorrect assumption that Nicholas Stone built this house was no doubt based on entries for work on Tart Hall that appear in Stone's Account Book in 1639.[4] The undeveloped twelve-acre site had been purchased by an Alphonsus Fowle in 1611, and a depiction of an

167

unnamed building on the site is shown on a plan dated 1614.[5] This tiny, naïve drawing does have specific detail probably indicative of an identifiable structure, and although now somewhat unclear, implies that the house originally may have been E-shaped.

The land and house passed, in 1617, to Fowle's son-in-law, William Bennett, and his son, Alexander Bennett sold the house to the Arundels on 1 December 1633. The conveyancing document clearly states that the building was 'now in the holding or occupacõn of the … Earle' at the time of the purchase, suggesting that they may have been leasing the house for sometime beforehand.[6]

The Countess appears to be mentioning two separate building projects in a letter to her husband on 11 October 1633. This reads: 'I believe Mr Page that he never sawe so fine a plase as Gowborough …; and for a lodge, I hope y^u will let me be the architichte when we are opon the place' (this latter statement an important point in the context of the Countess's design ambitions). A post script to the letter states that 'Mr Gage sayeth that the field can not be had unlesse the man that o[wn]eth it have leave to make a great newe building'.[7] The 'lodge' mentioned was probably connected with a house the Arundels were apparently considering building at Gowbarrow Park on the north side of Ullswater. The Gage postscript, however, may be referring to the planned London house, given that the Building Proclamations specifically concerned restrictions in and around the city.

An anonymous copy (dating from after the mid 19th century) of a now lost 1633 plan of Tart Hall indicates a stage of building planning, with inscriptions mentioning the 'Count^{ss} of Arundell' several times. This is entitled 'A plan of the Estate of Tarthall Pimlico showing the Division of the Parish of St Martins & St Margarets by Richard Baynes 1633', indicating the relationship of the house to the all-important parish boundaries, probably to settle the apportionment of rates payable on a newly-built house between the two parishes. A further inscription states, 'Copied from a Plan drawn by Richd Baynes 1633'.[8] The U-shaped footprint indicated on the plan does not appear to be of a finished structure, and its status and any implications – other than it indicates a stage of planning – remain unclear. A survey-plan is unlikely to show projected buildings, but may do if they were clearly marked out or half-built. Perhaps this is the basic ground plan of the Arundels's new house (superimposed upon almost the entire old structure), shown immediately before, or in the early stages of construction. There is no indication of a rear, central tower, but, faintly highlighted, is a square area inscribed 'The old kitchen' under a superimposed, skewed, north-west arcaded wing. A 1641 inventory mentions 'south' and 'north' parts of the 'Old House', containing some rooms that seem to have been located on the ground floor in the two wings to the south and north-west of the 'New House'.[9] The inventory indicates that the south-east rear wing, at least, had a ground floor loggia, but not along the full length as the copied 1633 plan shows. Ancillary buildings are indicated by a narrow building of lesser construction stretching from the north-west side, and perhaps by 'unfinished wall lines' shown to the south-east.

Over a period of nearly a century, the 1633 plan, and two others – Morgan's map of London from 1682, and a copy of a drawing executed by Nicholas Stone's nephew, Charles Stoakes, in 1725 – clearly show a related progression of accretions with the house being enlarged from an original U-shape.[10]

Hollar's house and the Countess

Speculation has arisen concerning the identity of the house that appears in the background of Wenceslaus Hollar's 'Spring', from the set of four full-length etchings of *The Four Seasons* executed in the early 1640s. Analysis shows that it is most likely that Hollar's house is, as previously mooted by some, a depiction of Tart Hall.[11] It is a generously fenestrated building of three storeys with an attic, but with the rear roofline of the house lower than the front. With no discernible indication of the rear layout visible, this makes it completely possible that the back section of the house consisted of two subservient wings, extending further at ground floor level as a loggia – or, at least, something like the feature shown on the copy of the 1633 plan.

Hollar's house shows an ancillary building to the (probable) north-west in the same position as the ancillary building on the 1633 plan, and there may have been another at the opposite end of the house hidden behind 'Spring'. Further ancillary erections in the right front of Hollar's view – which apparently did not survive to appear on the 1682 Morgan map – occupy almost exactly the same position as the

169

'Welcom sweet Lady you doe bring Spring That makes the Earth to looke so greene
Rich presents of a hopefull Spring As when see first began to treeme.

'Spring' from *The Four Seasons* by Wenceslas Hollar, 1643, showing Tart Hall in
the background and its walled garden to the left (*The Royal Collection © 2007.
Her Majesty Queen Elizabeth II*).

'Fountain Court' to the right front of the 1633 plan. The initial
planning for this feature, in the inhospitable north–west angle of the

house, was possibly abandoned and the area used instead for more mundane purposes. It can probably be assumed that all of the structures shown in the right-hand corner of Hollar's view – from which the coach and horses are departing – were service buildings. To the far left of Hollar's etching is an elaborate walled Italianate garden, complete with fountain, and more or less in the same favourable, south-eastern position as a garden noted on the 1633 plan as the site of 'The Count[ss] of Arundell's … Court Yard and Garden'.

Two sloping ramps, on the 1633 plan, at the north and south-east corners of the house in the front courtyard, lead up to two sets of garden steps and terraces abutting the wall along St James's Street. These ideas were, it seems, also abandoned or changed in the ten years between 1633 and when Hollar executed his etching.

It must also be considered most probable that a small circular object on the balustrade of the south-eastern terrace – complete with what seems to be a gnomen when looked at with strong magnification – was a 'little Brass sonne Dyall' on the 'Top of the

A detail from Hollar's 'Spring', showing the lower roof-line of Tart Hall. Note the tiny sundial-type object on the left roof-terrace railing.

New house' at the south end, as listed in the 1641 inventory of Tart Hall that was taken to assist in the removal of Lady Arundel's effects to the continent.[12]

Wenceslaus Hollar's association with Lord and Lady Arundel began in 1636 when the Earl was visiting Vienna in his ambassadorial role to the Emperor Ferdinand II, and the artist was commissioned to record the Embassy and its environs.[13] Hollar stayed in their retinue when they returned to England, and later married Margaret Tracey, one of Lady Arundel's waiting women.[14] It seems that the Arundels commissioned Hollar to also produce views of their various homes and environs in England around the time they left in 1641.[15] Some of the resulting etchings are dated by Hollar as having been executed between 1641 and 1646. Hollar followed the Arundels to Antwerp, and his name appears among the members of the Guild of St Luke, entered in the Register for 1644-5 as a 'free-master', painter and etcher.[16] There are six views of the environs of Albury, two dated 1645, along with an etching of the house at Albury itself which Pennington dates to 1642-6. Nicholas Cooper states that the Albury views are 'cabinet pictures … for private contemplation'.[17] There is also one of Arundel Castle dated 1644, and two domestic courtyard scenes at Arundel House in London, one dated 1646. Hollar's three-quarter length 'Summer', from 1641, shows a view, through a window, of Lambeth and Westminster that was probably an aspect from Arundel House, while another shows a further view of London apparently taken from the roof.[18]

The Four Seasons

It seems logical then, that Lady Arundel would also have desired a view of Tart Hall which, Howarth writes, was her most favourite of all their properties. Evidence later given to the Committee for Advance of Money shows that the Countess actually continued with some financial upkeep of the house for many years after she left England, and even made plans to return to the house around 1652.[19] An astrological note recorded by Elias Ashmole refers to the birth of James Hollar, the son of Wenceslaus Hollar and Margaret Tracey, the Countess's servant, born at Tart Hall in spring 1643.[20] The young woman depicted as the personification of 'Spring' in Hollar's etching, is probably his pregnant wife, with the held tulips and the rose in her hair symbolizing love and fertility. The allegorical verse reads:

> Welcom sweet Lady you doe bring
> Rich presents of a hopefull Spring
> That makes the Earth to looke so greene
> As when she first began to teeme.

That is, he compares the fecundity of the first spring with his wife producing their first child at Tart Hall, the verb 'to teem', now archaic, meaning 'to bring forth, produce, give birth to, bear (offspring).'

The topographical backgrounds to the other three Seasons in this set can also be compellingly linked to the Arundels. Firstly, the perspective to the right of the figure in 'Summer' must have been taken directly from the front of Tart Hall towards the north-east, across the rectangular Rosamond's Pond (which appears on Baynes's 1633 plan), to the Banqueting House at Whitehall, the Holbein Gate, and the restored St Paul's Cathedral beyond.[21] Lord Arundel was on a specially formed 'Commission for the [rebuilding of the] Banqueting House' formed by James I, and both the Earl and Lady Arundel personally participated in Masques held there. As the Earl Marshal, Arundel supervised the displays of honour and nobility and sacred processions occurring around these buildings. Moreover, the earl supplied, from his own quarries in Ireland, some of the Drean marble used by Inigo Jones for the spectacular new classical portico to the old medieval cathedral.[22]

'Autumn' is linked, quite obviously, to the Arundels, as the background building is of the grotto in the grounds of their Surrey estate at Albury. Mary Hervey states that '[It] became the favoured resort of the family for many years [and] Lord Arundel hoped to have drawn his last breath [there and] delighted to sit and discourse [in] the grottoes [he] caused to be cut in the sandy hills about Albury'.[23]

It is less clear what the exact connection of the Arundels with the Royal Exchange in the City is meant by its depiction in the final etching, 'Winter'. The earl was closely associated, however, with Sir Henry Garway, 'a great merchant prince of the City … a friend of both Arundel and Inigo Jones'; his business interests certainly would have involved many visits to the exchange,[24] a main centre for information on mercantile transactions and not just a large, 17th-century shopping centre. The Earl was also one of the King's alnagers (mercery was a large part of the exchange's business); it might be pertinent that 'Winter' faces in the direction of the Mercers' Hall.[25] Relevantly, one of Hollar's etchings done in 1644 is of the Royal Exchange, while the 1641 inventory of Tart Hall lists 'a Print of the Exchange at Amsterdam', on which the Royal Exchange in London was closely modelled.[26]

Nicholas Stone and George Gage

Nicholas Stone has long been a prime nominee for authorship of the design of Tart Hall, a not unreasonable assumption considering firstly the recorded payments to Stone for work carried out at Tart Hall in 1639, and secondly that Hollar's building, like other of Stone's work, shows a distinct Serlian influence. The number of rooms in the 'New House', however, on the inventory from 1641, indicates that it had been a relatively major building project. Nicholas Herman, in a letter dated [Tuesday] 2 August 1639, to Lionel Cranfield, states that 'since Mr Conns departure … on ffridaie last … her honor … hath not come from Tarthall', indicating that the house was quite habitable around the middle of the period that Nicholas Stone was working there.[27] In the second half of the decade Lady Arundel was frequently at Tart Hall, and the implications of the 1633 plan are that the major structural alterations to the house were begun in the early to middle years of the decade. The identification by George Con, in a letter to Cardinal Barberini in March 1637, of the house where he had dined as a *casino* (that is, a small Italian pleasure house) also implies that the Italianate conversion had already been carried out by then.[28] The regular payments made to Stone may imply that he was acting as surveyor for building works at that time, but it is conceivable that by this stage these may have been interior decorative masonry, garden statuary and terracing, or ancillary buildings.

Moreover, David Howarth has cited a letter, dated 1 October 1638, from the Arundels's agent, Nicholas Herman, to Cranfield, a longstanding and intimate friend of the Arundels, which reads: 'That Ned Savage is a jolly widower, that Mr Gage (the Architect of Tart halle) is in Purgatorie, or that Baron Pagett of the exchequere is dead,

I believe is no newes to your Lo^{PP}'.[29] George Gage, a Catholic priest, was a close and long-standing friend of Lord and Lady Arundel. The Countess was described as 'always in the company of Gage', who by 1637 'had settled down as [her] chaplain.'[30] According to Dodd's Church History, he was 'of graceful person, good address, well skilled in music, painting and architecture', the latter a point that is emphasised by his portrait by Van Dyck, in the National Gallery, in which he gracefully leans on a classical pier, with classical columns in the background.[31]

Confusingly there was yet another Catholic priest named George Gage, as well as a prominent Lambeth soapmaker of the same name who added to the confusion by dying around the time Stone was carrying out work on Tart Hall in 1638-9.[32] It may be that Herman was confusing the priest's demise with his soapmaker namesake, although his reference to 'Tart-halle' was presumably to distinguish this George Gage from the other two. In any case, whichever George Gage died in 1638, the implications are that the major works were carried out at least several years before.

There is no doubting the Countess's close relationship with Gage, or her strong association with the Catholic 'goings-on' in and around Westminster (including dinners with priests at her 'casino'), which dismayed both the king and her husband.[33] Interestingly, the 1641 inventory lists all the goods at Tart Hall 'Except of Six Roomes at the Northend of the ould Building (wch the Right Honourable the Countesse of Arundell hath reserved unto her peculiar use)'. It is not unreasonable to speculate that one of these private rooms secreted some devotional objects and paintings.[34]

Two contemporary observations by Gage certainly show him as an architectural pundit. The first is in a letter to Toby Matthew from Gage when he was in London, which Matthew re-sent to Doncaster. This reads: 'I have seene Inigo Jones his banqueting house, which is a good lustie peece saving that it hath some blemishes here and there…But though Architects may differ in opinion about ornaments, I am glad in substance to see good building begin to get into this Island.'[35] The second is in a letter of George Garrard's to Lord Conway, dated 4 September 1636, where Garrard tells that he 'went to viewe [Laud's] new Quadrangle [at St John's, Oxford], built wholly by himselfe, a noble building, for soe Sr Tobye Mathewe, and Mr Gage would stile yt …'.[36]

The Venetian Link

Thus, notwithstanding Stone's eligibility as 'architect' of Tart Hall, a cluster of clear indicators point to another proposal. As Dr Richard Goy states,[37] the style of Hollar's house can be seen as a 'rather fascinating hybrid: part Venetian palazzo, part Brenta villa and part English.' The balcony fenestration, for example, is somewhat evocative of the central bays of the Palazzo Mocenigo-Nero, where the Countess rented apartments in 1620-2.[38] But the countess also rented a villa, probably at Dolo, *en route* to Padua where the two Arundel boys attended university, and it is when one realises that Tart Hall would not have looked out of place on the Brenta canal in the Veneto, that the probable inspiration for the Countess's *casino* becomes apparent. It has been suggested as very likely that Gage was with Lady Arundel in the Veneto for some of this time.[39] It seems they were expected to travel home together, for Sir George Chaworth, on 27 June 1623, wrote to the English agent in Brussels, 'Mr Gage is comed [from abroad]; but not my Lady of Arundel …'[40] With the combination, therefore, of the Countess's love of Italian culture and Gage's apparent architectural expertise, very likely he later produced some architectural drawings for her from which evolved her Westminster *casino*.

If the Countess rented her Dolo villa also from the Mocenigo family, there are three that might be possible candidates; the Villa Mocengio di San Samuele, the Villa Mocenigo delle Perle, and the Villa Mocenigo at Fiesso d'Artico.[41] The façade on Hollar's house facing St James's Park is strongly evocative of the most common style of the Brenta villas: two- or three-storeyed pavilion-like structures, which often had Serlian-influenced, balconied, central fenestration on the *piano nobile*, roof gables containing rooms, and rows of tall, single-light, round headed, imposted windows.[42]

Notwithstanding the evocative feel of Hollar's house, however, comparison also highlights a hybrid nature. As Goy states, the façade of Tart Hall 'has a very strong … urban … Venetian influence … more palazzo-like than villa-like'; the 'main entrance portal looks distinctly

Venetian, with chunky rustication in the manner of Sanmicheli'. It is the compact pavilion-like structure of the front of the house that strongly echoes the Brenta villas, while the U-shaped plan, with a courtyard and arcaded loggia towards the rear, clearly resembles yet another Mocenigo villa on the Giudecca.[43]

The regular row of windows on the *piano nobile* of Hollar's house is an unusual feature in Venetian *palazzi* and villas, which usually have two spaced, large single lights, one near the outer corner and the other close to the spine wall that divides the outer corner room from the central *portego*. An exception is the fenestration of the 16th century Villa Vendramin at Stra, close to Dolo.[44] More relevantly, perhaps, the façade of the Mocenigo house on the lagoonal island of Giudecca has, Goy says, this 'unusual example of this type of regular single-light fenestration [and so] the Mocenigo family link appears again.' Furthermore, he points out that square-headed windows were common on the ground storey, and simple square or rectangular lights were also almost universally used for the topmost storey; and 'thus only on the piano nobile … of the *palazetto* … the more complex

Detail of 'Veduta del Palazzo del Signor Santorio', by G.F. Costa (1711-72). A typical example of the many scores of villas on the banks of the Brenta Canal (*Conway Library: Courtauld Institute of Art*).

window types are found', just as at Tart Hall.[45] As Goy observes, the three parallel double roof pitches have 'more of London than Venice about' them, but the façade of the house is distinctly '*alla veneta*' if one covers up the two outer gables.

It is interesting also to compare John Thorpe's design for 'Sir Jo. Danvers, Chelsey' with Tart Hall, as there are similarities in the central façade fenestration of the two houses. Aubrey wrote that Danvers (who was in the Arundels's circle) 'travelled France and Italy and made good observations'; he built Danvers House at Chelsea and began to lay out an Italianate garden in the early to mid 1620s. Cooper states that '[few] who visited Venice … can have been unaware of the villa culture of the *terra firma* …', and makes the acute observation that 'if [Danvers] had been to Venice, the setting of the house on the banks of the Thames could have reminded him of the Brenta.'[46]

Although Gage probably did advise Lady Arundel, it also seems likely that much of the design of Tart Hall was influenced by the Arundels' own observations in the Veneto.[47] It must be relevant that Venetian touches had also been added to the Arundels' Albury House. Hollar's view shows a classical doorway and balcony tucked in between the flat-roofed end of the house and gabled section, and the

'Albury' by Wenceslas Hollar, *c.*1642–6. Detail of etching, showing classical columns on the porch, topped with pinnacles and surmounted by a scrolled, pedimented gable (*The Royal Collection* © 2007. *Her Majesty Queen Elizabeth II*).

two-storeyed porch is embellished with classical columns topped with pinnacles, surmounted by a scrolled, pedimented gable, features truly evocative of many Brenta villas.[48]

The end of Tart Hall

The Countess of Arundel died in Amsterdam in 1654, eight years after her husband's death in Padua in 1646. Tart Hall passed to the Arundel's fifth son, William Howard, Viscount Stafford (1614–80), and then to his son, Henry Stafford-Howard, 1st Earl of Stafford (1648–1719). A '… Catalogue of the Pictures, Prints, Drawings. Etc., … of the Old Arundel Collection and belonging to the Late Earl of Stafford', refers to a sale of contents of Tart Hall that took place in 1720. George Vertue visited the house *c.*1740-1, and made notes on the few remaining paintings there at the time.[49] Two years later, William Mathias Stafford-Howard, the 3rd Earl of Stafford (1718-51), sold Tart Hall, and this unique hybrid of Venetian-vernacular and English architecture was then demolished.

10

Kew Palace

Lee Prosser and Lucy Worsley

Kew Palace (**Plate 7**) is one of the principal surviving early-17th-century villas in the London region. Built by Samuel Fortrey, a City merchant, in 1631, it was adapted for use by the royal family during their occupation from 1730-1818. It is this late-Georgian period of use that gives the building its rather dark and melancholy reputation as the place where King George III was confined during his episodes of 'madness'. The survival of Samuel Fortrey's house has much to do with chance and the failure of the other royal buildings of its type. Yet, at the same time, the 1631 villa was surprisingly convenient for the needs of the new kind of royal household developed by George III: a tight-knit, domestic set-up of husband, wife and daughters, living in semi-retirement from the court.

Kew Palace is a typical 17th-century villa, and provides insights into both the history and development of the villa as an architectural form, and of the subsequent uses that were considered appropriate for buildings of this kind. In the absence of extensive documentary evidence, despite its royal use, physical analysis has answered many questions about the early house. While its exterior architectural form has been the subject of much interest in the past, the surviving parts of its early interiors have, until recently, remained almost completely unexplored.

The palace has been open to the public since the late 19th century. Today the building is looked after by Historic Royal Palaces, an independent charity funded purely by visitor admissions and donations, with no financial support from the government or the royal family. In the spring of 2006, Kew Palace was re-opened, after nearly ten years of closure, with a new presentation scheme. The results of the building analysis informing this extensive conservation and presentation project form the substance of this article.

The 17th century

The Palace represents the last survivor of a number of suburban houses that were dotted along the banks of the Thames from the late 15th century. Courtiers were drawn to the magnet of Henry VII's rebuilt royal palace of Richmond a mile upstream from Kew, and began to construct convenient, semi-rural retreats on modest parcels of land at a remove from the hustle of court itself.[1] One notable nearby house (now completely lost) was owned by the Earl of Devon, and was used to lodge the Spanish princess Catherine of Aragon when newly widowed after the death of the heir to the throne, Prince Arthur. Of the other houses in the immediate vicinity, however, almost nothing is known, except for some brief archaeological insights gained from excavations. Kew Palace itself provides the most extensive remains in the shape of a still-surviving undercroft, constructed as a series of vaulted brick chambers dating from around 1550. A series of land transfers and indentures suggests that this property was owned by Robert Dudley, the favourite of Queen Elizabeth, and took the form of a modest lodge, used for occasional accommodation and entertaining. The disappearance of these many houses along the river may have been due to the abandonment of Richmond Palace. The several that were later rebuilt include the small house enlarged by Frederick, Prince of Wales (1707-51), into the building that became known as the White House, standing just to the south of Kew Palace.

By the early 17th century, several pieces of land in the vicinity of the modern Kew Gardens passed to merchants of the City, and the site of the Palace itself was leased by Samuel Fortrey. Fortrey is an enigmatic man of Huguenot parentage, who, with his brother, followed his father into business. It is likely that he dealt in all sorts of commodities, and it is known that he owned a part share of a ship, the *Pearcey*.[2] With his wife Catherine, he built the existing mansion in 1631, presumably after demolishing the earlier lodge on the site.

This is attested by a brick-carved monogram and date-stones over the entrance, but it is likely that he had taken a lease on the property by 1620.[3] Archaeological investigation has uncovered much about Fortrey's lavish treatment of the interior of his new house, but the family's tenure was relatively brief. After his death in 1643, Fortrey's heir Samuel Fortrey junior seems to have taken little interest in the villa, instead decanting the family to the Isle of Ely to reclaim land from the Fens and concentrate on agriculture. After several changes of hands, the lease was sold in 1697 to Richard Levitt, sometime tobacco merchant and Lord Mayor of London.[4] Following Levitt's death in 1710, the house languished in obscurity until it caught the eye of Queen Caroline, consort of George II (r.1727-60). She took out a long lease in 1729-30 for her daughters, the princesses Amelia, Caroline and Anne.[5]

The plan of Kew Palace (see p. 48) is of a typical double-pile type, brick-built and marked by a curious mixture of Mannerist motifs: a Tower of the Orders, projecting bays, rusticated window surrounds and ogee gables, all expressed in a *virtuoso* treatment of cut and rubbed brick. It is little appreciated how common this idiom was once in the London region, and its striking appearance is now given greater prominence by a relative lack of contemporary comparisons. The building has attracted much speculation. Since the 19th century, the palace has also been known as 'The Dutch House', a name stemming from the assumed links between its Flemish bond brickwork, the so-called Dutch gables and the origins of Fortrey himself, implying continental tastes and influences. This is perhaps too simplistic an interpretation, and instead the building's design draws on much more subtle sources closer to home. Flemish bond was never the predominant bond of the Low Countries, occurring primarily in late medieval contexts, and then failing to re-emerge until after it had become widespread in England. Examples contemporary with Kew, however, occur across East Anglia, including church porches, and most significantly, the service wing of Blickling in Norfolk, dated to 1623. Ogee gables are similarly distributed widely across East Anglia, with an ultimate derivation perhaps from the continent, but at Kew they are flaunched with tiles, rather than the stone-capped examples found in the Netherlands. There is still much work to be done in identifying the wider sources for the building, including the Baltic and Hanseatic influences exerted on East Anglia at this date. Cut and rubbed brickwork was once extensive in London, as were curved gables, dispelling the image of Kew as being particularly exotic and Dutch. Instead, it lay far more in the mainstream of architectural developments elsewhere in the region, and it is more relevant to interpret these characteristics as the conspicuous expressions of wealth and cosmopolitan fashion.

The interiors of the palace (**Plates 10a–d**)) have received far less study than its brickwork. They reflect distinct periods of occupation and refitting but the house today is overwhelmingly the result of a comprehensive remodelling for the occupation of Queen Caroline's daughters between 1730 and 1734, some of which was undertaken under the supervision of William Kent and Thomas Ripley. Modifications comprised the insertion of extra chimney stacks, new doors and panelling throughout the lower floors, the replacement of the earlier staircase and the enlargement of the roof for servants' accommodation. Another, more subtle, remodelling took place for King George III *c*.1800-4, while later phases of redecoration and minor changes can be dated to the mid 19th century, the late 1890s, when the palace was being prepared for public opening, and as recently as the 1970s, when it was refurbished by the Department of the Environment. The building is therefore very much a palimpsest, but important earlier elements have been retained. They reveal much about the tastes and attitudes of the 18th and 19th centuries as superimposed upon a villa of the 1630s.

There are still 17th-century architectural features scattered throughout the house. The original transom and mullioned casement windows were replaced by sashes in 1730. However, the window embrasures, where exposed, show no sign of cutting back, suggesting that the earlier windows were set in timber frames. Much evidence of this kind was observed during the extensive repairs to the building that were undertaken following the closure of the palace from 1997. This provided a unique opportunity to remove areas of panelling and floorboards, and Historic Royal Palaces embarked on a number of studies such as a comprehensive paint survey.[6] This programme of analysis showed that much of the internal timber skeleton survives, and that the plan-form of a central through-passage on each floor remains essentially unchanged. Of the 17th-century decoration,

Modern view of Princess Amelia's bedroom, showing inserted Georgian arch (*Nick Guttridge, © Historic Royal Palaces*).

overmantels survive in two principal ground floor rooms, together with the carved chimneypiece of Tournai marble and alabaster in the Queen's drawing room, which was originally the principal dining room of the house. Panelling survives in the King's breakfast room (probably the parlour of the early house) though the room was, regrettably, stripped of its paint history in 1932 in a misguided attempt to re-create its historical appearance. Repositioned Tudor linenfold panelling adorns the ante-room to the library, while the King's library itself retains important 17th-century elements.

184

The King's library holds particular interest, both from an historical perspective, and in terms of recent discoveries from the original decorative schemes of the house. The room was the setting for a peculiar historical drama, played out one day during April 1801. A footman announced visitors to the ailing King George III. Two doctors, John and Robert Willis were accompanied by 'four of Warburton's men' (experienced asylum attendants) determined to seize the king and place him under restraint. By tricking the king to show them into the dining room across the corridor, ostensibly to show them a prized portrait of Van Dyck, they announced that for his own good he would be 'put under control'.[7]

The room is a curious mixture of 17th- and 18th-century features. Two walls of original panelling and a decorative timber overmantel

Recently-uncovered 17th-century wall painting in the King's Library (*Cliff Birtchnell,* © *Historic Royal Palaces*).

185

frame an over-large Portland chimney piece by William Kent, flanked on one side by a cupboard and the other by a niche for books, both of which have carved 'green men' as their keystones. Paint analysis initially suggested that these curious features were probably repositioned components from a dismantled hall screen, but the removal of a fitted 1960s bookshelf from the niche exposed an original theatrical painted scheme of brown with yellow ochre swirls and shells surviving in the upper recesses, which had once dominated the entire room. More extensive analysis, undertaken in 2005, revealed three 17th-century schemes, suggestive both of occasional change and rich decorative effect. The overmantel and green men were shown to be part of the same construction and not derived from elsewhere in the house. They were decorated with a figurative painted scheme in grisaille with extensive use of black marbling and gilding, clearly emulating expensive stone and carved work. A section of the 'painted lady of Kew' has now emerged from beneath 22 layers of paint as one of the more important indicators of the early building. It is clearly of the highest quality, likened to the techniques of Antonio Verrio, although probably too early in this context for his hand.

The first floor now represents an elegant interior of the 18th century, but there are important archaeological traces of the earlier schemes, particularly in the Queen's drawing room. This room is celebrated as the place where the parents of Queen Victoria, and the future King William IV and Queen Adelaide were married in a double wedding in 1818. As well as being the most important space in the building, it retains a strapwork frieze in addition to its Stuart chimneypiece. The will of Samuel Fortrey mentions gilt leather hangings in this room. The walls now have later bolection-moulded panelling, which must form a modification undertaken during the short tenure of Richard Levett at the end of the 17th century.

Plasterwork survives rather less well at Kew than in contemporary buildings in London such as Boston Manor and Forty Hall, but the two principal surviving elements are important in their own right. The Queen's boudoir, possibly a music room in the original house, retains a fine ceiling depicting the five senses in medallions, set within a ribbed lattice. On the ground floor, the door from the high end of the hall (now the King's dining room) to the original parlour retains a magnificent overdoor with shells, a mustachioed bust and grotesques, modelled with great skill.

Few observers have examined the second floor and attics of the palace, where more early evidence, though fragmentary, is preserved. One half of the second floor was used by the daughters of George III as suites of bedrooms and dressing rooms in the early 19th century, while the western half of the house seems to have been used for storage, and as an office by the housekeeper. Here there is much 17th-century panelling, often reused as simple wainscotting and most probably redistributed throughout the upper, less important, floors during the refurbishment of 1730. To date thirteen different moulding profile types have been recorded. Two unusual pine doors of the 1630s survive *in situ*, with clear traces of upholstered or fabric-hung backs and grained panelled fronts; they are now painted stone grey. Meanwhile, traces of decorative structural pillars also remain, with late 17th-century fragments of wallpaper.

The roof structure is now largely exposed after the remedial work undertaken in the recent past, which necessitated the removal of ceilings in the garret rooms. The original triple oak roof of 1631 survives intact, together with a second phase of augmentation from the 1730s, when the open valleys of the original structure were spanned by new roofs to create more space. The whole structure was then protected by a flat roof in the 1930s, solving endless problems of blockages in the gutters. Most interestingly, the pattern of doors and studwork partitions show that the roof was divided into a number of small suites for servants or possibly bedrooms for children or members of the household in the 1630s. Two original doors survive at this level, as well as a third from about 1660. The whole roof is also marked by a number of apotropaic or ritual protection marks, clearly cut with a race-knife into the soft, new oak. They include a variety of circles, and the letters 'M' or 'MR', representing invocations to the Blessed Virgin Mary. Marks of this type have been recorded on many vernacular buildings by Tim Easton and Linda Hall but rarely on houses of this status.[8] The attics also preserve a crucial reminder of the lavish interiors of the building's earliest phase. In 2005, a section of a *tromp l'oeil* scheme which once decorated the lost 17th-century staircase was found to have survived beneath later layers of distemper. This open-well stair had newels two metres in height, piled up with turned decorative finials, a heavily moulded handrail and precocious vase-balusters.

The 18th century

The palace passed into royal use in 1730. The banks of this stretch of the Thames had become lined with fashionable residences, almost like the Loire valley, with houses like Richmond Lodge, Kew, Ham House, Marble Hill and Hampton Court scattered along its length. George II's wife Queen Caroline was the first member of the royal family to take an interest in Kew Palace. She leased the small brick villa for her daughters because of its proximity to her own country house at Richmond Lodge, while her son Frederick, Prince of Wales, in turn took over the building later known as the White House across the lawn from Kew Palace. Queen Caroline and Prince Frederick subsequently developed the surrounding gardens with curious and exotic features such as Merlin's Cave and a Hermit's Grotto. Queen Caroline's estate (known as Richmond Gardens) and Prince Frederick's land (known as Kew Gardens) were later united by George III, and now form the basis of the Royal Botanic Gardens. Frederick's great project to transform the old White House into a new residence was William Kent's earliest complete country house commission. Frederick's widow, Princess Augusta, continued to embellish the gardens with the help of Sir William Chambers, designer of many of the surviving 18th-century garden buildings such as the pagoda and orangery.

Frederick died young and never reigned, but his son, the future George III, plays the most prominent role in the history of Kew Palace. By 1758, the rooms in the palace were listed as a great room, waiting room, bedchambers and dressing rooms, all of which were richly appointed. On 25 October 1760, the twenty-two-year-old prince was riding out from Kew when he was intercepted by a messenger who informed him of his grandfather's death that morning at Kensington Palace. The new King George III appeared grave and thoughtful, though a later account added that 'it might be perceived by his countenance that he was not sorry to be a king'.[9]

The new king was soon married to Charlotte of Mecklenburg-Strelitz. The couple moved initially to Richmond Lodge, and in 1772, after the death of George's mother, to the White House at Kew.

George III became celebrated for his modest and happy family life. He preferred tea to coffee, did not eat between breakfast and dinner at 4pm, usually dined on a simple meal of mutton and vegetables, and loved the society of his wife and children: habits well suited to life in the quiet domesticity of the houses in Kew Gardens. Kew Palace was pressed once again into service to educate a future monarch, this time as the schoolroom of the Prince of Wales, the future George IV.

From the late 1770s, Kew became the setting for the major melancholy drama of the reign, that of the king's 'madness'. Although his contemporaries thought he was suffering from a mental disorder, it is now known that George III was actually experiencing the metabolic illness porphyria, with its symptoms of blue urine, uncontrollable shaking and 'incessant loquacity'. Between November 1788 and March 1789, George III was kept at Kew. His doctors described his symptoms: his heartbeat was 120 times a minute, his eyes were 'like blackcurrant jelly, the veins in his face were swelled, the sound of his voice was dreadful'.[10] He often spoke until he was exhausted, while foam ran out of his mouth. Though the king made a good recovery, his second major bout of illness in 1801 saw him taken once more to Kew. Though on this occasion he was put into rooms at the White House, the Queen and her daughters were now housed in Kew Palace itself.

By this time the White House was gradually disintegrating, having been neglected in anticipation of the completion of a grander, castellated palace nearby. This grandiose scheme was never finished, and was demolished in 1828.

The key to understanding the Georgian use of the villa at Kew lies in its *ad hoc*, haphazard nature: the available rooms were hurriedly allocated to provide short-term accommodation for various household members. Haste lies behind the decorative schemes within the palace, though when the queen and princesses came into residence their apartments were fitted up in some style. The princesses Elizabeth, Augusta and Amelia were given fashionably-appointed rooms on the first and second floors, and flimsy wooden architectural features such as curved niches were constructed within the shells of 17th-century rooms and decorated with green verditer wallpapers (of which dated fragments survive) and pink paintwork. Soft furnishings included black and red curtains with yellow and black patterns for other textiles. Princess Amelia's bedroom retains its original pink painted finishes of *c.*1809 with a 16th-century fireplace inserted to add a Gothic touch. This and the other rooms on the second floor, left undisturbed by later generations, are particularly redolent of the Georgian period.

Queen Charlotte died at Kew in 1818, an event that may have saved the Palace from destruction. George IV planned to demolish and rebuild it, but lack of money gave it a stay of execution. Despite a number of worrying structural problems and the cost of maintenance, Queen Victoria held a sentimental attachment to the palace as the scene of her grandmother's death, and it was preserved from depredation and neglect. Although further marginalised by the transformation of the gardens from a historic royal pleasure ground to a scientific institution, Kew Palace was opened to the public for the first time in 1898. As a rather drab and sparsely furnished museum, the building was nonetheless generally popular, and was overhauled in the 1930s, 1950s and 1970s. In the 1990s, serious structural problems once again emerged, and the displays had to be dismantled. At this time, research revealed that much of the existing decorative scheme, paint colours and wallpapers to be imaginative but essentially 20th-century creations. As a result of extensive recent analysis, a new and more authentic presentation of the palace has been developed, anchored around the year 1804: the period in which the house took on a national prominence as a place of recuperation for the king, and a domestic refuge for the royal family. Crucially, the palace's new interpretation also combines this Georgian story with the stories about the conservation of the house, and about its origin as an early-17th-century villa. Some of the approaches have been controversial. Conservation of the external brickwork revealed traces of an original coloured wash. This was reinstated in 1999, allowing the building to be seen in its original architectural form for the first time in centuries.

The structural works necessitated by the parlous condition of the palace showed that the building was rather poorly constructed, and has survived only because of concerted and expensive efforts to maintain it in good order. Structurally, the roof used middling oak to the best technological advantage while the brickwork, as impressive as it first appears, conceals deeper structural shortcomings. Without the interest of Queen Caroline and subsequent royal attention, it is unlikely that the building would have survived long into the 18th century.

Conclusion

Examining the archaeology of the building has revealed Samuel Fortrey's country villa to have been nothing less than lavish. It was decorated sparingly and selectively with expensive marble, a parsimony compensated for by painted schemes imitating more expensive materials, the use of fabric hangings, and varied panelling in Baltic oak and pine. The interior was as dazzling and conspicuous as the exterior, which must have presented visitors with a breathtaking amalgam of mannerist motifs and extraordinary workmanship. A considerable amount of Fortrey's wealth must have been invested in this bauble on the banks of the Thames. Like other villas, however, the house was not seen as a vital part of the family inheritance, and after Samuel's death, it is likely that interest waned and the site was soon seen as an asset to generate revenue.

The remodelling of the building undertaken for the Georgian Royal Family involved a curious split approach. Painted decorative schemes were obliterated without exception by more sober Georgian colours, but structurally the modifications were much more conservative. Externally, the house was not altered, apart from the addition of sash windows. Although expense may have been a factor, there was no decision to disguise the early origins of the house with render as was done at the nearby White House by William Kent. Internally, the approach was careful and selective. Several important Stuart decorative features such as overmantels, decorative plasterwork and panelling were retained, though clearly much was destroyed and the criteria for retention have yet to be understood.

Kew Palace has many more stories to tell beyond its tale of royal madness. Notwithstanding its dramatic later history, this 17th-century villa provides an important example of Renaissance domestic taste, yet remains something of an enigma.

11

Country Retreats in Seventeenth-Century Hertfordshire

Paul M. Hunneyball

One of the most common definitions of the 17th-century English villa is a lodge-like building constructed near London by a wealthy merchant seeking temporary respite from the pressures of city life. In 1700 Timothy Nourse described the typical villa as 'a little House of Pleasure and Retreat'.[1] He supplies a convenient summary of the scale and function of such buildings, but offers no clues about their stylistic character. The word 'villa' tends to conjure up the image of a compact and stylistically progressive structure, but the reality in the 17th century was both more complex and more varied than this. The merchants who created and occupied country retreats in London's environs were not a homogeneous group, but rather represented a broad cross-section of English society, with contrasting aspirations and financial capabilities. The fact that they could afford these second homes indicates that they had enjoyed economic success, but this of itself was no absolute guarantee of a taste for the new fashions circulating in the capital. The end product of their building activities was indeed sometimes the stereotypical villa form, but, depending on individual circumstances, they might equally opt for a much larger house, or an old but upgraded one. The discussion which follows seeks to elucidate these issues by examining the full range of merchants' building projects in one particular county, Hertfordshire.

Before considering the houses themselves, it is necessary to outline the geographical environment in which these developments occurred. In the 17th century there was already a kind of 'stockbroker belt' around London, with Middlesex, Surrey and Kent in particular providing convenient rural retreats for people whose main base was the City or the court. Hertfordshire sat on the far edge of this zone. On horseback it was possible to cover the fifteen or so miles from London to a district such as Watford in just a few hours, so day or weekend trips to at least the southern end of the county were a real possibility. In an age of mounting urban pollution, Hertfordshire was famous for its air quality, as Robert Morden reported just at the end of this period: 'this county being so near the City of London has abundance of fine houses of gentry and citizens, who flock hither in summer for the benefit of the air, and recreation.'[2]

Defining a 'country retreat' is nevertheless problematic. It is tempting to adopt Morden's account as the fundamental explanation for the creation of Hertfordshire's villas, and, as will be seen, some of these Londoners did indeed acquire houses as just temporary retreats. However, when owners engaged in substantial reconstruction of their properties, they were likely to be contemplating longer-term residence, and perhaps even the establishment of a new gentry line. Lawrence Stone's analysis of Hertfordshire's social elite indicates that around ten per cent of people entering his sample between 1580 and 1699 were merchants and financiers from outside the county, mostly from London, and the trend was upwards during this period. On that basis, a measure of caution is advisable in assessing the precise function of a country house.[3] In the ensuing case-studies, the builders were all merchants or financiers seeking a home outside London, and in that sense their houses were all country retreats. Even so, the architectural consequences varied considerably according to the owners' personal circumstances and priorities. Three main categories will be considered: remodelled properties, moderately large new structures, and finally compact villas.

Not all City businessmen found it appropriate to build entirely new houses. Some acquired country seats and left them substantially unchanged, while others opted for a limited upgrading of their properties. Pishiobury, near Sawbridgeworth, a moderate-sized courtyard-plan house, was originally constructed in the 1570s or

1580s, so it was still a relatively modern building when purchased in 1612 by Lionel Cranfield, a prominent London mercer who was recruited by the government in the following year as Surveyor-General of the Customs. Cranfield's account books reveal that he constructed an elaborate new classical porch for Pishiobury, and also renovated the gardens, though initially he was otherwise satisfied with the property. Meanwhile, he advanced rapidly through the government's ranks, becoming Lord Treasurer in 1621, and Earl of Middlesex a year later. However, peers and senior ministers were expected to live in a style appropriate to their rank, and Pishiobury was now far too compact for Cranfield's needs. Rather than rebuild on this relatively small estate, he began hunting for a larger seat elsewhere. Thus work at Pishiobury was suspended within five years of the initial improvements being completed, and the house was finally sold in 1635.[4]

Total reconstruction did not necessarily happen even when the owner was a long-term resident. For example, Brent Pelham Hall was built about 1608 on a traditional manor-house plan, with a central hall flanked by parlour and service wings. It was bought in 1626 by Francis Floyer, a London mercer and a leading figure in the Levant trade, specifically so that he might enjoy 'a private life in the country'. His son-in-law, the antiquarian Sir Henry Chauncy, who lived there for a time, recorded that once Floyer 'had adorned this house, he furnist it with all things so that nothing was wanting to make it pleasant and delightful'. However, in structural terms Floyer's changes were limited. He certainly upgraded the heating provision, and installed a fashionable new staircase which presumably provided access to first-floor reception rooms. However, there is no evidence that he significantly enlarged the house, and almost certainly he left the exterior of the building more or less untouched. The present brick casing was added by Floyer's grandson several decades later, and the original walls were either timber-framed or at best of mixed brick and timber construction.[5]

There again, some owners aspired to wholesale reconstruction, but lacked the money to fulfil their ambitions. For example, Salisbury Hall was remodelled by the London financier, Sir Jeremiah Snow, about 1670. Snow was on friendly terms with Charles II, who is said to have visited the house several times, so he was not lacking in motivation to modernize this early Tudor property. However, his intermittent cash-flow problems forced him to compromise, and rebuild a little at a time. Naturally he started with the main entrance and reception rooms, but effectively he reproduced the old floor plan, right down to the traditional, and now very old-fashioned arrangement of a hall and screens passage. The detailing was brought up to date, with modern fenestration, a classical entrance doorway and a partially hipped roof. Had the work been completed, the entrance façade at least would have resembled other compact Hertfordshire seats of the late 17th century. In the event, though, the Tudor kitchen wing adjoining the screens passage was left substantially unaltered, and indeed survived in this state right through to the early 19th century.[6]

Salisbury Hall demonstrates clearly the potential disadvantages of a limited budget. However, it should not be assumed that those merchants and financiers who could afford to build from scratch automatically opted to construct modest country retreats. Hertfordshire's best example of a more lavish approach is Balls Park (see p. 117), just outside Hertford, which was built for John Harrison sometime around 1640. Harrison, who hailed from Lancashire, began his career as a clerk in the London customs house, but graduated in the 1630s to the more exalted role of customs farmer, joining several consortia which contracted to collect customs dues on the Crown's behalf. This was a high-risk but generally very lucrative activity, and the farmers were necessarily on very intimate terms with the government. When Harrison bought the Balls Park estate in 1637, he had risen from humble stock to become a man of real substance and position, and accordingly he commissioned a house which would reflect his wealth and status.[7]

The result was predictably not a compact villa, but rather a spacious, courtyard-plan country seat, with the most sophisticated classical façades yet erected in the county. Moreover, as Sir Henry Chauncy observed in the 1690s, 'every side [was] equally fronted and exactly uniform'. This description of four perfectly matching façades was only a slight exaggeration, and a display of symmetry on this scale was still a real novelty in England in the mid-17th century, when most houses had just one or two show fronts. The use of a hipped roof with dormer windows also gave Balls Park the stylistic edge over

Hertfordshire's existing country houses. Taken as a whole, this building was so advanced for its date that when the inspectors from the Royal Commission on Historical Monuments visited at the start of the 20th century, they assumed that it must be Georgian, and excluded it from their survey of the county.[8]

Nicholas Stone, the king's mason, has been suggested by John Newman as the designer of Balls Park, on account of similarities between the mouldings around the windows there and those recorded at Goldsmiths' Hall in London. Certainly, other details such as the ornamental brooches on the pilasters flanking the main doorway tie the house firmly in with the latest ideas circulating in the capital (the same device appeared, for example, on the late 1630s houses in Great Queen Street). Given Harrison's ties with the government, it is feasible that he turned to the Royal Works circle for a surveyor. At this date, there were very few designers even in London who were capable of producing such a confidently classical façade without smothering it in pilasters, so Nicholas Stone is a plausible candidate, given his close working relationship with Inigo Jones.[9] As if to confirm the exclusive origins of Balls Park, the house's stylistic novelty was underpinned by expensive craftsmanship. Most of the original interior decoration disappeared long ago, but Chauncy noted 'the ceilings within the house wrought with several and distinct patterns of fretwork, the steps in the great staircase wainscotted in pares, [and] the hall paved with black and white marble'. Harrison ran into major financial difficulties during the Civil War period, and it is not clear whether the whole of the interior was ever finished as intended, but the quality of the external detailing still provides a sense of what has been lost. The only significantly retrograde element of the house was in fact its fairly conventional courtyard plan, the main entrance leading into a sort of screens passage, with a large hall off to the left, beyond which lay the staircase hall, and beyond that reception rooms.[10]

Balls Park demonstrated very effectively the ability of wealthy and well-connected London merchants to tap into the capital's construction market, and create a house which was a match for Hertfordshire's best gentry seats. Around twenty years later the point was made again at Kimpton Hoo. The builder this time was Jonathan Keate, the son of a London grocer, and a merchant and financier in

Kimpton Hoo in *c.*1700, drawn by Jan Drapentier for Chauncy's *Historical Antiquities of Hertfordshire* (*Bodleian Library, University of Oxford, Gough Herts. 14, p. 510*).

his own right, who married the heiress to the Kimpton estate. Keate was not in the same league as Harrison financially, but he seems to have shared his ambition of retiring from the commercial world and setting himself up as a country gentleman.[11] Kimpton Hoo was another almost square house, narrower than Balls Park but boasting an extra storey. It was much altered before its demolition in 1958, and the original plan is difficult to establish, but it certainly featured a small inner courtyard. Services were probably contained in the basement, with major reception rooms on the first floor. Stylistically, the input of current London ideas was unmistakable. The windows on the three main floors were linked vertically by projecting panels, while the window frames in the entrance façade's central bay were given a more elaborate decorative treatment, two features popularised by the leading London surveyor, Peter Mills, during the previous decade. These progressive elements were somewhat undermined visually by Kimpton Hoo's distinctly old-fashioned gabled skyline, which suggests that Keate obtained elevation drawings from the capital, but employed craftsmen who were not well practised in the latest fashions. Nevertheless, the house easily outshone most other recent gentry projects in the county.[12]

The final example in the category of lavish construction, Oxhey Place, is the least well recorded of these three houses, but it was significant for providing Hertfordshire with what was probably its first overtly Baroque entrance façade. Two builders were involved this time, a father and son, both of them London financiers. Sir William Bucknall claimed descent from the Northamptonshire gentry, though his immediate background seems to have been relatively humble. He spent his early career in the London Salters' Company, but like John Harrison of Balls Park he found it was more profitable to collect government revenues, in this case the excise tax. At the time of his death he is said to have been worth £113,000. Bucknall purchased the Oxhey Place estate in 1668, the year in which he doubled the scale of his excise farm, and according to Chauncy he built a house there prior to his death eight years later. However, Sir William's son Sir John is also credited by later authors with a construction project in 1688. Virtually the only source for the building's appearance is an 18th-century drawing by H.G. Oldfield, which seems to show the elder Bucknall's house of c.1670 after it was remodelled by his son. The end result was a very substantial pile, three floors high, with an eleven-bay entrance façade, of which the two outer bays at each end and the third storey in between them may represent the younger man's additions. Whatever the building's precise evolution, its most conspicuous feature was an ultra-fashionable, flat, balustraded roofline, a motif then still associated primarily with Royal Works projects, which on stylistic grounds is unlikely to date much earlier than 1690. Oxhey Place was demolished in 1799, but the Bucknalls' private chapel, a free-standing Jacobean structure, still survives, complete with the late-17th-century fittings that they installed there. This high-quality woodwork is strikingly similar in design to the joinery created around the same time for the new churches built in London after the Great Fire of 1666. The basic fabric of Oxhey Place may be difficult to reconstruct with certainty, but if the chapel fittings are representative of the interior of the house, then one can say with some confidence that the Bucknalls were again responsible for a significant injection of the capital's latest design trends.[13]

Having considered the extremes of Hertfordshire's merchant projects, remodelling exercises on the one hand, and substantial new seats on the other, one might reasonably argue that the final category of activity, the fashionable compact retreat, represents a happy median between the two. Nevertheless, it remains important to consider the individual circumstances behind each example, in order to understand the shape that these buildings took. The first case-study in this section concerns Rawdon House at Hoddesdon, a small town on the main road from London to Cambridge. Although scholarly opinion is divided over this building's early history, it was most probably constructed in the early 1620s by Marmaduke Rawdon, a Yorkshireman who made his fortune in London through the wine trade. Sufficiently prominent that his fellow merchants employed him to represent their interests to the government, he came to be highly regarded by the king, James I, and his great favourite, the Duke of Buckingham. Rawdon's main base was the City, but he acquired through marriage a small estate at Hoddesdon, 'where he had a fair house of his own building, a place of much recreation'. This was in fact a particularly strategic location for a country retreat. Not only

Rawdon House, Hoddesdon, as recorded in 1833 by John Buckler (*Hertfordshire Archives and Local Studies, Buckler drawings, iv, f. 46*).

was Hoddesdon a relatively easy journey up from London, but it also lay close to the king's favourite country residence, the palace of Theobalds. According to family tradition, James often used to call in at Rawdon House on his way back from hunting at Royston. Rawdon also on one occasion entertained another important neighbour, the second Earl of Salisbury.[14]

The structure one sees today, although extensively restored, convincingly matches the profile of its presumed builder. One reason why it has perplexed some observers is precisely the fact that it does not fit the normal Hertfordshire pattern of small country houses of this date. The plan is extremely compact, essentially five bays wide and one range deep, with a large staircase turret at the rear; and the models on which Rawdon and his surveyor drew were recent projects in the London suburbs, such as Nottingham House in Kensington or Eagle House at Wimbledon. The standard local pattern still involved an old-style hall entered at one end through a screens passage, but at Rawdon House the hall was rotated 90 degrees so that it could be placed centrally within the house, with the main entrance porch superceding the screens passage. In stylistic terms, this reorientation made it much easier to achieve an entirely symmetrical entrance façade, something which had apparently not been attempted before in Hertfordshire in a house of this size. A symmetrical façade in turn could be much more readily articulated by classical ornament, in this case two prominent entablatures at first- and second-floor level, with pilasters below them to mark the bay divisions.[15] This was never the most sophisticated of schemes. The third-floor fenestration is not precisely aligned with the bay windows of the two lower floors, and the individual bays of the façade are themselves of irregular widths. Even so, the stylistic ambition of this project is unmistakeable. The Doric and Ionic pilasters have a pedantic, scholarly feel to them, which implies that someone involved with this design was at the very least accustomed to using pattern books of the classical Orders. Moreover, the very concept of ordering a façade in this manner was at this date normally associated with much larger buildings, such as the Earl of Salisbury's own home, Hatfield House. Add in the expensive brick construction, which in Hertfordshire was still normally reserved for major seats, and what one has here is in effect a grand mansion in miniature, the city come to the country, in short a villa. Little can be reliably stated about the interior decoration, but the main reception rooms appear to have been spacious, albeit few in number. In other words, Rawdon House was too small to serve satisfactorily as a principal residence, but it made perfect sense as a country retreat for a city magnate who expected important visitors.[16]

During the 17th century, Hertfordshire probably boasted a number of buildings in the same class as Rawdon House. Robert Morden drew particular attention to the large number of seats in the county's southern districts which provided retreats for London's citizens.[17] Little trace now remains of most of these properties, but one rare survival of compact design from the middle years of the century is Codicote Bury, which was built by George Poyner during the 1650s. The son of a minor Shropshire gentleman, Poyner was apprenticed as a London ironmonger in 1629. However, he also engaged in the overseas cloth trade, particularly with the eastern Mediterranean, which is probably how he made most of his money. He acquired Codicote manor in 1653, and took enough interest in the local community to provide a makeshift Presbyterian chapel on his estate three years later. Indeed, once the house was built, he seems

Codicote Bury, as recorded in 1840 by George Buckler (*Hertfordshire Archives and Local Studies, Buckler drawings, iv, f. 154*).

to have shifted his family there, as three of his children were baptised in the village. Nevertheless, Codicote was clearly intended as a country retreat, since Poyner was briefly appointed a London alderman in 1661, and served as Master of the Ironmongers' Company in the following year.[18]

Codicote Bury's top floor was altered in the 18th century, and the original appearance of the roof is difficult to establish. However, the two-storey elevations were certainly of an advanced character. The entrance façade is divided into nine narrow bays. Of these, the three central ones are distinguished from the rest by a somewhat crude classical frontispiece, while the outer bays consist of single windows flanked by blank recessed panels. The recesses possibly once also contained windows, though in that case the effect must have been rather cramped. In many ways this frontage looks rather clumsy, but it is best understood as a transitional design. While lacking the relative sophistication of Balls Park, it was still an advance on the concept of a classical frontage articulated entirely by pilasters, such as that erected at Rawdon House. Instead, the sharp relief of the central frontispiece is contrasted against the shallow articulation of the recessed panels in the flanking bays. Arguably, this formula anticipated the dominant pattern in small English country houses in the decades following the Restoration, which was of two-storey façades, divided horizontally into three, with the central section emphasized by a pediment. This analogy should not be pushed too far, but Codicote Bury as a whole was architecturally more innovative than conservative, which suggests that Poyner employed a London designer rather than a local one.[19] In constructional terms, the house was evidently a compromise. The plan was quite advanced for its date, a compact square with reception rooms and perhaps also closets at the front, and a large staircase hall at the rear. The sheer scale of the staircase suggests that there were also important rooms upstairs. However, it is unlikely that Poyner hired his joiner in the city. The carved ornament on the stairs is an elaborate version of a fairly common Hertfordshire gentry pattern of the period which ultimately seems to derive from the great Jacobean staircase at Hatfield House. In all likelihood, then, Poyner economised on some aspects of his country retreat, commissioning the basic design from a surveyor or bricklayer familiar with London patterns, but relying on good-quality local craftsmen to fit out the interior.[20]

The compact square plan adopted at Codicote Bury was one of the more popular layouts for late-century villas, but other options were available. A more elongated model was tried out by John Culling 'of London' when he built Hertingfordbury Park sometime between 1681 and 1687. Apparently the son of a prominent London mercer and alderman, Thomas Culling, he married the daughter of another local merchant, lived in the City parish of St Andrew Holborn during the 1670s, and was eventually buried at St. Helen Bishopsgate. It is not clear whether Culling himself engaged in trade, but his close ties to the capital and its merchant community make it highly likely that he commissioned Hertingfordbury Park from a London designer.[21] With its hipped roof and two-storey, nine-bay entrance front with projecting central bays, the building broadly resembled the post-Restoration country house format popularised by Hugh May and Sir Roger Pratt. However, the project also featured several distinctly urban twists. The treatment of the wall surfaces, particularly the flat arches over the windows, was quite typical of London's late-century domestic fashions, apart from the lack of a plat

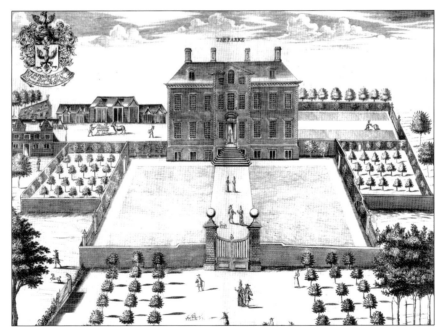

Hertingfordbury Park in *c.*1700, drawn by Jan Drapentier for Chauncy's *Historical Antiquities of Hertfordshire* (*Bodleian Library, University of Oxford, Gough Herts. 14, p. 272*).

band between the ground and first floors. More surprising was the continuation of the central bays up above the roofline as a full attic storey. An unusual motif in 17th-century English architecture, it was probably inspired by one of the Dutch pattern-books which circulated in London at the time. The precise design of the attic storey, an arched window pushing up through the base of the crowning triangular pediment, and flanked by smaller rectangular windows, could have been copied from a print of the Escorial Palace in Spain, but it was more likely borrowed from a similar and recently built example in the capital, the church of St Peter Cornhill. Equally intriguing is the large-scale presence of sash-type windows, which were still a luxury item at this date, and most commonly found in buildings associated with the Royal Works. That is not to say, of course, that Culling necessarily possessed contacts at Court, because so many of the Crown's craftsmen and surveyors also found work in the City, but it gives a sense of how expensive the house must have been. Regrettably, nothing is known in detail of the building's plan. The designer of Hertingfordbury Park also remains unidentified, though the decidedly handsome appearance of the building strongly suggests that Culling hired one of the more accomplished architects of the day, and certainly someone based in London.[22]

Taken as a group, these nine houses provide a fair cross-section of the forms that a 17th-century London merchant's country retreat might take, but how well do they resolve the question of what the typical villa envisaged by Timothy Nourse actually looked like? At first sight, the sample seems simply to confuse the issue. Because no two merchants approached a project with precisely the same objectives and opportunities, the buildings that they created or adapted were equally individual. Marmaduke Rawdon and John Harrison both dealt professionally with the wine trade, and almost certainly knew each other, yet their Hertfordshire homes, Rawdon House and Balls Park, represent virtually the polar extremes of the projects under consideration. One conclusion must then surely be that while villas might well be places of rural retirement, not all country retreats were in fact compact, lodge-like buildings. Clearly, a different approach to the problem is required. The one common factor running through all these examples, with the possible exception of Jeremiah Snow's Salisbury Hall, is that the merchants concerned were all affluent enough to be able to choose freely which style they wished to adopt. Although there were elements of compromise at Codicote Bury and Kimpton Hoo, these patrons were all in a position to hire progressive craftsmen and surveyors. Moreover, finding themselves in that situation, they all opted for the latest styles circulating in London. On that basis, one might tentatively suggest that a villa in Nourse's sense was not simply an agreeable place of retreat, but a house where a wealthy merchant might show off his urban sophistication in a rural setting. In effect, a villa combined the taste of the city with the smell of the country.

Acknowledgements:

I am grateful to Hertfordshire Archives and Local Studies and the History of Parliament Trust for permission to use the unpublished materials cited in this discussion.

12

Forty Hall and Tyttenhanger

Elain Harwood

This chapter is very much a work in progress. Forty Hall and Tyttenhanger were both the subject of study days organised for the Society of Architectural Historians of Great Britain, and these accounts began as summaries drawn from those days. Since then I have found more archives relating to Tyttenhanger, and Paul Drury and Richard Peats are undertaking a thorough survey of the fabric of Forty Hall. They are but two houses from the early-17th century looked at as part of an occasional series of study days in recent years, in the hope that close study will draw out a consistent pattern of planning and design details from this period of transition. While ostensibly Forty Hall and Tyttenhanger have little in common, although only fifteen years and fewer miles apart, an understanding of the plan and detailing of one may in some measure aid the other.

Forty Hall

Forty Hall is a small country house of 1629-32 lying in the north of the London Borough of Enfield. It has been a local authority museum since the 1950s, until a brief closure in 2000 prompted English Heritage to commission research and a conservation plan. It has hitherto remained enigmatic, in part due to a paucity of documentation, in part because of its transitionary place in the history of the small country house – a puzzling mix of traditional and modern elements. New research by Paul Drury and Richard Peats will help us understand its plan more thoroughly.[1]

Forty Hall, showing the entrance (north) and principal garden (east) elevations. The hipped roof is original, despite the later cornice. The garden elevation lost its projecting bays early in the 18th century, and its central section (save for the doorcase) was radically remodelled in 1897 (*Author*).

Nicholas Raynton or Rainton was born in Lincolnshire, and became a prominent member of the Haberdashers' Company, importing satin and taffeta from Florence and velvet from Genoa, just when the role and finances of the City companies were expanding from dealing in home manufactured wares to international trading. Raynton bought the manor of Worcesters in 1616, but it was only in 1629 that he began to build a house, on a new site at the top of Forty Hill. Lysons records this site as being not part of Worcesters but a separate land holding, 'sometime Hugh Fortee's and late Sir Thomas Gourneys'.[2] The date 1629 appears on a brick at the north-east corner of the house, and in a ceiling in the south-east room on the first floor. Richard Gough and William Robinson record a date of 1632 on another brick near the top of the house, now gone.[3] Raynton's City career culminated in his serving as Lord Mayor of London in 1632-3 and a knighthood. In 1632 he was elected chairman of the London feoffees of impropriations, a Puritan body which aimed to install more godly clergy, and in 1639 he refused to

207

lend money to Charles I, and to disclose the wealth of his associates, actions which landed him in the Tower for five days. Few senior City figures expressed such avowedly Puritan sympathies, yet Raynton was no popularist. When the City's merchant oligarchy broke down in 1642 he pleaded other commitments and retired to Forty Hall, where he died in August 1646, aged 77.[4] A handsome tomb in the parish church also depicts his wife Rebecca, son and daughter-in-law (also Nicholas and Rebecca), and their seven children, all of whom predeceased him. The inscription records his 24-year involvement with St Bartholomew's Hospital, an area deserving further research, and his support for 'the republic of London'.

Raynton's successor was his great nephew, also Nicholas Raynton, whose additional land acquisitions included the site of the royal palace of Elysinge. The outbuildings to the west may have been added at this time. Thence it passed to this Nicholas's daughter, Mary Wolstenholme, who in turned settled the house on her son – another Sir Nicholas – and his wife Grace.[5] Sir Nicholas Wolstenholme was the first of a series of occupants to fall seriously into debt, although not until he had, as Lysons noted, 'repaired and modernised' the house in about 1700 – the date of 1708 recorded on 'lead-pipe heads' with the initials W/GM, according to Robinson. Wolstenholme's work almost certainly included the sash windows, the cornice that abuts those on the attic floor, as well as fireplaces and panelling on the first floor.[6]

Work by subsequent 18th-century owners is harder to ascribe. After Sir Nicholas's death Grace Wolstenholme married William Ferdinand Carey, Lord Hunsdon, who is said to have improved the estate, but his life interest in Forty Hall ended on Grace's death in 1729. Sir Nicholas's nieces inherited the house, as is recorded in a series of indentures from 1739 onwards.[7] Mary lived there until her death in or before 1770, while the other, Elizabeth, married Eliab Breton of Norton in Northamptonshire in 1740. Although Breton is alleged to have been more interested in his Norton estates, he and Elizabeth seem to have made improvements to Forty Hall in the 1760s before attempting unsuccessfully to sell it in 1773, after Mary's death and thought to be the date of a surviving estate plan.[8] The estate comprised some 1,440 acres of land in Enfield and Waltham Holy Cross, all of it enclosed and demonstrating evidence of improvement in descriptions of woodland having been turned to pasture. But in 1787 – two years after Breton's death – the estate was sold in 65 lots, seemingly to pay off the debts of his three sons. Forty Hall was bought by Edmund Armstrong, who Robinson records as laying out about £4,000 in repairs and alterations, including covering the house with lime-wash and improvements to the grounds, before also running into debts that necessitated the sale of the house after his death by the Court of Chancery, in 1799.[9] The first known view of the house is dated 1793, and it was illustrated in the *Gentleman's Magazine* in 1823.[10] The view in the Guildhall Library, London (**Plate 9**), shows the house limewashed, with a dentilled cornice rather different to that presently existing, with clear eared surrounds above and to the sides of all the storeys – the attic floor crashes into the present cornice.[11]

No significant alterations appear to have been made to the house for much of the 19th century. In 1800 it was acquired by James Meyer, a merchant of Dutch extraction whose initials appear on the hopper heads on the north and south façades and who re-assembled much of the estate.[12] It was subsequently occupied by his brother Herman, their nephew Christian Paul and, between 1837 and 1894, by the latter's son, also James Meyer. The house was then bought by Henry Carington Bowles, who lived at the adjoining Myddelton House, for his eldest son, Henry Ferryman Bowles, the local MP. In 1897 the house underwent a radical modernisation programme, tantalisingly described in the local paper. It was in this condition that the house was surveyed by the Royal Commission on Historical Monuments, who published its report in 1937, and was sold to Enfield Urban District Council in 1951 to become a museum.[13] In 1952 there were five flats, which were remodelled in 1957 to create a museum in the principal ground and first-floor rooms. The adjoining stable yard to the west, with its stores, harness room and stalls, was rebuilt between 1964 and 1966 and remodelled into tea-rooms and a banqueting suite *c.*1968.[14]

The roof

What makes Forty Hall so interesting is its combination of typical Jacobean decoration with elements of classical simplicity. Historians long found it difficult to accept as original the hipped roof: in fact not

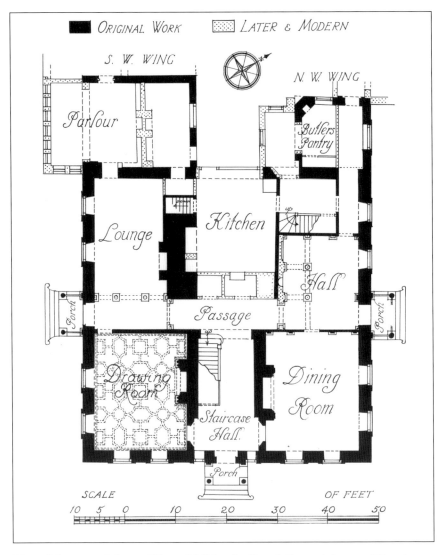

Plan of the ground floor of Forty Hall by the Royal Commission on Historic Monuments, 1937 (NMR / *English Heritage*).

an all-embracing hip but a narrow roof running right round a central well. This form can be seen in many houses from the mid-17th century, for example at Leadenham Old Hall, Lincolnshire; Tyttenhanger is a good example of the mid 1650s and the original form of The Grange, Hampshire, from the 1660s was probably similar. At Forty Hall, the heavy modillion cornice of *c.*1700 has led to a long-held assumption that the roof was remodelled at this time.

210

However in 1991 Andor Gomme and Alison Maguire determined that the roof must be original; not only does its butt purlin construction bear no trace of having been disturbed, but plaster faces set in the cove of the south-east attic room are clearly of the early 17th century, as Claire Gapper has confirmed. The position of these faces, one in each corner of the coved ceiling, cannot be squared with a gabled roof such as is still found at Boston Manor or Swakeleys. Robinson's note of rainwater goods dated 1708 would seem to confirm the stylistic attribution of the cornice to this time.[15]

The principal elevations

There are only a few clues to the original form of the glazing on the principal elevations. In the small yard on the west side rather more of the original fenestration can be seen, for the small attic casements appear to be survivals from the 17th century, both in their form and mouldings. The first-floor windows here are broader than are found elsewhere in the house, and may be another clue to the

The residual great hall at Forty Hall, shown as the dining room on the 1937 plan, looking towards the screen, infilled in the mid-18th century (*English Heritage – Nigel Corrie*).

211

earlier shape of the rest.[16] One basement window survives on this front, in line with those above. A study of the position of the basement windows on the south elevation, which no longer match those above, may indicate the original arrangement on the principal floors, with more closely spaced windows in the centre, and broader, shallower windows to either side more appropriate to the mullion and transom form. Later brickwork around the windows seems to confirm this.

The east elevation was altered as part of the remodelling of the staircase hall in 1897. An oblique photograph taken before this work began shows pairs of sashes at first and second floor level similar to those on the remainder of the façade, and that the segmental-headed porch below had arched cheeks to the sides.[17] There survive at ground floor level narrow windows either side of this central porch. Sir Howard Colvin has provided two pieces of evidence to indicate the form of this east elevation, which contains the principal rooms. He has compared the plan of Forty Hall with that of Thorpe Hall, outside Peterborough, of 1654-6 but described by Nicholas Cooper as still having an 'old-fashioned plan'.[18] Thorpe Hall has the same pattern of principal rooms either side of a staircase, and these rooms have small, square bays placed symmetrically. Pete Smith has additionally drawn attention to West Dean, Wiltshire, which also had shallow bays to its side elevations. West Dean was remodelled some time after its purchase by the Evelyn family in 1618 and two watercolours of it hung until recently at Forty Hall, showing the bays.[19] Disturbed areas of brickwork in similar positions on the east front of Forty Hall suggested that there may have once been such an arrangement here. To confirm this suggestion, Sir Howard has found Richard Gough's annotations of Lysons's *The Environs of London*, held at the Bodleian Library, which record that at Forty Hall 'the foundations of 2 bow windows in the E front were laid open in repairing it 1800'.[20] An excavation by the Enfield Archaeological Society in the summer of 2005 discovered the foundation of these bays, which have relieving arches in the basement.

The internal plan

The house Raynton created was almost completely square, but a small spur was added to the north-west corner shortly after it was completed, for an incised brick is dated 1635. A wing on the south-west corner existed by 1760 and was extended southwards into the grounds. In plan the house may best be described as being three rooms deep around a central core, or what Drury has called 'the compressed courtyard' type. The principal rooms on the ground floor are on the left or eastern side of the entrance. The plan of Thorpe Hall, built for another Parliamentarian, Oliver St John, makes a useful starting point for discussing the plan of the eastern side of the house. At Forty Hall the screens passage leads from the main entrance into a residual hall, later known as the dining room, which in turn is linked to the staircase by a door at the high end of the room. There is a corresponding door on the other side of the stair hall to a similarly sized room beyond, which may have served as a parlour to a suite on the south front. Above the ceiling of the Raynton Room, the remodelled 18th-century room occupying the south front, Drury and Peats have discovered the remains of a partition – with differing ceiling heights to either side – suggesting a chamber and closet here.

The western part is more difficult to sort out, but the enormous stack indicates that the kitchen was always in the centre of this range, with butteries to the north, on the opposite side of the main entrance from the hall. The present entrance hall is an 18th-century creation, the columns supporting an early-18th-century fireplace and stack. Crucial to an understanding of the house is the position of the back stair. The 1773 and 1787 sales particulars – with estate agents' economy, the descriptions are the same – state clearly that 'staircases are centrally placed'.[21] An examination of the floor framing in the centre of the house by Drury and Peats suggests that it took its present form in the 18th century, and a service stair here would have easily served the suites of rooms around it. There is also good evidence to support Peter Guillery's suggestion of a tight newel stair on the west side of the main kitchen stack, where there would have been a window until the 18th century and where there is still a stair leading to the basement. Paul Drury has discovered plasterwork in the void between the ground-floor ceiling and first-floor floor indicating that there was a service stair in this position, even though it could only conveniently serve the first-floor panelled room over the kitchen on the west front, perhaps the principal bed chamber.

Drury and Peats have interpreted the first floor as consisting of two suites of inter-connected rooms, one to the south side and the other on the north. The principal room was that in the south-east corner of the house, whose scale and importance is indicated by the design of the dated ceiling. This would have led to a withdrawing chamber in the south-west corner of the house, and in turn to a principal bed chamber on the site of the panelled room. Their examination of this panelling shows that it has been *in situ* since the mid-17th century and that this room originally extended further north. The sequence was probably completed by an unheated closet in the north-west corner of the building, on the site of the current back stairs. The northern suite is thought to have consisted of a chamber (the current north-east room, with a complete plaster ceiling), which led to an inner chamber and closet. Traces of the original chimneybreast heating the inner chamber can be found in the late-19th-century corridor leading to the north-east room and evidence of a partition between this room and the closet is visible in the panelling of the northern room.[22]

For too long historians have regarded the presence of a vestigial hall to one side of the entrance as old fashioned. Yet the idea of a progressive trend towards a centrally placed hall is as simplistic as suggesting a linear progression towards modernism. Forty Hall was advanced for its date in having four generally symmetrical façades under a hipped roof, but the different sizes of room within led to awkward spaces in the centre of the house that fall short of Palladian ideals. Particularly awkward is an unfinished void in the centre of the house, clearly not intended to be seen. Awkward central spaces are not unusual in early-17th-century houses. At Balls Park, Hertford, there was an open courtyard, elsewhere are small halls, and at Forty Hall the centre seems to have been blocked to provide purely service space.

The principal staircase

The main staircase is set between the two principal rooms on each floor, which were served by pairs of doors next to the windows. It seems likely that the staircase was an open well, and began by the garden door at the upper end of the hall. There are blocked doors to the principal first floor rooms above those leading to the staircase on the floor below, and they are slightly higher than the present half landing level, indicating a landing on the eastern side. The strapwork ceiling over the staircase hall does not extend as far into the centre of the house as does the present staircase, supporting the argument that the centre of the house could have housed the secondary stair. An article of 1897 in *Meyer's Observer and Local and General Advertiser* tells us that 'the easternmost hall, from whence the staircase springs, has been opened up by the removal of the brickwork which partly closed up the fine arched entrance to the hall from the main passage in the centre of the house. This admirably-designed and well-executed work has vastly improved this portion of the interior, and has added materially to the utility of the upper floors.'[23] This suggests that the ground floor remained blocked, even though the back stair had been removed to provide better access between the first-floor rooms. The first floor demonstrates how large 17th-century suites of rooms were cut down into self-contained bedrooms, seen in the dated ceiling that indicates the south-eastern room to have been much larger. The dated centrepiece is no longer central, and there is more of the ceiling in a cupboard off the adjoining lobby. Drury suggests that, with its grand, dated ceiling and evident large scale, this was the great chamber of the house. Christies' particulars state that by 1773 there were ten principal bedchambers and dressing rooms, a number that suggests that some must have been in the attics with the 'sufficiently numerous' accommodations for the servants.

Later work to the house

The house was extensively remodelled in the early 18th century, when the present fenestration pattern was introduced, and the first floor remodelled into self-contained bedrooms as shown by the panelling. The north-west stack was inserted at this time. Drury and Peats also argue that the back stair was manufactured at this time to fit into the wing, although it is described centrally in the 1773 sales particulars. These also describe a drawing room, dining room, breakfasting parlour and study on the ground floor. This would correspond with a suite running around the north, east and south sides of the house, assuming the south-facing Raynton Room could serve as a breakfast parlour and the small wing beyond was a study. There is a fire insurance plaque dated 1760, and this would seem a suitable date for these two rooms – Drury and Peats suggest that the south-west wing was added around this time – along with the central doorcase and first floor window surround of the south elevation. A similar date would seem appropriate for the remodelling of the passage between the Raynton Room and the north entrance, described in the sales particulars, and for the Gothick decoration with which the screen to the Great Hall was infilled – although Robinson clearly states that this last was only inserted by Edmund Armstrong, who also remodelled the fireplace here (the ceiling is shown by the Royal Commission as modern). Some support for the first-floor fireplace and stack put in during the early 18th century would have been needed in the hall, but the decoration is later. The 1773 sales particulars, the earliest description of the house, give particular attention to what may have been these improvements, describing how 'the Singularity and Coldness of the original Ornaments are ingeniously opposed to the *petite* neatness of the present.'[24] They give particular attention to the 'HALL adorned with a Screen of Columns, Mosaic Pavement, and elaborate Designs in Stucco, and to the several Doors are magnificent Porticos.'

Although Edmund Armstrong is recorded as spending heavily on the house, Land Tax returns between 1788 and 1800 record no great increase in rateable value; the critical years of 1785-8 are hard to interpret because the values are not recorded, but suggest that any work undertaken by Armstrong must have been in 1787-8. The value of the house increased by a third between 1802 and 1804 following its purchase by James Meyer, whose initials are recorded on the hopper heads.[25] The extent of further work by him, however, is unclear. The house reached its present form in 1897, with the insertion of the current stairs by Henry Ferryman Bowles. For a definitive analysis we must await the completion of Paul Drury and Richard Peats's research, and a further publication.

Tyttenhanger

Tyttenhanger (**Plate 11**), spelled Tittenhanger until around the 1830s, substantially survives as a house of *c.*1655-60, replacing a house associated with St Alban's Abbey first recorded in the 1320s and made more substantial around 1400. It was large enough for Henry VIII and Queen Katherine to stay for a fortnight in 1528 and, while a part was demolished in 1620, its near-continuous occupation by the Pope and

Blount families suggests that much of the structure may have survived until after the present house was completed.[26] Recent excavation work associated with gravel extraction, led by Jonathan Hunn, has identified a gatehouse, probably of the 15th century, and a range to the south-west of the present house.[27] Part of a moat system survives, both east and west of the house, with the remains of a large fish pond to the north, and the way the house is set slightly higher than its surroundings may indicate that the land has been made up with rubble.

Tyttenhanger was granted in 1547 to Thomas Pope, Treasurer of the Court of Augmentations and Founder of Trinity College, Oxford. He died in 1559 and the house was occupied until 1593 by his widow Elizabeth. Her brother William Blount had married Thomas Pope's niece, Frances Love, and in 1593 Tyttenhanger passed to their son, another Thomas, who added the name Pope to that of Blount. In 1639 the house passed to his eldest son, also Thomas, and on his death without issue in 1654 to Sir Henry Blount, his other son to survive infancy.

Sir Henry had lived an extraordinary life. He had travelled in France and Italy, and in the 1630s had made a great journey from Venice to Sarajevo, Belgrade, Bulgaria and Constantinople, partly in the company of a Turkish army sent to invade Poland. He had subsequently visited Alexandria and Cairo with the Turkish fleet. His *Voyage to the Levant* went through seven editions in his lifetime, and he was knighted in 1640. Politically he was a radical, but a trimmer noted for his legal brain; he was a member of the Hales Commission appointed to revise the criminal code in 1652 and served the Restoration as Sheriff of Hertfordshire in 1661. In 1647 he had married a wealthy widow, Hester Mainwaring, née Wase.[28] Sir Henry must have seen great architecture and now he had the means to create it. The date given for the house of 1655-60 is supported by a certificate of 1684 recording the chapel as having been dedicated by Ralph, Bishop of Exeter 'in the time of the late rebellion.'[29] His will, in 1682, records that he has already made over Tyttenhanger to his son Thomas, having previously passed it to his wife Hester to avoid reparations.[30]

That Tyttenhanger survives so well is due to the fact that it was tenanted for much of the 18th century. Henry's son Thomas, created

217

a baronet in 1679, died in 1697 and his son Sir Thomas Pope Blount lived mainly in Twickenham. Subsequently the house passed through the latter's daughter and granddaughter to the Yorkes, Earls of Hardwicke. It was reported as being in poor repair in the 1790s, but after 1800 was tenanted firstly by the Rev. Charles Lindsay and from 1805 by James Yorke, cousin of Philip, the third earl. After Philip's death in 1834 the house was occupied by his widow, Elizabeth, until her death in 1858, and by their widowed daughter, Catherine, Countess of Caledon, who lived there until 1863. The entrance was turned from front to back in around 1834, and Elizabeth worked on both the house and the grounds.[31] The house survived in limited occupancy through the 20th century until in 1973 it was sold to John S. Bonnington, a former partner of Sir Basil Spence, who converted it into architects' offices.

The elevations

The elevations are quite crude in their proportions. The house is of brick, resting on a plinth of clunch and harder limestone that may have been salvaged from the medieval works. The south elevation is symmetrical and this was the entrance front until the 19th century; indeed it is much the most significant elevation, the west elevation looking on to a series of walled enclosures as late as 1767, the date of an estate map, the east elevation giving on the service court and the north elevation encumbered by having the windows for the two disproportionate staircases. There are a number of inconsistencies between the south elevation and a drawing made of it some time in the middle or later 18th century now in the Hertfordshire Archives.[32] This does not show the central five bays as having alternating round-headed and triangular pediments to the first floor windows, and it shows the ground-floor windows of the projecting end bays having aprons like those found only in the upper storeys of the house we see today. These are, however, likely to be inaccuracies, as Oldfield's tiny engraving of *c.*1790 shows the present formation.[33] Pete Smith noted that the alternating short and broad quoins, found at all the corners including the re-entrant angles, have a short quoin at the top of the main elevations, an unusual feature that prompted speculation that the eaves may have been changed. Looking into a roof space, Paul Drury found a painted rafter with a simple cyma curve that may have been reused from an earlier, smaller cornice. The eaves are shown in their present form on the 18th-century survey.

A similar drawing survives for the west front, although with a proposal for a canted bay stuck over the right-hand half of the elevation that was clearly never carried out. This elevation is uneven, with five irregularly placed windows. The 1767 estate plan shows that the west front gave on to a small enclosed ground with beds, or possibly the fruit trees described in the particulars of the house in the 1780s. Accompanying plans of the house dated 1802 is an unrealised design for a raised terrace along the west front by the architect Henry Parsons of King William Street, London Bridge, where he practiced between 1854 and 1857.[34] Garden gates placed nearby are dated 1873. Today several windows on this elevation are blocked, particularly on the ground floor, and photographs in *Country Life* show the three ground-floor openings (and the adjoining two on the south elevation) as long casements, – one was a door with steps.[35] There is no 18th-century elevation for the north front, which is in many ways the most complex and interesting. Its end two bays project forward much less than those on the south front. There is a blocked cellar door to the right, the main door is a 19th-century aggrandisement and the main stair windows were remodelled to take 19th-century stained glass.

The interior

Although not long occupied as a principal seat, Tyttenhanger has undergone two major changes to the interior in the 19th century, and many changes of use to its sequence of generally small rooms that have resulted in the moving of panelling and fixtures. The plan is H-shaped, the first floor marked as the principal floor as late as 1802. The roof has a central well, with a gable running all around, as at Forty Hall. Leadwork is dated 1818, i.e. from shortly after the death of James Yorke. Looking in a cupboard on the floor below revealed a line of cruck rafters, alternating in direction, which carried the twin roofs down to the central crosswall.[36] We know more about the plan of Tyttenhanger thanks to the discovery of two sets of survey drawings; one undated set from the mid-18th century and one from 1802.[37] The earlier set shows a number of proposed works – that for the ground floor is marked 'the hall floor as at present', which the second shows not to have been carried out. An attempt can be made to relate the plans to an inventory made at the death of the first baronet in 1697, and to two schedules accompanying leases of the estate to Edward Coke of Holkham made in 1702 and 1725. That little work had been done to the house latterly is suggested by a lease of November 1701 where Sir Thomas Pope Blount agreed to undertake a list of repairs to the exterior and outbuildings.[38] The plans show that the present entrance hall was unconnected to the main stair, and so could only have served the service quarters on the north and east sides of the house. Its ceiling and reused linenfold panelling are clearly part of a 19th-century remodelling. The form of the vestigial screen in the original hall is also different from that shown on both sets of plans, which has columns. Adjoining it is a 'back parlour' or winter parlour, snugly situated next to the kitchen. By the second half of the century, when the house was advertised for lease, dining is firmly on the ground floor and the winter parlour has become a breakfast room.[39] One of the plans of 1802 shows proposals for moving the kitchen from the south side of the east wing to the north, where the housekeeper's room was, but this seems not to have been done. Two small butteries or pantries in the southern end of the wing made the great fireplace in the west wall of the kitchen more centrally placed, as John Smith suggested.[40]

The main rooms were in the west wing, with a great parlour and a withdrawing room listed in 1697 and 1702, though by 1725 they are the parlour and parlour-or-dining room. It was only in 1973 that the west windows were unblocked by John Bonnington to create the very bright office we have now, and plans suggest that two bays were always intended to be blind. In the rear rooms on both the ground and first floors very narrow side alcoves have been blocked. Even in 1725 a dining room continues to be listed on the first floor, along with a bedchamber – the rear of the two rooms is still shown as such in the mid-century plan, while a very large opening is shown leading from a lobby off the great staircase (**Plate 12**) into the bigger room to the south. It is this lobby that today has an overwhelming array of doorcases squeezed into it. The plans show that the bedroom on the south front, to the left of the lobby, had no door, but was entered through the anteroom. The segmental arched doorways would thus seem original but the pedimented ones were added later. At the other end of the house there was a bedchamber 'over the kitchen' together with a closet, described as Lady Blount's chamber in 1697 and adjoining a chamber for Lady Busby, her husband's step sister. While there is a clear reference to the room over the little parlour, with no bedstead, the locations of the other rooms remain uncertain, save that Mr Coke's dressing room of 1702 was probably that 'on the north front' in the 1725 schedule.

The mid-century plan of the second or 'attic' floor shows the chapel on the north front with a gallery along the southern half of the central range roughly divided into rooms on an overlain sheet of paper. That this alteration was not made at that time is revealed by the 1802 plans, which still show a gallery. In *A History of Tyttenhanger*, written in 1895 at the behest of her brother, the fourth Earl of Caledon, Jane van Koughnet describes how 'there used to be a music room on the second floor, but when Lady Hardwicke came to reside permanently here, part of the music room was partitioned off into bedrooms, leaving only the narrow passage. Lady Stuart [her aunt, and one of Lady Hardwicke's daughters] could recollect that the place where the orchestra stood was ornamented with gilt leather.' The 1702 schedule duly describes a 'gilt leather gallery' with 'gilt leather chairs', though the 1725 schedule has both a gilt leather room and a long gallery. This schedule places a white room at the high end of the second floor, with a nursery probably at the other. There is also a 'paper room', and Jane van Koughnet recounts that 'on this floor is Sir Henry Blount's private study, and over the door is written *Hoc Age*. This motto was placed there by Sir Henry, and the room always bears that name. His coat of arms is on a panel near the window, still clear and well preserved.' This duly survives today, in the centre of the east wing.

Only the 1802 set of plans includes the top or 'garret' floor, also with a gallery – and called the 'gallery over the gilt room' in the 1725 schedule. Van Koughnet described 'a curious corridor under the roof, stretching along the whole front' with a lattice pane in an east window, 'broken only recently' inscribed with the names Judith Wase and Anne Bagnall, 1656. Judith would have been a relative of Sir Henry's wife, and the early schedules suggest the floor contained bedrooms for the family or named retainers, including in 1702 a 'Mr Longstrath'.[41] The servants seem to have then slept close to the

221

kitchen or in the basement, though they are in the attic by 1802.

Acknowledgements:

I am particularly grateful to Paul Drury and Richard Peats for being so generous with their findings from opening up parts of Forty Hall in October 2005. The study days were made possible through the generosity of the owners, the London Borough of Enfield and John S. Bonnington respectively, and for the help of Geoffrey Gillam of the Enfield Archaeological Society. I am grateful to all those who attended, and in particular to Sir Howard Colvin, Paul Drury, Andor Gomme, Peter Guillery, Jonathan Hunn, Frank Kelsall, Alison Maguire and Pete Smith for their contributions to the days and for subsequent discussions and correspondence.

13

Winslow Hall

Pete Smith

Winslow Hall in Buckinghamshire may seem an unexpected choice of subject for a book concerned specifically with the design of the villa in the 16th and 17th centuries. For the house is not usually described as a villa, and its architect, Sir Christopher Wren, is rarely if ever linked to general discussions about the design of the villa. But, since Wren was arguably the most important English architect of the 17th century and since Winslow Hall is the closest he ever came to designing a country house on the villa scale, it seems pertinent to examine this well preserved and well documented house in an attempt to explain if, and why, it is not a villa, and perhaps at the same time gain some insight into Wren's attitude to the design of country houses.

Wren and Domestic Architecture

Amongst the many official documents detailing Wren's career which have come down to us, and his musings on the theory of classical architecture that were largely published by his son in *Parentalia*, not one single word concerns the design of domestic architecture, let alone the much more specific topic of the villa.[1] This does not mean that Wren was not interested in the design of houses. A number of design drawings and plans for houses do exist amongst the surviving Wren drawings at All Souls College, Oxford. And, when he visited Paris in 1665, Wren not only studied the new public

223

buildings and churches then being constructed in the city, he also visited and recorded many of the châteaux in the Ile-de-France area, by architects such as Salomon de Brosse, Louis Le Vau and François Mansart. Interestingly the only occasion on which Wren actually uses the word 'villa' is to describe these châteaux in a letter written to a friend from Paris in 1665:

> After the Incomparable **Villas** of Vaux and Maisons, I shall but name Ruel, Courances, Chilly, Essoane, St. Maur, St. Mande, Issy, Meudon, Rincy, Chantilly, Verneul, Liancour, all which … I have survey'd.[2]

Edward Browne, who accompanied Wren on one of these visits, also recorded in a letter that

> The next day wee saw Rinsy [Le Raincy],[3] an house belonging to the Duchesse of Longueville … the house is small but extremely neat, and the modell pleased Dr Wren very much: the chambers are excellently well painted, and one roome with an handsome cupola on it is one of the best I have seen'.[4]

But on his return to England Wren became so preoccupied with his official duties and architectural commissions that he rarely found

Tring Manor. North façade engraved by John Oliver and published in 1700.

time to design any country houses. In Howard Colvin's *Biographical Dictionary of British Architects*,[5] which contains the most complete summary of Wren's known works, there are entries for only two new country houses: Tring Manor in Hertfordshire and Winslow Hall. It is not at all surprising that Wren had so little time for the design of country houses, considering his vast output in other areas. So the question then arises: why did Wren choose to design these two relatively minor houses? What made these two patrons so special that Wren would take time out from his myriad official duties to design them? One could perhaps understand it better if he had chosen to design one of the many great houses being built at this time, like Chatsworth House or Blenhiem Palace.

Henry Guy (1631-1711) [6] and William Lowndes (1652-1724), [7] for whom Wren designed Tring Manor and Winslow Hall respectively, had one thing in common; they were men in positions of great financial power. In fact, they were both consecutively Secretary to the Treasury, Guy from 1679 to 1695 and Lowndes from 1695 to 1711. This not only brought them into regular personal contact with Wren in his official capacity as Surveyor of the King's Works, it also gave them enormous influence and power over the Treasury's spending, including the financing of most of the major public building projects which Wren was concerned with at that time. From this, one must conclude that Wren was prepared to make an exception and design houses only for those few men who had the power directly to ensure that spending on his major public works would continue. This is perhaps not surprising in an architect wise in the ways of the world, who was so dedicated to the completion of all his major official commissions.

Henry Guy

Even though Henry Guy and William Lowndes occupied the same post at the Treasury, they could not have been more contrary in their characters and life-styles. Consequently the houses that Wren designed for each of them are completely different. For this reason it is worth looking briefly at the life of Henry Guy and the design of Tring Manor, as well as Winslow Hall, in order to understand just how clearly each house reflects the individual requirements of their disparate owners. Henry Guy was born in 1631, the only son of

Henry Guy, a tenant farmer on the Tring Manor estate. He was educated at Greys Inn and the Inner Temple. On coming of age in 1652 he received £1,800 which he used to attach himself to the exiled Court, eventually becoming a personal friend of the future King Charles II. After the Restoration Guy gained a post in the queen's household, eventually becoming a groom to the bedchamber. Through his uncle Francis Wethered he became associated with farming excise taxes in Yorkshire, eventually becoming MP for Hedon, a seat he held from 1670 until 1702. In 1679 he was appointed Secretary to the Treasury. In the words of his biographer: '[The] office was lucrative, and Guy's own estimate of his fees as £2,570 was almost certainly too low. He was probably receiving at least £3,500 p.a. before the death of Charles II and possibly as much as £5,000 p.a. after 1685'.[8] He had to resign his office after charges for corruption were brought against him in 1695, though he still continued to receive the profits of the office after William Lowndes was appointed Secretary in his place. Henry Guy died unmarried on 23 February 1711, at the age of 80. He left a fortune estimated at £40,000 in cash and £500 per annum in land. He was described by one of his contemporaries as 'a polished figure, thoroughly acceptable at Court'.[9]

Tring Manor

The Tring Manor estate was acquired by Henry Guy in 1680 and the new house was built sometime in the 1680s.[10] The exact date of its construction is not known. In a letter dated 14 May 1682 Wren himself refers to a proposed visit to Tring, and in June 1690 King William III is recorded as dining with Guy at Tring Manor, so presumably the house was constructed some time between 1682 and 1690. The earliest record of the house's appearance is an engraving by John Oliver of one façade – the north front – published in Chauncey's *Historical Antiquities of Hertfordshire* in 1700 (see fig. p. 224). The house that was built at Tring to Wren's designs survives today, though it is now encased within a late-Victorian brick skin added by Lord Rothschild. It was a medium-sized country house, relatively unexceptional on the exterior but having a complex triple pile plan with a combined two-storey hall and staircase at its centre. This central hall and staircase, though radically altered in the late-

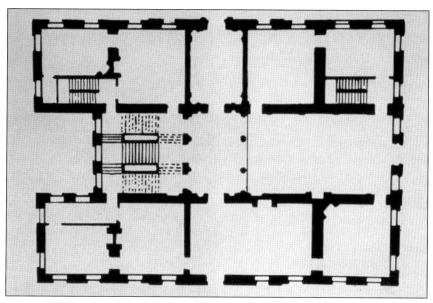

Tring Manor. Reconstruction plan (*Kerry Downes*).

Victorian period, still dominates the interior of the house, occupying nearly one-third of its total volume. It was clearly intended to reflect Guys' status as a courtier and friend of kings, and was presumably used by him for entertaining and impressing his many friends and visitors. The remaining rooms in the present house have also been altered, confusingly in the Wrenaissance style. Though at least two original plaster ceilings with wreathed and foliate decoration survive in two of the lesser ground-floor rooms,[11] which shows the high standard of workmanship that was presumably lavished on all the original interiors. The only contemporary descriptions surviving of the interior were made by Roger North in his architectural notebooks, published by Howard Colvin and John Newman.[12] Roger North was an amateur architect and architectural critic, and a contemporary of Wren. From his writings it is possible to tell that he made a study of contemporary country house design and he mentions in the text a number of well-known houses which he had obviously visited. These include Tring Manor, which he states three times was designed by Sir Christopher Wren.[13] Presumably he was in a position to know, for he was acquainted with Henry Guy, and he had met Wren and discussed architectural problems with him on a number of occasions.

Roger North does not, unfortunately, discuss the internal decoration of the house; instead he concentrates his attention on how the house was planned. Confirming the arrangement of the hall and staircase either side of a central hall, he mentions a

> double order of columns which makes a screen, and carrying a floor upon the entableture of the first, which is a gallery above. This gallery is the landing of the great staires [and] the gallery to the hall, there was a very great defect in the height; which the surveyor hath helped by sacrificing the garratt; and from the seiling a shell is lifted up cuppulo-wise over the gallery.[14]

North recognised the modernity and experimental nature of its triple pile arrangement, and he noted that its three-range plan, arranged horizontally rather than vertically as in the Palladian 'triple pile', was derived from a plan type found at Melton Constable Hall in Norfolk, and Thorpe Hall in Northamptonshire. Wren's major innovation at Tring was to make the central range slightly broader than the flanking ranges and to place the hall within it, approached through an entrance vestibule from the main (north) door. North especially notes Wren's attempt to combine both single- and two-storey rooms within what he calls a 'compact' house. Interestingly he also notes that this design was moving away from the villa-type plan, which North thought was inappropriate to the English climate, and towards a house built *alla moderna*, as he puts it,[15] or, as we would describe it today, a more Baroque type.

William Lowndes

In comparison with Tring, Winslow Hall is a remarkably modest and simple house. Its owner, William Lowndes, could not have been more different from Henry Guy, the builder of Tring Manor. Though they worked together for many years and occupied the same position as Secretary to the Treasury, they had very different outlooks and expectations that go a long way to explaining why their houses looked and were planned so differently. William Lowndes's beginnings were slightly more humble than Guy's. He was the son of impoverished minor landed gentry who had settled in Winslow in the 16th century. His only schooling was at the local free school, and at

Winslow Hall. South front (*Author*).

the age of fifteen he was sent to London, where he eventually gained employment as a clerk at the Treasury in about 1675, probably through the auspices of a relation, Thomas Lowndes. He remained at the Treasury, becoming Chief Clerk in 1689, Secretary in 1695 and Senior Secretary from 1711 until his death in 1724. He held a number of other official government appointments, and was a Commissioner for the Royal Hospital for Seamen at Greenwich from 1694 to 1704, during almost exactly the same period that Sir Christopher Wren was working as Surveyor to the Hospital. Lowndes was also an MP during the last twenty years of his life. He married four times and had four sons and four daughters.

> Lowndes occupies a position of pre-eminence in the annals of the Treasury … An outstanding civil servant, he is justly seen by modern

historians as 'one of the stabilising factors in the financial history of the period', and as having 'masterminded the technical framework of the financial revolution'. He was steeped in the world of the Treasury minutiae, and his financial expertise and inventiveness made him indispensable to any administration.[16]

William Lowndes was also, according to Lord Chesterfield, the author of the phrase 'take care of the pence, for the pounds will take care of themselves'. He was largely independent of party politics, a strongly religious man, hardworking and scrupulously honest, unlike Guy. In fact it was Guy who recommended Lowndes as his successor, and Guy continued to guide him through the political complexities of such a senior post. Lowndes even agreed that Henry Guy should continue to have the profits of the office, whilst he retained only the official salary of £1,000 a year, later increased to £1,200, a relative meagre sum for such a senior position. This official income and the shrewdness with which Lowndes managed his personal finances enabled him to acquire an estate at Chesham in Buckinghamshire as well as property in Westminster. In 1697 he was able to purchase the manor of Winslow, and he later acquired further property in Hertfordshire and Chelsea. Unlike Guy, Lowndes was not a courtier with high ambitions, and consequently the house that he commissioned from Wren was much smaller and less pretentious than the house Wren had designed for Henry Guy at Tring.

Winslow Hall

As we have seen, Winslow was Lowndes's birthplace, and though he must have spent most of his busy working life living in his house in Margaret Street, Westminster, he obviously purchased Winslow Manor, in 1697, as a country retreat. Winslow Hall is not set at the centre of a vast estate; in fact it is sited just on the edge of the relatively large village of Winslow.[17] It is not a particularly large or unusual house, but it is a striking one nonetheless, due partly to its height, but most especially to the four huge chimney stacks that dominate its roofline. It is a bold piece of design carefully weaving the standard architectural features of the period into a quietly original country house.

The surviving building accounts for Winslow Hall were quite

miraculously found by a previous owner, Norman McCorquodale, in a second-hand bookshop on the Charing Cross Road in the 1920s. This book, entitled 'Accompts of the Charge of Building the house att Winslow – with the Offices, Out Houses and other Edifices belonging thereunto and making the Gardens there in the years 1699, 1700, 1701 and 1702 by Mr. Wm Lowndes', was published by the Wren Society in 1940.[18] It is extraordinarily detailed, including not only a general abstract of the all the works, broken down into materials and construction costs, but also a series of very detailed annual bills from each of the craftsmen, together with copies of the articles drawn up between the two major craftsmen, Richard Mapletoft, the mason and Mathew Banks, the carpenter and William Lowndes himself. It includes the names of all the craftsmen employed:

> Richard Mapletoft, Mason
> John Yemans, Bricklayer
> Mathew Banks, Carpenter (King's Master Carpenter)
> Charles Hopson, Joyner (King's Master Joiner)
> Robert Adams, Glazier
> Stephen Big, Smith
> Robert Greenway, Locksmith
> Mathew Roberts, Plumber (King's Sergeant Plumber)
> Charles Coates, Painter

And it itemises every penny spent on the destruction of the old house and the building of the new one. For instance, we learn that the house and gardens cost a total of £6,585.10s.2d, and that 1,140,300 bricks were used, of which 35,000 were re-used from the old house. The accounts even specify exactly who made the various types of bricks, where they came from and how much they cost. For example, ordinary bricks cost an average of 17s.5d per thousand and rubbing bricks £1.8s.10d per thousand when all extra charges were included. 48,000 roof tiles were needed, plus 260 'hyp' tiles and 50 ridge tiles, all at a cost of £68.4s.1d. Everything is itemised and priced: the stone, the glass, the lead, the various types of timber beams and boards, the lime mortar, even the hair used in the mortar, six quarters and two bushels of which were purchased at a cost of £1.9s.2d. The smith's bill includes cramps for the masons and bars for the windows, plus 36 pairs of hinges and 231 pairs of shutter hinges. The locksmith's bills include bolts, various different types of locks and keys and even the screws to fasten them to the doors. The plumber's bills include lead and 'soder', as well as all sorts of different sized nails. The painter's bill specifies each of the window lights and even the individual glazing bars that were to be painted. The joiner's bills include panelling charged for by the yard – Hopson charged £648.7s.10d for 1178 yards of 'Wainscott wrought with a fair Bolection, the Cornice and Dore Mouldings measured in'. This was the most expensive of three different types of panelling used in the house. Other items include shutters, banisters, doors and sashes. The two circular or 'Compass sashes in the Pedim[en]ts', cost 30s. each.

Nowhere in these accounts is an architect or designer mentioned by name. Mr John Churchill, is described as a 'Surveior', though he was only paid for measuring and examining the bills.[19] The accounts also record that 'Sir Christopher Wren, Surv[eyo]r Gen[era]ll of his Ma[jesty's] Works' examined and abated many of the workmen's bills, but nowhere is he actually named as the designer of the house. And Howard Colvin, in his *Biographical Dictionary*, goes no further than saying that the house was 'probably' designed by Wren. Yet the fact that many of the craftsmen, including the carpenter, joiner and plumber, were tradesmen habitually employed by Wren, strengthens the case for him as the designer. The account book also records that George London and Henry Wise, the royal gardeners, who had worked alongside Wren at both Hampton Court and Kensington Palace, laid out the gardens.[20] All these factors, together with the complexity and ingenuity of the internal planning and the quality of the external elevations, very strongly suggest that Sir Christopher Wren did in fact design Winslow Hall.

The exterior

Winslow Hall has identical entrance and garden façades, each seven windows wide, with a slightly projecting central three-window section topped with a pediment (see fig. p. 229). The pediments contain small circular windows. The hipped roof is topped by four broad brick chimney stacks which rise up from the top of the flat ridge. The house stands on a full height, but half-buried basement, the ground and first floors are of equal height, and there is a lower top

Winslow Hall. Anonymous painting of the south front, *c.*1700 (*Private collection*).

floor. The corners are defined by ashlar quoins, the basement has a moulded stone plinth, the top storey is separated by a plain stone band and the hipped roof has a wooden dentilated eaves cornice. The central doorways each have ashlar doorcases with curved pediments, that to the south inscribed 'WILLIAM LOWNDES, A. D. MDCC'. The south entrance front retains its stone steps, though those on the north front were removed early in the 20th century, when the garden terrace outside the north front was raised. The walls of the house are faced in a rich dark brown brick whilst the windows and doors are delineated with contrasting bright orange brick surrounds. This orange brick is used for the jambs and lintels of the windows, though not for the sills, which are of stone. These window openings are defined by rubbed-brick staff mouldings to the jambs and lintels. Both these details, the coloured brick and the staff-mouldings, are features that Wren often used on his buildings; they feature prominently on the Royal Hospital at Chelsea, built between 1682 and 1692.

The present owner of Winslow Hall restored the tall sash windows by renewing their glazing bars in the 1950s. Early photographs of the house show that though the frames and sash windows were never removed, the sashes had their glazing bars reduced in the 19th century to allow for the insertion of sheets of plate glass. Sliding sash

233

windows became very popular in the last years of the 17th century, and it is not surprising to find that Wren, who was probably involved in their development, used them for all the windows of this house. One early painting of Winslow Hall survives (see fig. p. 233), and this confirms that the house had sashes in all the windows from the start.[21] This very useful picture also shows that the building was built with symmetrical service blocks at either side, which were accessed across small rectangular walled courts. These side blocks were the laundry and kitchen building on one side and the brewhouse and stable building on the other. These small brick single storey buildings still survive today, though the former stable on the east side was radically altered and directly linked to the house itself, filling in the former courtyard, in 1901. This is the only major alteration to the original layout of the house.

The east and west façades of the house are also symmetrical, with the same decoration as the main façades. They are each five windows wide, and again, like the main façades they have a central three-window section which projects forward, though these projections are deeper on the side elevations. Each façade also has a central doorway, placed at a lower level, between the basement and ground floors. These doorways have simple brick surrounds, like the windows. These are obviously service doors, which actually lead into the staircases, allowing direct access down to the basement and also up onto the main ground floor of the house itself.

The plan

The house itself is rectangular in plan, approximately 70 feet wide and 45 feet deep. Internally it has a most unusual plan form. Each of the floor plans of the house is dominated by a thick central cross wall, which contains the chimney flues, and which also links the two rectangular staircase spaces. Together these form the solid structural core of the house with the main façades wrapped around the rooms of the house. This basic structural outline rises right through the house from the basement to the top floor, and within this the remaining spaces are divided up as required for each of the different floors. The staircase towers at either side project forwards on the side façades. These staircases are not exactly the same size; that to the east side is slightly larger. It projects nearly two feet further into the house

Winslow Hall. North-south cross-section drawn by J. Brandon Jones and Mary Crowley, 1940.

making the eastern closets deeper as well. This houses the main stair, whilst the slightly smaller space to the west contains the servants' stair.[22] The central wall, which carries all the chimney flues up to the central stacks on the roof, can be clearly seen in the north-south cross-section drawing produced by J. Brandon Jones and Mary Crowley for the Wren Society. This formed the structural spine of the

235

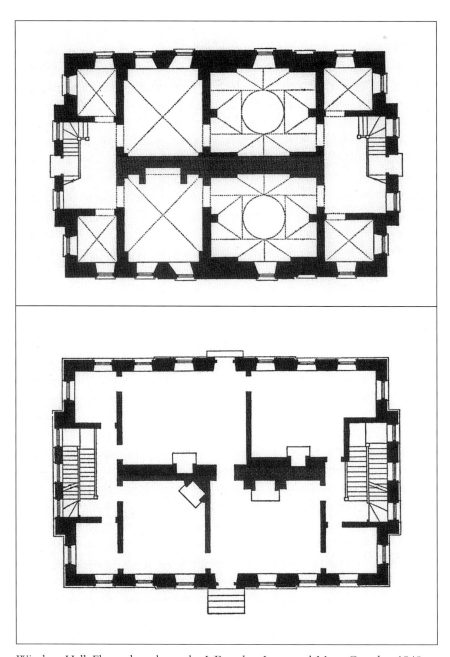

Winslow Hall. Floor plans drawn by J. Brandon Jones and Mary Crowley, 1940.
Top: Basement.
Bottom: Ground floor.
Top right: First floor.
Bottom right: Second floor.

236

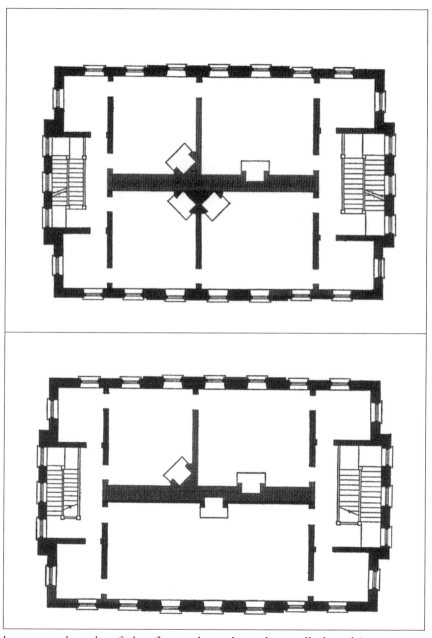

house, and each of the floor plans show how all the chimneys are placed against this wall.

The ground-floor plan also indicates how the house originally worked. The main entrance from the south leads directly into the hall; this room then gives direct access to all the other rooms on this

237

floor, as well as access to the main staircase and the upper floors. Three of the four main rooms have a closet, which can be accessed both from the room itself and from the staircases, allowing servant access. The north-east room incorporates an alcove rather than a closet. A somewhat similar arrangement is found on the first floor (see fig. p. 237), though here the rooms could be interpreted as a pair of north and south apartments, in the French manner. The larger rooms, or *anti-chambres*, are accessed from the main staircase, these then lead to the bedrooms, or *chambres*, with closets, or *cabinets*, beyond, both with servant access from the service staircase. The top or second floor has a further identical apartment arrangement on the north side and a single large saloon on the south (see fig. p. 237). This large room, the largest in the house, was presumably a gallery or saloon, used for social gatherings. This extremely compact and practical arrangement of rooms allows for maximum access without the necessity for wasteful corridors, yet it also allows for privacy: all the rooms can be individually accessed from the staircases without the necessity of passing through other rooms. The fact that this house has survived almost completely unaltered for over 300 years does suggest that it is a house which functions successfully.

The interior

The rooms themselves also survive remarkably unaltered. In the basement, described as cellars in the accounts, all the rooms have brick vaulted arches, which support the floors above (see fig. p. 236). In the two largest of these cellars, to the east, the brick vaults support beautifully crafted shallow domes. Most of the other rooms have simpler brick groin vaults and retain some of their original four-panel doors with arched tops. The south-west room originally contained a large fireplace, so it probably had a use other than as a cellar, perhaps it was the servants' hall. Unfortunately no early inventories have as yet come to light for this house, so it is not known for certain what uses the individual rooms were put to. From the west end the service staircase rises through two flights to each floor; it has simple turned balusters and a moulded handrail. On the upper floors the stair has been screened off from the landings at a later date.

The house was originally entered through the main south door into the entrance hall. Like all the other rooms on the ground floor the hall retains all its original full height bolection mould panelling and a polished marble fire surround. This is exactly the type of interior decoration that one would expect to find in a building by Wren. Comparable rooms with almost identical panelling can be found in the less grand rooms at either Hampton Court Palace or the Royal Hospital at Chelsea. However, it would be equally true to say that these are exactly the type of interiors one finds in houses by contemporary architects, and that by the later 17th century this type of bolection mould panelling, arranged with small panels at the bottom, a dado rail, then large single panels above and topped with a continuous moulded cornice, had become absolutely standard throughout England. This entrance hall has the equally standard type of bold bolection mould fire surround, with two moulded panels above. The first contains a long narrow mirror and the one above a painting. The wall between this room and its closet has been removed in recent years.

To the west of the hall is a smaller room, now the dining room, though probably used as a parlour or business room originally. It has exactly the same panelling to the hall, and a smaller cross corner fireplace with the same over mirror and painting. All these rooms have six-panel doors set in 'bolection mould' frames with their

Winslow Hall. The dining room (*Author*).

239

original brass locks intact. These can be identified with the entry in the accounts which reads 'Ffor Locks, Keys, and Bolts. Paid Rob Greenway. H[is] M[ajesty's] Locksmith including 3sh carriage … £52.9sh'. Similarly the panelling can all be identified as the work of Charles Hopson, 'his Matjs Joyner', who charged for this type of panelling or 'wainscott' by the yard. The accounts also record that this panelling was 'Measured and Cast up per Mr John Churchill, Survr in Nov 1701', which suggests that the actual arrangement of the panelling was decided by Churchill rather than by Hobson or Wren. Perhaps this is not surprising, since John Churchill was himself a carpenter employed on the royal palaces and at Marlborough House.

The largest room on the ground floor is the drawing room, to the north-west. It has similar panelling, which is now painted. The detailed painter's bill recorded in the accounts only mentions external paint works, so it seems very unlikely that any of these panelled rooms were originally painted. Being on the north side of the house, this room would never have been over-lit, and it was presumably in an attempt to lighten it that it was painted by later owners, who also attempted to solve this problem by inserting mirrors into the panels on either side of the fireplace. Interestingly, the panelling in this room is not symmetrically arranged, certainly not on the east wall, though

Winslow Hall. The drawing room, showing the unsymmetrical arrangement of the panelling on its east wall (*Author*).

Winslow Hall. The study (*Author*).

it is on the west wall with three panels between its balancing doors. The doorway on the right, to the closet, has been converted at a later date into an alcove. The study, the final room on the ground floor, and perhaps the original dining parlour, is the only room where the closet was never separated off from the rest of the room. Again retaining its full height panelling, again painted, this room has an equally unsymmetrical arrangement of panels. All the rooms on the ground floor, indeed all the rooms in the house, have plain flat plaster ceilings, and the limited expenditure recorded in the accounts on plasterwork suggests that the house never had ornate plaster ceilings of the type which survive at Tring. This is another clear indication that Lowndes wished for a comfortable, rather than an ostentatious house.

The slight extra depth allowed for the eastern stair, less than two feet, gives a far more impressive impact to the main staircase, which is also enhanced with the slightly bolder turned balusters (see fig. p. 242). On the first floor the apartment on the north side, overlooking the garden, must have been the most important. The largest room has exactly the same type of panelling as the rooms on the lower floor, but here the four main wall panels above the dado rail are filled with large painted panels (Plate 13). There is no mention of these panels in the accounts, but the fact that they are of such high quality does

.Winslow Hall. Main staircase (*Author*).

Winslow Hall. The saloon on the top floor (*Author*).

suggest that they were most likely painted in London and only installed here after the house was completed. The fact that they fit their panels so exactly also indicates that they were originally painted for this room. In an era which loved painted rooms and especially painted staircases, these might not seem to be unusual. But their subject matter, or more exactly their lack of it, does make them different from most similar schemes. These pictures are like huge picture frames through which one can see distant gardens or ideal rural landscapes. These strange frames are made up of hermes or caryatids and other classical devices, with elaborate grotesques and curtains, like some theatrical proscenium. They are definitely pastoral in theme, though with none of the scenes of gods disporting themselves, which might give a clue as to their allegorical meaning. The fact that this room looked directly down on to the main garden, may have had some bearing on the meaning of these elaborate wall decorations. Whatever their meaning, they again show that Lowndes wished for the very latest type of fashionable decoration in his otherwise relatively modest house. The remaining rooms on this floor are slightly plainer, they have the dado panelling, the cornice, and the bolection mould fire surrounds with overmantel panels, but the upper wall panels are missing. These could have been removed at a later date, or they may simply have been designed for paper or hangings.

On the top floor the ceilings are lower, eight feet rather than the twelve feet of the floors below. This floor contains the saloon, which occupies the central five windows on the south side of the house (see fig. p. 243). This is a most unusual room to find at the top of a late 17th-century house. It seems more like the type of prospect room or high great chamber that one might expect to find in a house of the late 16th or early 17th centuries. Winslow Hall has no cupola or viewing platform on the roof, like many of its contemporaries, and this room may well have been intended as a type of prospect room used for winter exercise or for viewing the hunt. This room has full height panelling, with broad upper panels and a fine, if plain, grey marble fire surround. It would presumably have been used as an occasional ballroom for dances or larger parties, and it makes a very interesting contrast with Tring, where the two-storey hall, no doubt sumptuously decorated, would have been the setting for such entertainments. The saloon at Winslow with its simple panelled decoration, was intended more as the setting for family celebrations and local entertainments, rather than the type of courtly extravagances which Henry Guy's house was designed to accommodate. The remaining rooms on this floor, including the closets, are panelled in a similar fashion. The rooms on the north side probably provided accommodation for Lowndes's many children and their nursery or schoolroom. The pediments with their circular windows provided very limited attic space and servants' accommodation. The service wings probably also provided some servants' rooms but the close proximity of the house to the local village meant that few servants were required to live on the premises.

Conclusion

It is obvious from this brief study of the surviving house at Winslow that it was not intended as a status symbol like Tring Manor. William Lowndes was no courtier, like Henry Guy; William III never called to dine at Winslow Hall, and was never likely to. Consequently the house had no complex triple-pile plan incorporating a large double-height hall for lavish entertaining. William Lowndes was an altogether more modest and unassuming man, wishing for a simple house in the country, close to the local community from which he had risen: modest, but with all the most modern and up-to-date features, carried out by the best craftsmen to the best possible design. No expense was spared on the London workmen or the best quality materials, but neither was money wasted on unnecessary carved ornament and decoration. The accounts show that the house was completed in four years and at a cost of £6,585, a very fair price for such a fine quality house. It is a plain but striking house, for a plain and rather unassuming gentleman who in his quiet way carried out a much needed revolution in the workings of the Treasury.

So, what does this tell us about Wren's attitude to house design? Primarily, that Wren considered each commission as a separate problem which required its own solution. In other words, he was not interested in the idea of a model solution; instead he chose to look at each new commission as a separate challenge. Winslow Hall and Tring Manor are both houses with individual and original plans, and the few other surviving house plans known to be by Wren show an equally individual and original approach to country house planning. Wren's well known fertile imagination combined with his eclectic Baroque interest in all types of architectural sources led him to explore many new solutions to the problem of house design. We know that he was aware of the work of architects like Palladio and Scamozzi, for he mentions them by name in his theoretical writings, but their ideas about villa planning certainly do not seem to have been influential on any of his house designs, and especially not on his designs for Winslow Hall. Instead, Wren chose an entirely original solution using a simple structural outline which allowed within it a freedom of choice about the arrangement of rooms on each individual floor.

Winslow Hall could in some ways be seen as an ideal late 17th-century villa. It was designed as a small country retreat for Lowndes and his family, and it has a number of features found in other villa designs. The symmetrically arranged flanking service wings, for example, are derived originally from Palladio's villa designs, and the lack of servants' quarters and of any formal state rooms inside the main house emphasises the informal nature of life at Winslow. Even the pastoral or garden images on the walls of the painted chamber could be interpreted as symbolic of the bucolic rural idyll that all

245

villas aspired to. But, however much this house may have shared functions with the villa, Wren chose consciously not to follow any of the prescribed villa plan formulas. Instead, he produced an entirely original and exceptionally compact plan in order to provide William Lowndes and his family with a practical and comfortable house. Ironically, the fact that Sir Christopher Wren used the word 'villa' to describe such a diverse group of French châteaux, from the compact type at Le Raincy to the enormous courtyard type at Écouen, suggests that to him the word simply meant a country house. If this is true, then presumably Wren would have referred to both Tring Manor and Winslow Hall as villas.

Acknowledgements:

This paper began life as a brief lecture entitled 'Wren's Domestic Architecture' given at a day conference held at Ardington House in Oxfordshire in 2004, organised by Dr Nicola Smith. This was then adapted and expanded for this conference on the 17th-century villa. I would like to thank both Malcolm Airs and Nicola Smith for their encouragement and Kerry Downes and Anthony Geraghty for their assistance. I would also like to thank Sir Edward Tomkins for his kind generosity in allowing me access to Winslow Hall and its account book, and for his permission to reproduce photographs.

CONTRIBUTORS

Malcolm Airs was Professor of Historic Conservation at the University of Oxford until 2006 and is now Vice-President of Kellogg College. He has directed the annual series of conferences on the architectural achievements of the elite, of which this volume is a part, since their inception in 1994.

Nicholas Cooper spent much of his professional career with the Royal Commission on the Historical Monuments of England. He is now an independent historian and consultant. His book on the *Houses of the Gentry, 1480-1680* was published in 1999.

Dianne Duggan is an independent scholar who studied at the Courtauld Institute of Art and who researches early-17th-century architecture.

Andor Gomme is Emeritus Professor of English Literature and Architectural History at Keele University. He is a past Chairman of the Society of Architectural Historians of Great Britain and editor of *Architectural History.* He is the author of *Smith of Warwick.*

Elain Harwood is a senior investigator with English Heritage. She is writing a book on English architecture 1945-75 and researching for a PhD on buildings for the arts after 1945.

Paula Henderson is an independent scholar with a PhD from the Courtauld Institute of Art. Her book *The Tudor House and Garden: Architecture and Landscape in the 16th and early 17th centuries* was published by Yale in 2005.

Gordon Higgott is an architectural historian at English Heritage who has published on the drawings and design theory of Inigo Jones

247

and the design history of St Paul's Cathedral. He is currently preparing a catalogue of the English baroque architectural drawings at Sir John Soane's Museum.

Paul Hunneyball is a senior research fellow at the History of Parliament Trust. He specialises in the social, economic and cultural context of 17th-century British architecture, particularly the processes of stylistic change.

Sally Jeffery is an architectural and garden historian. She lectures at Birkbeck College on garden history and is currently researching later-17th-century houses and their garden setting.

Caroline Knight is an independent architectural historian who runs the 'High Renaissance – Baroque' course at the Victoria & Albert Museum. She is writing a book on the suburban villas around London for publication in 2008.

Charles McKean is professor of Scottish Architectural History at Dundee University. He is author of a number of books including *The Scottish Thirties, The Making of the Museum of Scotland* and *The Scottish Chateau*. He is series editor of the RIAS/Landmark Trust illustrated architectural guides and has written a number of the individual volumes.

Lee Prosser is Curator (Historic Buildings) at Historic Royal Palaces. He studied at Lampeter and Bristol, where he specialised in landscape archaeology. He also teaches courses for the Board of Continuing Education at Cambridge University.

Patricia Smith is a freelance writer and architectural historian who received a PhD from the Courtauld Institute of Art for her analysis of spatial aspects of late-Stuart and early-Georgian country houses. She is currently restoring Crowcombe Court in Somerset.

Pete Smith is a Senior Architectural Investigator with English Heritage who has lectured and published extensively on various aspects of the English country house.

Geoffrey Tyack is a fellow of Kellogg College, Oxford. He wrote the entries on the Renaissance and post-Renaissance villa in the *Dictionary of Art*, and is also the author of *Warwickshire Country Houses*, *Oxford: an Architectural Guide*, and a chapter on John Ruskin and the English house in *Ruskin and Architecture* (Spire Books, 2003).

Lucy Worsley is Chief Curator at Historic Royal Palaces. She has degrees from the universities of Oxford and Sussex, is a Fellow of the Royal Historical Society, and is currently Senior Research Fellow at the Institute of Historical Research.

NOTES

Preface (Pages 7-8)
1. One exception is D. Arnold (ed.), *The Georgian Villa* (Stroud, 1996).
2. See, however, N. Cooper, *Houses of the Gentry 1480-1680* (New Haven & London, 1999).

Chapter 1 (Pages 9-24)
1. Timothy Nourse, *Campania Felix* (London, 1700), p. 297.
2. Roger North, *Of Building: Roger North's Writings on Architecture* (ed. H.M. Colvin & J. Newman), (Oxford, 1981), p. 62.
3. John Evelyn, *Diary* (ed. E.S. de Beer) (Oxford 1955), IV, 143-4.
4. Ibid., II, 108, 112, 234-6.
5. Thomas Coryat, *Coryat's Crudities* (first published 1611) (Glasgow, 1905), II, 282.
6. Sylvia Thrupp, *The Merchant Class of Medieval London* (Chicago, 1948), p.125.
7. Ibid., p. 144 & n.
8. Anon, 'The English Courtier and the Country-gentleman: of Cyvile and Uncyvile Life' in W.C.H[azlitt] (ed.), *Inedited Tracts* (London, 1868), n.p.
9. John Norden, *Speculum Britanniae: The First Part … Middlesex*, (London 1593), p. 12.
10. *Calender of State Papers, Venetian, 1617-19* (London, 1909), p. 245.
11. William Bedwell, 'A Brief Description of the Town of Tottenham Highcrosse' (first published 1622) in W.J. Roe, *Ancient Tottenham* (Tottenham, n.d.), p. 107.
12. The MS map is preserved at Syon House. The plate is taken from an anonymous late-19th-century reproduction published by Stanford & Sons, London; this appears reasonably accurate and is easier to read than the original.
13. William Angus, *The Seats of the Nobility and Gentry of England and Wales* (Islington, 1787), XL; Daniel Lysons, *Environs of London* (London, 1795), III, pp. 565-6.
14. William Robinson, *History and Antiquities of the Parish of Hackney* (London, 1843), p. 91.
15. John Stowe, *A Survey of London* (ed. C.L. Kingsford) (Oxford, 1908), II, p. 78.
16. Leon Baptista Alberti, *On the Art of Building in Ten Books* (eds J. Rykwert, N. Leach & R. Tavernor) (Cambridge, Mass. & London, 1988), p. 294.
17. Keith Thomas, *Man and the Natural World* (London, 1983), p. 248.
18. Sir Philip Sidney, *The Duchess of Pembroke's Arcadia* (1590), I, ch. 2.
19. Daniel King, *The Vale Royal of England* (text by William Webb, *c.*1622) (London, 1656), p. 67.

20. Maren–Sofie Rostvig, *The Happy Man: Studies in the Metamorphoses of a Classical Ideal, 1600-1700* (Oslo, 1954), p. 82.
21. Ben Jonson, *Poems* (Ian Donaldson, ed.) (Oxford, 1975), p. 280.
22. Abraham Cowley, *Of Greatness* in A.B. Gough (ed.), *Abraham Cowley, The Essays and Other Prose Writings* (Oxford, 1915), p. 183.
23. James Turner, *The Politics of Landscape* (Oxford, 1979), p. 1.
24. Kevin Sharpe, *The Personal Rule of Charles I*, (New Haven & London, 1992), p. 210.

Chapter 2 (Pages 25-37)

1. An earlier version of this chapter appeared in my article, 'Secret Houses and Garden Lodges; the Queen's House, Greenwich, in context', *Apollo*, 146 (July 1997), pp. 29-35. Here I have expanded the number of buildings discussed and emphasised what information was available to English builders about villas, all of which I hope strengthens my original argument.
2. Coryate's book, *Coryat's Crudities hastily gobled up in Five Moneths Travells* (1611) was not published until 1905 (2 vols, Glasgow, 1905), I, p. 13.
3. *Sandys travels, containing an history of the original and present state of the Turkish Empire: their laws, government, policy, military force, courts of justice, and commerce: The Mahometan religion and ceremonies: a description of Constantinople, the Grand Signior's seraglio, and his manner of living: also, of Greece, with the religion and customs of the Grecians. Of Ægypt; ... A voyage on the River Nylus: ... the former flourishing and present state of Alexandria. A description of the Holy-Land; of the Jews, and several sects of Christians living there; of Jerusalem, sepulchre of Christ, Temple of Solomon; and what else either of antiquity, or worth observation. Lastly, Italy described, and the islands adjoining; Illustrated with fifty graven maps and figures* (London, 7th ed., 1673), iv, p. 274.
4. William Thomas, *The History of Italy*, (1549) (ed. George B. Parks, Ithaca. 1963), p. 177.
5. Ibid., p. 15.
6. Ibid., pp. 95-6.
7. Robert Dallington, *Survey of the Great Dukes of the State of Tuscany* (London, 1605), pp. 12-13, 19, 23, 42.
8. Fynes Moryson, *An Itinerary written by Fynes Moryson gent. First in the Latine tongue, and then translated by him into English: containing his ten yeeres travell through the twelve dominions of Germany, Bohmerland, Sweitzerland, Netherland, Denmarke, Poland, Italy, Turky, France, England, Scotland and Ireland* (1617), republished as *An Itinerary* (Glasgow, 1907).
9. Pliny the Younger, *Letters and Panegyrics*, (I.E.H. Warmington, ed, and Betty Radice, translator, Loeb Classical Library, Cambridge, Mass., 1969), I, pp. 141-3.
10. Quoted in James Ackerman, *The Villa: Form and Ideology of Country Houses* (London, 1990), pp. 72-3.
11. *Of Building: Roger North's Writings on Architecture* (ed. Howard Colvin & John Newman) (Oxford, 1981), p. 62.
12. For illustrations of Burghley's various houses, see Paula Henderson, *The Tudor*

House and Garden: Architecture and Landscape in the 16th and early 17th Centuries (New Haven & London, 2005), figs 9, 52, 104, 106. Discussions of all these buildings and plans can be found in the text.

13. Francis Peck, *Desiderata Curiosa* 2 vols. (London, 1732-5), I, p. 50.

14. On the 'Great Standing', see Howard Colvin (ed.), *The History of the King's Works*, (London, 1963-82), IV, p. 16. The lodge has been restored by the Corporation of London.

15. Paula Henderson, 'Maps of Cranborne Manor in the 17th Century', *Architectural History*, 44 (2001), pp. 358-64.

16. *As You Like It*, II, i.

17. Secret Houses were first discussed by Mark Girouard, *Life in the English Country House* (London, 1978), p. 76.

18. See Henderson, *Tudor House and Garden*, fig. 93, and Howard Colvin, 'Royal Gardens in Medieval England', in *Medieval Gardens* (Dumbarton Oaks Colloquium on the History of Landscape Architecture, IX (ed. Elisabeth B. MacDougall, Washington, D.C., 1988), pp. 18-20.

19. One of the lodges at Hampton Court survives as the 'Tilt-yard Café', and the mount can still be seen at Nonsuch. Wyngaerde's drawing of the tilt-yard at Hampton Court is illustrated in Henderson, *Tudor House and Garden*, fig. 180.

20. Northamptonshire Record Office, Finch Hatton 272; both are reproduced in Henderson, *Tudor House and Garden*, figs 108, 109.

21. John Summerson (ed.), 'The Book of Architecture of John Thorpe in Sir John Soane's Museum', *Walpole Society,* 40 (1964-6). The plan of the banqueting house is T182 (pl. 84, p. 93); T34 (pl. 14, p. 52), T141 (pl. 64, p. 83) are both based on plans of villas in Palladio's *Quattro Libri*. Summerson discusses the Palladio-derived plans on p. 29.

22. Summerson, 'Book of Architecture of John Thorpe', T56 (pl. 26, p. 60).

23. Thomas Fuller, *History of the Worthies of England* (London, 1662), quoted in Summerson, 'Book of Architecture of John Thorpe', pp. 60-1.

24. Paula Henderson, 'A Shared Passion: the Cecils and their Gardens', in Pauline Croft (ed.), *Patronage, Culture and Power: the early Cecils,* (The Paul Mellon Centre for Studies in British Art and The Yale Center for British Art, Studies in British Art 8) (New Haven & London, 2002), pp. 108-9 and fig. 51.

25. On Sheffield Manor, see Mark Girouard, *Robert Smythson & the Elizabethan Country House* (New Haven & London, 1983), fig. 65, pp. 118-9. See also Ruth Harman and John Minnis, *Sheffield* (New Haven & London, 2005), pp. 204-6.

26. Summerson, 'Book of Architecture of John Thorpe', T56 (pl. 100, p. 101).

27. An argument against this theory has been put forward by Gordon Higgott; see Chapter 8. If there were no kitchens in the basement, food could easily have been brought from the palace itself.

28. Ackerman, *The Villa*, p. 1.

29. A fuller discussion of this garden is found in Paula Henderson, 'Sir Francis Bacon's Water Gardens at Gorhambury', *Garden History*, 20:2 (1992), pp. 116-31.

30. British Library, Add MS 27278, fols 24-5.

31. Illustrated in Henderson, *Tudor House and Garden*, fig. 154.

32. All quotes from Aubrey come from Bodleian Library, Oxford, Aubrey MS 6, fols 68–74.
33. Pliny the Younger, *Letters and Panegyrics*, (Loeb Classical Library, 1969) I, p.7.
34. Ibid., p. 29.

Chapter 3 (Pages 38-63)
1. James Ackermann, *The Villa: Form and Ideology of Country Houses* (London, 1990), p. 9.
2. John Varley, 'New Light on the Red Hall at Bourne', *Lincolnshire Historian*, 12 (1965), pp. 17-18.
3. John Summerson (ed.). 'The Book of Architecture of John Thorpe', *Walpole Society,* 40 (1964-6), pl. 11.
4. Nikolaus Pevsner & Ian Nairn, *The Buildings of England: Surrey* (2nd ed., Harmondsworth, 1971), pp. 406-7.
5. *Of Building: Roger North's Writings on Architecture* (ed. Howard Colvin & John Newman) (Oxford, 1981), p. 72.
6. *John Leland's Itinerary* (ed. J. Cameron) (Stroud, 1993), p. 491.
7. P. Slocombe *et al.,* 'Study day report to Wiltshire Buildings Record on the Hall, Bradford-on-Avon' (unpublished typescript, 15 March 2004).
8. *Country Life*, 18 October 2004.
9. Mark Girouard, *Robert Smythson & the Architecture of the Elizabethan Era* (London, 1963), p. 154.
10. Anthony Wells-Cole, *Art & Decoration in Elizabethan & Jacobean England* (New Haven & London, 1996), pp. 38, 60.

Chapter 4 (Pages 64-87)
1. 'The Country Seat', National Archives of Scotland, MS NAS/GD/18/4404/1, transcribed by Vanessa Stephen. I am indebted to James Simpson for the chance to study this.
2. I am indebted to Chris Whatley for information about Clerk.
3. 'The Country Seat', p. 18.
4. This figure is purely hypothetical, based on a discussion with Bob Harris on late-18th-century villas around Dundee.
5. G. Crawfurd, *Genealogical History of the Family of the Stewarts, and General Description of the Shire of Renfrew* (Edinburgh, 1710, revised Sempill *c.*1780).
6. Ibid, p. 33.
7. [J.O. Mitchell], *The Old Country Houses of the Old Glasgow Gentry* (Glasgow, 1870), XII.
8. Ibid., LVIII.
9. Ibid., V.
10. Ibid., XC11.
11. 'The Country Seat', p. 22.
12. One of two brothers who founded Hutcheson's Hospital.
13. Quoted in full in J. Napier, *Notes and reminiscences relating to Partick* (Glasgow, 1873), pp. 23-43.
14. National Archives of Scotland, Sketchbook of J.C. Nattes (1799), sketch of

Partick.

15. Napier, *Partick* , p. 42, quoting from Craufurd's *Renfrewshire*.

16. C. McKean, 'Timothy Pont's Building Drawings' in I. Cunninghame, (ed.), *The Nation Survey'd* (East Linton, 2001).

17. *Registrum Magni Sigilii Regum Scotorum* (J.M. Thomson *et al.*, eds) (Edinburgh, 1878-1902), V1, no. 746 (8 August 1598), p. 250. I am very grateful to Michael Pearce for finding and translating this.

18. P. Hume Brown, *Early Travellers in Scotland* (reprint, Edinburgh, 1973), p. 93.

19. For example, the dolphin fountain at Ravelston.

20. Their owners vary from craftsmen – e.g. goldsmiths – to lawyers like Laurence Scott who built Bavelaw in 1628; lord provosts; merchants like William Cairns who built Pilmuir in 1624; bankers like Sir William Dick of Braid who modified Grange in 1631; minor scions of greater families doing well in Edinburgh; and officials of the State.

21. J. Wallace, *The Historic Houses of Edinburgh* (Edinburgh, 1998), *passim*.

22. 'Timothy Pont's Building Drawings' in Cunninghame (ed.), *The Nation Survey'd*, pp. 111-24.

23. There were many variations in how people referred to their principal ancestral house, but this had become the normal expression by the time of John Macky's *Tour* in 1723.

24. That is how she referred to herself on the armorial panel on her belvedere in the palace of Dunfermline.

25. For more on Schaw, see D. Stevenson, *The Origins of Freemasonry – Scotland's Century 1590 – 1710* (Cambridge, 1990), chapter 3; J.W. Saunders, 'William Schaw, Master of Works to King James VI' in *Ars Quatuor Coronatorum*, *50* (1937), pp. 220-6; and A. Mackechnie, 'James VI's Architects' in M. Lynch & J. Goodacre, (eds), *The Reign of James VI* (East Linton, 2000).

26. See M. Lee, 'King James's Popish Chancellor,' in M. Lee, *The 'Inevitable' Union* (East Linton, 2003), pp. 145-58.

27. E. Henderson, *Annals of Dunfermline* (Glasgow, 1878), p. 753.

28. Ibid, p. 252.

29. R. Chambers, *Domestic Annals of Scotland* (Edinburgh, 1858), 1, p. 358.

30. J. Macky, *A Journey through Scotland* (London, 1723), p. 173.

31. I am indebted to Stephan Hoppé for information on German practice on this. It is obvious in the Schloss at Neuburg, Bavaria.

32. D. Howard, *Scottish Architecture from the Reformation to the Restoration* (Edinburgh, 1995), p. 28.

33. 'The Country Seat', p. 24.

34. A. MacKechnie, personal communication.

35. Royal Commission on the Ancient and Historic Monuments of Scotland, *East Lothian* (Edinburgh, 1924), p. 103.

36. Translated and quoted in M. Bath, 'Alexander Seton's Painted Gallery' in L. Gent, (ed.), *Albion's Classicism: The Visual Arts in Britain 1550-1660* (London, 1996), pp. 102-3.

37. Howard, *Renaissance to Reformation*, p. 102.

38. Based on the Isaac Miller drawing of Hamilton Palace in the 1670s.

39. Based on the drawing by Capt. John Slezer of the coast of East Lothian.

40. It is very clear from the stonework on the gable with the bay window.

41. Bath, 'Alexander Seton's Painted Gallery,' pp. 79-108.

42. Cuninghame was royal architect after Schaw's death, and was knighted in 1604. Alexander Edward's drawings of the windows in the Castlestead gallery so much resemble those of the Earl of Cassilis' town house in Maybole (near Robertland) as to imply the same hand. If so, this is the first building that we might attribute to him.

43. I am enormously indebted to Michael Pearce for introducing me to Castlestead.

44. See A. MacKechnie, 'Scots Court Architecture of the early 17th century' (Ph.D thesis, Edinburgh University, 1993).

45. A. MacKechnie, 'Evidence of a post-1603 court architecture in Scotland?', *Architectural History*, 31 (1988), pp. 108-16.

46. *Register Privy Seal* (1625-7), I, p. 14; III, p. 101. I am hugely indebted to Charles Wemyss for this information.

47. Tyninghame, which was a conversion, is an exception.

48. Sir W. Fraser, *Memorials of the Earls of Haddington* (Edinburgh, 1889), pp. 300-2.

49. See C. McKean, 'The Wrichtishousis – a very curious edifice' in *Book of the Old Edinburgh Club*, NS, 3 (Edinburgh, 1994).

50. There is no written evidence for this distinction. However, the west wing has the smarter staircase, grander windows, and stair with a belvedere on top, and the assumption has been made that this was the wing for public rather than private activities.

51. There is no record of what it looked like.

52. Ian Campbell has suggested that it was not originally built on a U-plan but may always have been intended to be so.

53. A loggia was not unusual at this time. The villa built in 1606, possibly by Sir James Cunninghame of Robertland in the grounds of Falkland Palace for the Earl of Athol, had just such a feature.

54. A term devised by Andor Gomme, and used by Matt Davis to characterise a group of houses in the north-east which were extended upwards in the early 17th century, one particular feature being the location of a gallery at a high level and a belvedere.

55. 'The Country Seat', p. 12.

56. Ibid., p. 19.

Chapter 5 (Pages 88-110)

1. The plans accompanying this chapter are reconstructions or redrawings of the original room arrangements of the ground floors, as far as they can be sensibly ascertained. Sources are given for original plans of houses that were not executed, no longer exist, or have been altered beyond recognition. All the other reconstructions have been produced after consulting a wide range of documentary evidence, and/or through physical survey. All plans have been redrawn to a common scale. In order to focus on spatial aspects rather than architectural detail, simplifying conventions have been applied, notably to

features such as windows, pilasters and chimneypieces.

2. *Shorter Oxford Dictionary*, usage from 1611. The entry also gives the later use of villa to mean 'a residence in the country or in the neighbourhood of a town, usually standing in its own grounds'.

3. Charles Middleton, in *Picturesque and Architectural Views for Cottages, Farm Houses, and Country Villas* (London, 1793), distinguished the 'elegance, compactness and convenience' of the villa from the 'magnificence and extensive range of the country seats of nobility and opulent gentry'.

4. John Summerson, *Architecture in Britain 1530-1830* (Harmondsworth, 1953), chapters 4-5.

5. John Summerson (ed.), 'The Book of Architecture of John Thorpe', *Walpole Society,* 40 (1966), T99 (Pl. 2a).

6. John Newman, *The Buildings of England: West Kent and the Weald* (Harmondsworth, 1980), p. 423, says this does not represent the remains of an earlier house; Timothy Mowl & Brian Earnshaw, *Architecture without Kings* (Manchester, 1995), p. 158, say that it does.

7. For a description of Honington Hall before the major changes of the mid 18th century, see Roger North, *Of Building: Roger North's Writings on Architecture* (ed. Howard Colvin & J. Newman), Oxford, 1981), p. 73.

8. John Thorpe was perhaps the first to design a central door into a central hall, at Holland House in Kensington in 1606.

9. Since I first made the case for inverting the plan further documentary evidence has been identified which corroborates the case for the original entrance front having been, as proposed here, to the south: see Andor Gomme, 'Chevening: the Resolutions', *Georgian Group Journal,* 15 (2005), p. 121.

10. Colen Campbell, *Vitruvius Britannicus* I (London, 1715), pls 78-9.

11. Summerson, 'Book of Architecture of John Thorpe', no. T218.

12. North, *Of Building,* pp. 71-3.

13. All Souls College, Oxford, Wren Drawings 11/108; reproduced in *Wren Society,* 12 (1935), pl. 2.

14. Eric Mercer suggested that the stair may have been in the hall itself, as at Hanbury Hall. However, if this was the case, it would pre-date similar arrangements by some twenty or thirty years and would have created awkward upper access.

15. Andrea Palladio, *The Four Books of Andrea Palladio's Architecture* (Isaac Ware, ed.) (London 1738), E.G. pls 32, 41, 42.

16. For the unexecuted version, see RIBA, Smythson drawings, no. 1/8.

17. Summerson, 'Book of Architecture of John Thorpe', no. T94.

18. Ibid., no. T202.

19. *Vitruvius Britannicus* I, pl. 17.

20. J. Woolfe & J. Gandon, *Vitruvius Britannicus* VI (London, 1771), pl. 86.

21. Campbell, *Vitruvius Britannicus* II (London, 1717), pl. 35.

22. Palladio, *Four Books of Architecture* (ed. Ware), pls 30, 33, 34, 40.

Chapter 6 (Pages 111-126)

1. Bodleian Library, Oxford, Aubrey MS 17, 'Designatio de Easton-Piers in Com:

Wilts'. Some of the sketches referred to are reproduced in John Dixon Hunt, *Garden and Grove* (London, 1986), pp. 154-7.

2. Richard Barber (ed.), *The Worlds of John Aubrey* (London, 1988), p. 228.

3. Andrea Palladio, *The Four Books of Andrea Palladio's Architecture* (Isaac Ware, ed.) (London 1738), p. 41.

4. See Caroline Constant, *The Palladio Guide* (London, 1988) for examples.

5. John Bridges, *History and Antiquities of Northamptonshire*, I (1791), p. 328.

6. Colen Campbell, *Vitruvius Britannicus*, III (London, 1725), pl. 9.

7. Tillemans was there in 1721. The drawings are in the British Library, Add MS 32467, fols 237, 238, and are illustrated in B.A. Bailey (ed.), *Northamptonshire in the Early Eighteenth Century: The Drawings of Peter Tillemans and Others*, Northamptonshire Record Society, 39 (Northampton, 1996), pp. 194-6.

8. It is clearly shown by Tillemans, and can be made out on 19th-century maps.

9. Bridges records that he sent to Genoa for tapestry designs in his capacity as head of the Mortlake factory.

10. Daniel Defoe, *A Tour Thro' the Whole Island of Great Britain*, vol. 3 (London, 1742), pp. 291.

11. By Samuel Wale, in R. & J. Dodsley (publishers) *London and its Environs Described* III (London, 1761), opposite p. 110.

12. The engraving shows the garden front with what appears to be the front court and its wall.

13. Wiltshire Record Office, Trowbridge, 944/1.

14. William Lawson, *A New Orchard and Garden* (London, 1618), p. 10.

15. E.S. de Beer (ed.), *The Diary of John Evelyn* (Oxford, 1959), entries for 4 Jul. 1652, p. 323, and 6 August 1674, p. 601.

16. Formerly at the house.

17. David Jacques, 'Garden Design in the Mid-Seventeenth Century', *Architectural History*, 44 (2001), pp. 365-76.

18. According to a plan by Arthur William Hakewill, and published in H. Avray Tipping, *English Homes, Late Stuart 1649-1714* (London, 1929), fig. 48, p. 33.

19. Drawing by Peter Tillemans, British Library, Add MS 32467, fol. 154.

20. The story is contained in entries in the 'Common Place Book Belonging to Sr Mark Pleydell of Coleshill in the County of Berkshire', fol. 63v. It has been quoted and discussed in: H. Avray Tipping, 'Coleshill House, Berkshire, *Country Life*, 26 July 1919, pp. 108-46; John Bold, *John Webb* (Oxford, 1989); Nigel Silcox-Crowe, 'Sir Roger Pratt 1620-1685: The Ingenious Gentleman Architect' in R. Brown (ed.), *The Architectural Outsiders* (London, 1985); Timothy Mowl & Brian Earnshaw, *Architecture Without Kings* (Manchester, 1995).

21. See Pratt's Notebook L, unnumbered folios on 'Scituation', in R.T. Gunther, *The Architecture of Sir Roger Pratt* (Oxford, 1928), pp. 55-6.

22. Berkshire Record Office, Reading, Pleydell-Bouverie papers, D/EPb/P1, 'A Platt of the Mannor of Coulsill and Parish of Coulsill in the County of Berks being the Lands &c of … Sr. George Pratt … By Wm. Brudenell'.

23. Celia Fiennes, *The Illustrated Journeys of Celia Fiennes 1685-c.1712* (Christopher Morris, ed.) (London, 1982), p. 47.

24. This process is well documented in weekly reports: Berkshire Record Office, D/EPb E25, weekly labour sheets, 1796-1801.

25. Berkshire Record Office, D/EPb A7/8, 1780/81.

26. The ovals on the inside faces originally contained classical busts. These are known from photographs, but are now missing.

27. Berkshire Record Office, D/EPb A 7/8, 1780.

28. Francis Bacon, 'Of Gardens', 1625, as quoted in John Dixon Hunt & Peter Willis (eds), *The Genius of the Place. The English Landscape Garden 1620-1820* (London, 1975), pp. 52-3.

29. British Library, K.Top. 7 45a, engraving by Boyce entitled 'Piers of Inigo Jones at Coleshill The Seat of Sir Mark Pleydell'.

30. At Ryston Hall. It is illustrated in Gunther, *Architecture of Sir Roger Pratt* (Oxford, 1928), opposite p. 169.

31. This garden is discussed in more detail in Sally Jeffery, '"The Flower of All the Private Gentlemens Palace in England": Sir Stephen Fox's "Extraordinarily Fine" Garden at Chiswick', *Garden History*, 32:1 (2004), pp. 1-19, which gives full references.

32. John Macky, *A Journey through England, in Familiar Letters from a Gentleman Here, to His Friend Abroad* (London, 1722), p. 73.

33. Evelyn, *Diary* (ed. De Beer), 30 October 1682, p. 464.

34. Robert Latham & William Matthews (eds), *The Diary of Samuel Pepys*, vol. 7 (London, 1972), p. 213.

35. Daniel Defoe, *A Tour thro' the whole Island of Great Britain*, (London, 1725), p. 19.

Chapter 7 (Pages 127-139)

1. John Norden, *Speculum Britanniae* (London, 1593), p. 12.

2. Count Magalotti, *Travels of Cosmo III* (London, 1821), p. 162.

3. Roger North, *Of Building:Roger North's Writings on Architecture* (ed. H.M. Colvin & J. Newman), (Oxford, 1981), p. 63.

4. A lithograph of 1842 after C.J. Richardson shows the chimneypiece with its elaborately carved overmantel still *in situ* at Canonbury.

5. John Evelyn visited the house in 1653, writing in his diary that he considered 'the prospect, which is doubtless for city, river, ships, meadows, hills, woods and all other amenities, one of the most noble in the world.' *The Diary & Correspondence of John Evelyn* (London, 1854) I, p. 285.

6. John Gurney 'Lady Jane Berkeley, Ashley House and architectural innovation in late-Elizabethan England', *Architectural History,* 43 (2000), pp. 113-20.

7. Nicholas Cooper discusses the plan of Charlton in his *Houses of the Gentry 1480-1680* (New Haven & London, 1999), p. 136.

8. John Newman, 'Strayed from the Queen's House?', *Architectural History,* 27 (1984), pp. 4-6

9. I am grateful to Claire Gapper for her opinions on the plasterwork in this house.

10. Anthony Wells-Cole discusses the print sources for this in his *Art & Decoration in Elizabethan & Jacobean England* (New Haven & London, 1997), p. 92

11. Recent examination of the fabric showed a small oval window in early-17th-

century brickwork in part of the roof-space, which may have marked an external wall of a four-bay house, rather than the six-bay house which we see today. I am grateful to Sally Jeffery for her help on this.

12. London Metropolitan Archives (hereafter LMA), Series 2/ACC 1360, Introductory Notes.

13. This painting was sold in 1922 for the large sum of 450 guineas, and has not been traced since then.

14. LMA, Series 2/ACC 1360/245/1-2.

15. Howard Colvin in his *Biographical Dictionary of British Architects 1600-1840* (3rd edition, New Haven & London, 1995), pp. 561-2, suggests that Ranelagh rather than Wren may have been responsible for the design.

16. North, *Of Building*, p. 9.

17. The house was bought in 1682 by his relative, the 1st Earl of Burlington.

18. John Bowack *Antiquities of Middlesex* (London, 1705), quoted by C.G.T. Dean, *The Royal Hospital, Chelsea* (London, 1950), p. 157.

19. Dean covers the building history of the site in depth.

20. A plan of the ground floor is among Wren's papers at All Souls College, Oxford, II, 86.

21. Dean, *Royal Hospital*, p. 154.

22. *The Builder*, 2 (1844), p. 571.

23. These are the 17th-century Lindsay House, and the 18th-century Argyll House.

Chapter 8 (Pages 140-166)

1. See James S. Ackerman, *The Villa: Form and Ideology of Country Houses* (Princeton, 1990), pp. 78-84; John Bold *et al.*, *Greenwich: An Architectural History of the Royal Hospital for Seamen and the Queen's House* (New Haven & London, 2000), pp. 45-6. The similarities between the Villa Medici and the Queen's House may be coincidental, as there is no evidence that Jones visited the building in 1613-14 and its design was not available to him in published form.

2. Mary Hervey, in *The Life, Correspondence and Collections of Thomas Howard, Earl of Arundel* (Cambridge, 1921), p. 76, notes that Lord Arundel stayed for several weeks at a villa 'two miles from Padua, on the way to Cattaio' in two periods between late July and late September 1613. This can only be the Villa Molin. Jones was familiar with the building, referring to it three times in his copy of Palladio's *I Quattro Libri dell'Architettura* (1601), now at Worcester College, Oxford; see Bruce Allsopp (ed.), *Inigo Jones on Palladio*, 2 vols (Newcastle upon Tyne, 1970) (transcript and facsimile, hereafter cited as Jones's *Quattro Libri*), Book II, p. 54 and Book IV, pp. 24, 105. For Jones's Italian tour, see John Harris & Gordon Higgott, *Inigo Jones: Complete Architectural Drawings* (London, 1989), pp. 52-7, and Giles Worsley, 'On the trail of Inigo Jones in Italy', *Country Life,* 18 November 2004, pp. 64-7.

3. George H. Chettle, *The Queen's House, Greenwich* (Survey of London Monographs, 14), 1937, pp. 25-8, 97-9 (transcript of works accounts); Howard M. Colvin (ed.), *The History of the King's Works, Volume IV, 1485-1660 (Part II)* (London, 1982), pp. 114-22; Bold, *Greenwich*, pp. 44-8.

4. Letter from John Chamberlain to Sir Dudley Carleton, 21 June 1617; see

NOTES to pp. 144-149

    Colvin, *King's Works*, p. 115.

5. Chettle, *Queen's House* p. 98; Bold, *Greenwich*, fig. 55.

6. Adriaen van Stalbemt & Jan van Belcamp, 'View of Greenwich', *c*.1632, in the Royal Collection; see Bold, *Greenwich*, fig. 73 and pp. 52-3; Harris & Higgott, *Jones Drawings*, fig. 16. The £5 15s. 10d. spent on stone masons' work in 1616-18 (Colvin, *King's Works*, p. 115) was far short of the sum needed to clad the ground floor walls in chamfered stone blocks and dress the openings, whose segmental heads survive exposed to view beneath the outer bridge rooms of both ranges.

7. Colvin, *King's Works*, p. 119; Harris & Higgott, *Jones Drawings*, pp. 322-3; Bold, *Greenwich*, p. 54-5. Jones's sketch for the door 'in to yᵉ voltes under yᵉ tarras' does not show the staircases on each side, which suggests that they had not been designed in 1635.

8. The drawing was lost – probably stolen – while on loan for the Inigo Jones *King's Arcadia* exhibition in 1973. It came from a collection of Colen Campbell's drawings at Newby Hall, Yorkshire. The legible inscriptions are 'Triomfo'(sic) and 'Sacrificio' above the outer first-floor windows, and 'Trofei' below the central pair. For further discussion of this drawing and the later phases of the design, see Gordon Higgott, 'The Design and Setting of Inigo Jones's Queen's House, 1616-40', *The Court Historian*, 11: 2 (December 2006), pp. 135-48.

9. Stone is the likely author of a precisely ruled ink elevation of the York Water Gate, *c*.1626, at Sir John Soane's Museum, in an interleaved copy of Pennant's *London*, III, no. 45 (p. 62).

10. For Alexander's work, see Bold, *Greenwich*, p. 88. The ground level before *c*.1935 appears in a photograph of September 1898 in the National Maritime Museum, published in John Charlton's guide book, *The Queen's House, Greenwich* (London, 1976), p. 16.

11. Julian Bowsher, 'The Queen's House: A Standing Building Report', Museum of London Archaeology Service Report, June 2000 (English Heritage, the Queen's House archives), pp. 92-102. The single surviving unaltered basement window is on the south side of the south-west corner room of the basement.

12. Van Stalbemt & van Belcamp show part of the eastwards view (n. 6, above).

13. See Mark Girouard, *Life in the English Country House* (New Haven & London, 1978), pp. 105-9; *Robert Smythson & The Elizabethan Country House* (New Haven & London, 1983)*, passim*; Paula Henderson, *The Tudor House and Garden* (New Haven & London, 2005), pp. 155-77.

14. See Giles Worsley, *Architecture in Britain: The Heroic Age* (New Haven & London, 1995), pp. 198-202.

15. For the examples by Palladio, see Bruce Boucher, *Andrea Palladio: The Architect in his Time* (New York, 1998), figs 88, 89, 198; Scamozzi's Villa Molin is best illustrated in Franco Barbieri & Guido Beltrami (eds), *Vincenzo Scamozzi 1548-1616* (Venice, 2003), pp. 368-75.

16. RIBA Drawings Collection, Jones & Webb 18; Harris & Higgott, *Jones Drawings*, pp. 66-7, where the drawing is assigned to the Queen's House in 1616 on the basis of its 40-feet square hall and adjoining round staircase. However, in functional terms it has little in common with the first and executed designs for

the building discussed here, and its formal rear elevation would not have been appropriate for a site next to a walled public road.

17. Ground Probing Radar Survey, Preliminary Report to English Heritage, March 2004, by Peter Barker, C. Eng. MICE MCIWEM MIFA. The survey examined the substructure to a depth of 0.5m below the marble floor.

18. See Bold, *Greenwich*, fig. 71.

19. National Archives, AOI/356/2487; see Chettle, *Queen's House*, p. 102.

20. Worcester College, Oxford, H & T 12, RIBA Drawings Collection, Jones & Webb 19; see Harris & Higgott, *Jones Drawings*, pp. 70-1, 66-8. I am most grateful to the Provost and Fellows of Worcester College for permission to reproduce material in their care, and to Dr Joanna Parker, Librarian, for her help on several occasions.

21. M. Whinney, 'An unknown design for a villa by Inigo Jones', in Howard Colvin & John Harris (eds), *The Country Seat* (London, 1970), pp. 33-5; Harris & Higgott, *Jones Drawings*, pp. 112-13.

22. Worcester College, Oxford, Jones's *Quattro Libri*, Book IV, p. 98.

23. RIBA Drawings Collection, Jones & Webb 206; see also Chettle, *Queen's House*, pp. 28-30.

24. See John Harris & Alan Tait, *Catalogue of the Drawings by Inigo Jones, John Webb & Isaac de Caus at Worcester College Oxford* (Oxford, 1979), p. 75, pl. 117, cat. nos 181, O and R, V.

25. The Prince's Lodging elevation has $3^{fo} - 2^y$ inscribed against the balustrade; see Harris & Higgott, *Jones Drawings*, pp. 89, 105, 257, 259, 261.

26. See Chettle, *Queen's House*, plates 50, 69. As internal floor levels have changed, the most reliable evidence for the loggia and window balustrade heights is John James's precise scaled drawing of the south elevation, *c*.1708; see Chettle, fig. 6, and Bold, *Greenwich*, fig. 118.

27. I am most grateful to Alan Fagan for his exceptional care in producing these line drawings and for his comments on the proportioning of the design.

28. Worcester College, Oxford, Jones's *Quattro Libri*, Book II, p. 64. He wrote 'loge Da Jo Sanci' against Palladio's plan of the loggia. For Houghton Conquest, see Harris & Higgott, *Jones Drawings*, pp. 84-5.

29. Worcester College, Oxford, Jones's *Quattro Libri*, Book IV, p. 94 (window 'C', annotated by Jones), and p. 127; Daniele Barbaro, *I Dieci Libri dell'Architettura di M. Vitruvio Pollio* (Venice, 1567), lib. III, cap. III, p. 154 (see modern reprint and commentary, edited by Manfredo Tafuri and Manuela Morresi for the *Edizioni il Polifilo*, Milan, 1997; Jones's annotated copy is at Chatsworth House, Derbyshire). For Jones's early use of Barbaro's Vitruvius, see John Newman, 'Inigo Jones's architectural education before 1614', *Architectural History*, 35 (1992), pp. 18-50.

30. See John Summerson, *Architecture in Britain 1530-1830* (9th ed., New Haven & London, 1993), pp. 120-1; Harris & Higgott, *Jones Drawings*, pp. 65, 70. The repair and refurbishment of the Queen's House from 1985-9 is described in Stephen Marks (ed.), *Transactions of the Association for Studies in the Conservation of Historic Buildings*, 14 (1989), pp. 3-15, 65-80.

31. See Howard Colvin (ed.), *The History of the King's Works, Volume 5 1660-1782*

(London, 1976), pp. 140-1; John Bold, *John Webb* (Oxford, 1989), pp. 126-7. The drawing may be the work of Willem de Keyser who was paid for 'draughts with the upwrights' of the bridge rooms in 1661. The projecting, wall-like blocks in front of the central doors represent middle steps, apparently shaded in error.

32. The doors are omitted without explanation from the reconstructions of the building in Bold, p.50; on p. 65 it is stated that the niche in the hall may have been used for the display of Bernini's bust of Charles I.

33. Worcester College, Oxford, Jones's *Quattro Libri*, Book II, pp. 8, 12, 22; Book I, p. 52 (and written in January 1615); Harris & Higgott, *Jones Drawings*, pp. 53-5.

34. In Book I, Chap. 21, 'On Loggias, Entrances, Halls and Rooms and their shapes', in Robert Tavernor & Richard Schofield (translators and eds), *Andrea Palladio: The Four Books on Architecture* (Cambridge, Mass., & London, 1997), p. 57.

35. Palladio illustrates two examples of such halls amongst his own house designs in Book II of the *Quattro Libri*, both of which Jones annotated in the period 1614-15: the design for the unfinished Palazzo della Torre in Verona (p. 11), and a design for a site in Venice (p. 72). See Jones's *Quattro Libri*; Tavernor & Schofield, pp. 87, 150; Boucher, p. 219.

36. Barbaro, *I Dieci Libri*, pp. 284-7; Palladio, *Quattro Libri*, pp. 24-35; Palladio illustrates this type of entrance-hall in his designs for two unexecuted *palazzi* in Book II, pp. 11, 72. For an important early discussion of Palladio's reconstructions of the Roman House, see Rudolf Wittkower, *Architectural Principles in the Age of Humanism* (London, 1962), pp. 76-82.

37. See the text and commentary in Ingrid D. Rowland & Thomas Noble Howe (eds), *Vitruvius: Ten Books on Architecture* (Cambridge, 1999), pp. 78-80, 256-8. In a long note dated 28 September 1625 on page 235 in Part I of his copy of Scamozzi's *L'Idea della Architettura Universale* (Venice, 1615) at Worcester College, Jones criticises Scamozzi for proportioning the atrium and aisles of his Roman Senator's House as one space, whereas 'Da: Barbaro and Palladio make ye atrio by itself […] and the alle [aisles] by themselves[.] this last I take to bee nearer the text of Vitrruvos'.

38. For datable features in Jones's handwriting from 1614 onwards, see Gordon Higgott, 'Varying with reason: Inigo Jones's theory of design', *Architectural History*, 35 (1992), pp. 73, 76, nn. 12, 67. The handwriting of these notes displays the secretary-style 's' with an upward flourish at the ends of words, a feature that disappeared from his hand by 1625 (as in the example cited above, n. 36). However, the script is more compact and cursive than in a group of notes dating from March 1619 (Worcester College, Oxford, Jones's *Quattro Libri*, Book II, p. 39; Book IV, p. 94).

39. John Summerson, *Inigo Jones* (New Haven & London, 2000), pp. 40-2, figs 13-15. However, at the Banqueting House all the compartments have full cornices. Jones appears to have refined his understanding of the detailing of such ceilings after he had finished the Banqueting House.

40. 'O is a pogiolo [balcony] or corritore scoperto [uncovered corridor] that from ye landing if the staires brings you to ye roome a parrte'.

41. *Ibid.*, Book II, p. 37. The earliest notes were written in Italy, and several on this

page and on p. 39 (the Corinthian Hall) date to March 1619, when Jones was designing the Banqueting House. This note is a few years later, and contemporary with those about the design of the Four Column Atrium, discussed above (see n. 38).

42. See Wittkower, *Architectural Principles*, pp. 80-1; Boucher, pp. 152-5; *Quattro Libri*, Book II, Chapter VI, pp. 29-32 ('Dell'Atrio Corinthio').

43. For the fullest illustrated history of Palladio's building, see Elena Bassis, *Il Convento della Carità* (Corpus Palladianum, volume VI, Vicenza, 1971). The staircase is illustrated at plates 48-56, and plates XC and XCI compare the Queen's House and Carità examples.

44. Jones's sketch shows the stone treads of the stairs in side view tapering slightly from front to back, and also in long view, where they taper in a shallow concave profile immediately behind the edge of the tread. He wrote next to the sketch, 'Sloping of ye Stones'. The cutting back of the tread reduced the weight of the stones. At the Queen's House he achieved this effect by cutting back the soffit of each tread in a concave profile (colour plate 6).

45. Worcester College, Oxford, Jones's *Quattro Libri*, Book II, p. 29.

Chapter 9 (Pages 167-179)

1. I am indebted to Elizabeth Chew, whose Ph.D. Dissertation, 'Female Art Collecting and Patronage in Seventeenth Century England' (University of North Carolina, 2000), inspired my research into the architectural history of Tart Hall.

2. See David Howarth, 'The Patronage and Collecting of Aletheia, Countess of Arundel 1606-54', *Journal of the History of Collections*, 10:2 (1998), pp. 125-37; see Karen Hearn (ed.), *Dynasties: Painting in Tudor and Jacobean England 1530-1630* (London, 1995), pp. 208-12.

3. National Archives, C54/20/2019/2; Wards 5/26/6; C54/3017/12.

4. Walter Lewis Spiers (ed.) 'The Note-Book and Account Book of Nicholas Stone', *Walpole Society*, 7 (1918-19), pp. 125-6.

5. This (now only partly legible) plan is in the Westminster Archives Centre listed as 'Plan of the Grosvenor Estate', 1049/12/115; a copy in the Crace Collection, British Library Maps (hereafter BLM) Crace X. 21, is entitled *A Plan of the Manor of Eybury and showing the Drainage from Oxford Street to the River 1614*.

6. See n. 3.

7. 'Mr Page' worked for the Arundels, and the 'Mr Gage' was almost certainly George Gage, who is discussed below. See M.F.S. Hervey, *The Life Correspondence and Collections of Thomas Earl of Arundel* (Cambridge, 1921), pp. 345-6, 374-6; Howarth, 'Countess of Arundel', p. 131.

8. BLM Crace XI. 61. Another inscription mentions the Equitable Gas Works which were built *c.*1829-50, giving an approximate date of the copy; see Walter Besant, *London in the Nineteenth Century* (London, 1909), p. 318.

9. Lionel Cust, 'Notes on the collections formed by Thomas Howard, Earl of Arundel & Surrey, K.G. – II', *Burlington Magazine*, 20 (Oct.– Mar. 1911-12), pp. 97-100, 233-6, 341-3 (hereafter Inventory), p. 99.

10. William Morgan, *Map of London & c.* [etc.] (1682), BLM, Crace Port. 2. 58; *A*

Plan of the Estate of Lord Stafford James St Pimlico late Tart Hall by Charles Stokes Senr 1725, BLM, Crace XI. 62. A Faithhorne mid-seventeenth-century view, in comparison with the three other plans, cannot be a faithful representation, even if drawn years before 1658; Faithorne and Newcourt, *An Exact Delineation of the Cities of London & Westminster & the Suburbs thereof* … (1658), BLM 183. P.1.(2.).

11. See John Harris, Stephen Orgel, Roy Strong, *The King's Arcadia Inigo Jones and the Stuart Court* (London, 1973), pp. 202-3; Anne Saunders, 'The Four Seasons by Wenceslas Hollar', *The Costume Society Extra Series* (London, 1979), pp. 10-12; Richard Pennington, *A Descriptive Catalogue of the Works of Wenceslaus Hollar 1607-1677* (Cambridge, 1982), (catalogue numbers) 606-609 (hereafter P + catalogue number); Richard Godfrey, *Wenceslaus Hollar: A Bohemian Artist in England* (New Haven & London, 1994), pp. 79-81. See also Antony Griffiths, *The Print In Stuart Britain 1603 −1689* (London, 1998), pp. 110-15.

12. Inventory, p. 236.

13. Richard Godfrey, 'Hollar's Prints for the Earl of Arundel', *Apollo*, 144 (Aug. 1996), p. 36.

14. Pennington, *Catalogue of the Works of Wenceslaus Hollar* , p. xxv.

15. Howarth, 'Countess of Arundel', p. 135.

16. Pennington, *Catalogue of the Works of Wenceslaus Hollar* , p. xxx.

17. P937-42, P954; Nicholas Cooper, *The Houses of the Gentry* (New Haven & London, 1999), pp. 324-5, pl. 335.

18. P937-42; P955; P1034-35; P154; P611; P1011, and p. xxviii. See also the Maggs Bros Ltd advertisement, 'Portrait of Alatheia, Countess of Arundel, from the 'Madagasca portrait' etching by Wencelaus Hollar. Antwerp, 1646', *British Art Journal*, 4:3 (2003), frontispiece.

19. See Howarth, 'Countess of Arundel', p. 131. The Countess's agent, a Theodore Taylor, paid 'the Gardiner of Tarthall' £10 from Lady Arundel, sometime after the death of the Earl in 1646, National Archives, SP19/143/52 v.; M.A.E. Green (ed.), *Calendar of the Proceedings of the Committee for Compounding, & c.1643-1660* (London, 1889-92), 4, p. 2463.

20. Pennington, *Catalogue of the Works of Wenceslaus Hollar*, pp. xxv-xxvi.

21. See Godfrey, 'Wenceslaus Hollar', pp. 79-80; Saunders, 'Four Seasons', pp. 9-10.

22. Stephen Orgel & Roy Strong, *Inigo Jones The Theatre of the Stuart Court* (London, 1973), I, pp. 131, 191-2, 205, ills 27, 28. See also David Howarth, *Lord Arundel and His Circle* (New Haven & London, 1985), pp. 116-17; Per Palme, *Triumph of Peace* (Stockholm, 1963), pp. 48n., 53-8, 104-5.

23. Saunders, 'Four Seasons', p. 10, Howarth, *Lord Arundel*, pp. 123, 215; Godfrey, *Wenceslaus Hollar* p. 80; Hervey, *Earl of Arundel*, p. 346.

24. See Lawrence Stone, *The Crisis of the Aristocracy* (Oxford, 1965), pp. 376, 428; Howarth, *Lord Arundel*, pp. 143, 203.

25. See *Acts of the Privy Council of England 1630 June − 1631 June* (London, 1964), p. 353 (1042, 28 May 1631); see Anne Saunders (ed.), *The Royal Exchange* (London, 1997), p. 95.

26. P1036; Inventory, p. 99.

27. Centre for Kentish Studies, Cranfield Papers, U 269/1, CB 105. Stone's Account Book records nine payments from 4 March 1638/9 to 30 November

1639; see Spiers, 'Note-Book and Account Book of Nicholas Stone', pp. 125-26.

28. British Library, Add. MSS, 15391, fols 166-7.

29. Centre for Kentish Studies, Cranfield Papers, U269/1 CB105; Howarth, *Lord Arundel*, p. 245 n. 38.

30. Edward Chaney, *The Stuart Portrait*, exh. cat. (Southampton City Art Gallery, 2001), p. 19.

31. Oliver Millar, 'Notes on Three Pictures by Van Dyck', *Burlington Magazine*, 3 (1969), pp. 414-17.

32. See Edward Chaney, *The Grand Tour and the Great Rebellion* (Geneva, 1985), pp. 19, 263-5; Susan Barnes, 'Van Dyck and George Gage', David Howarth (ed.), *Art and Patronage in the Caroline Courts* (Cambridge, 1993), pp. 1-11.

33. For copious evidence of this see British Library, Add..MSS 15390, fol. 146; Add..MSS 15391, fols 166-7; William Prynne, *Romes Master Peece or The Grand Conspiracy of the Pope* (London, 1643), p. 22; National Archives, SP23/36/13; Sir Edward Walker, *Historical Discourses upon Several Occasions* (London, 1705), 'Observations upon the Annals … At Amsterdam 1655', pp. 351-2; William Knowler (ed.), *Letters and Despatches of the Right Honourable Thomas Wentworth Earl of Strafforde* (Dublin, 1740), 2, p. 165 (with reference to Lady Maltravers, daughter-in-law of the Countess, and Lady Katherine Howard, (probably) a cousin of Lord Arundel); Green, *Calendar*, p. 2463; Hervey, *Earl of Arundel*, pp. 407-8; George Albion, *Charles I and the Court of Rome* (London, 1935), pp. 162, 203; Howarth, *Lord Arundel*, pp. 204, 209.

34. Inventory, p. 98. Relevantly it seems that Lord Arundel did not reside at the house in latter years, as his room was furnished more as a small sitting room, while his 'Bested … Tester, Valence, Curtaines' etc. were stored in the Wardrobe; see Inventory, pp. 100, 235.

35. J.P. Feil, 'Sir Tobie Matthew and his Collection of Letters', (Ph.D thesis, University of Chicago, 1962), p. 156. Feil does not give a date for this letter, but states that it is preserved among Doncaster's papers.

36. A. J. Taylor, 'The Royal Visit to Oxford in 1636', *Oxoniensia*, 1 (1936), p. 154. I am grateful to Sir Howard Colvin for both this and Dr Feil's reference to Gage.

37. In correspondence between Dr Goy and the author.

38. See Dianne Duggan, 'A Rather Fascinating Hybrid', *The British Art Journal*, 4:3 (2003), pp. 54-64 (ill. 13).

39. See Barnes, 'Van Dyke', p. 7; Howarth, *Lord Arundel*, pp. 158-9, 242 (n. 22).

40. Howarth, 'Countess of Arundel', p. 129.

41. Elena Bassi, *Ville Della Provincia Di Venezia* (Milan, 1987), pp. 379-80, 388-91, 398-9.

42. See Vaughan Hart & Peter Hicks, *Sebastiano Serlio on Architecture* (New Haven & London, 1996), pp. xi-xiii, for comment on the 'brief but potent' influence Serlio had on Venetian culture. See also Richard J Goy, *Venetian Vernacular Architecture: Traditional Housing in the Venetian Lagoon* (Cambridge, 1989), p. 136. See Bassi, *Ville Della Provincia Di Venezia*, pp. 349, 362, 409-11, 447-8, also pp. 373-5 (for the ground-floor central bay).

43. See n. 37, and Goy, *Venetian Vernacular Architecture*, p. 174.

44. Bassi, *Ville Della Provincia Di Venezia*, p. 434.
45. Goy, *Venetian Vernacular Architecture*, pp. 64, 229.
46. Cooper, *Houses of the Gentry*, pp. 128, 140-1.
47. John Harris has pointed out to me that there were two chests containing architectural designs of Scamozzi in the Arundel Inventory of 1655; see Hervey, *Earl of Arundel*. p. 487.
48. See, for example, Bassi, *Ville Della Provincia Di Venezia*, pp. 109, 296, 398 (the Mocenigo villa at Fiesso), 408, 414-15, 432, 446-7; see Cooper, *Houses of the Gentry*, pl. 335, for Hollar's full view of Albury. The timber-framed façade of Albury is asymmetrically decorated, implying that the scroll-work also may have been added later; see Ca Bembo, in Bassi, *Ville Della Provincia Di Venezia*, pp. 332-3. I have Nicholas Cooper to thank for suggesting that the Albury porch deserved a closer look.
49. George Vertue, 'Vertue Notebooks', *Walpole Society*, 24 (1935-6), pp. 166-7, 171; 26 (1937-8), pp. 26-7, 37.

Chapter 10 (Pages 180-191)
1. For a detailed examination of the various houses, see John Cloake, *Palaces and Parks of Richmond and Kew*, 2 vols (Chichester, 1996).
2. Will of Samuel Fortrey, dated 1641/2: National Archives, PROB11/202, RH226-7.
3. Samuel seems initially to have taken out the lease in his younger brother Peter's name. His son Samuel Fortrey junior was baptized at Richmond church in 1622: J. Challenor & C. Smith (eds), *Richmond Parish Registers* (Publications of the Surrey Parish Register Society, vol. 1, London, 1903).
4. The lease is contained in the Thoroton Hildyard of Flintham MSS, University of Nottingham (THF D3).
5. National Archives, CRES 2/1245.
6. Crick Smith Conservation: 'Kew Palace. Principal Interiors. Summary of findings' (unpublished typescript, Historic Royal Palaces archive, 1999, etc) documents the external colour-wash and other elements. See also Claire Gapper, 'Report on the Decorative Plasterwork at Kew Palace' (unpublished typescript, 1998); Alysson McDermott: 'Kew Palace Interiors. Investigation into the Use of Wallpapers. First and Second Floors' (unpublished typescript, 2001), both of which are kept, along with other unpublished reports, in the Historic Royal Palaces archive.
7. British Library, Add. MSS 41692-3, diary of Thomas Willis, April 1801, transcribed by Susanne Groom.
8. Linda Hall, *Period House Fixtures and Fittings 1300-1900* (Newbury, 2005). See also chapter 5 in Edward Roberts (ed.) *Hampshire Houses 1250-700: their Dating and Development* (Winchester, 2003); Tim Easton, 'Ritual Marks on historic Timber', *Weald & Downland Open Air Museum Bulletin* (Spring 1999).
9. From the memoirs of James, 2nd Earl Waldegrave, quoted in Christopher Hibbert, *George III* (London, 1998), p. 34.
10. The diary of Sir George Baker, November 1788, quoted in Hibbert, *George III*, p. 261.

Chapter 11 (Pages 192-205)

1. Nicholas Cooper, *Houses of the Gentry 1480-1680* (London, 1999), p. 128. See p. 10 for the full quotation.

2. John Evelyn, *Diary of John Evelyn*, (ed. E.S. de Beer) (Oxford, 1955), IV, p. 199; Robert Morden, *New Description and State of England* (London, 1704), p. 36.

3. Lawrence Stone & Jeanne C. Fawtier Stone, *An Open Elite? England 1540-1880* (Oxford, 1984), table 6.2.

4. J.T. Smith, *Hertfordshire Houses: Selective Inventory* (London, 1993), pp. 169-70; Menna Prestwich, *Cranfield: Politics and Profits under the Early Stuarts* (Oxford, 1966), pp. 50, 79, 89, 121, 254, 328, 412, 478, 497, 506.

5. Smith, *Hertfordshire Houses*, pp. 41-2; Henry Chauncy, *Historical Antiquities of Hertfordshire* (Bishops Stortford, 1826), 1, pp. 280-1; Robert Brenner, *Merchants and Revolution* (Cambridge, 1993), pp. 72-3.

6. Smith, *Hertfordshire Houses*, pp. 170-1; RCHME, *Inventory of the Historical Monuments in Hertfordshire* (London, 1910), p. 205; Hertfordshire Archives & Local Studies (hereafter HALS), Oldfield Drawings, VI, p. 38.

7. History of Parliament Trust (hereafter HPT), draft biography of John Harrison by Simon Healy; *Victoria County History: Hertfordshire* (London, 1912), III, p. 412.

8. Chauncy, *Historical Antiquities of Hertfordshire* (London, 1700), p. 264; (1826), 1, p. 520; Smith, *Hertfordshire Houses*, p. 81.

9. John Newman, 'Nicholas Stone's Goldsmiths' Hall: Design and Practice in the 1630s', *Architectural History*, 14 (1971), p. 34; Balthazar Gerbier, *Counsel and Advise to All Builders* (London, 1663), p. 14; John Summerson, *Architecture in Britain 1530-1830* (Harmondsworth, 1983), p. 164.

10. Chauncy (1826), 1, p. 520; Smith, *Hertfordshire Houses*, pp. 79-80.

11. B. D. Henning (ed.), *House of Commons 1660-1690* (HPT: London, 1983), II, p. 669; Stone & Stone, *Open Elite*, p. 204.

12. Smith, *Hertfordshire Houses*, pp. 160-1; Chauncy (1700), p. 510; Cooper, *Houses of the Gentry*, pp. 5, 230.

13. Henning, *House of Commons 1660-1690*, I, pp. 741-2; Eveline Cruickshanks, Stuart Handley & David W. Hayton (eds), *House of Commons 1690-1715* (HPT: Cambridge, 2002), III, p. 392; Chauncy (1826), II, p. 357; Smith, *Hertfordshire Houses*, p. 206; HALS, Oldfield Drawings, VII, p. 84; Nikolaus Pevsner & Bridget Cherry, *Hertfordshire* (Harmondsworth, 1977), p. 268; RCHME, *Hertfordshire*, p. 232.

14. Smith, *English Houses*, pp. 96-8; Paul M. Hunneyball, *Architecture and Image-Building in 17th-Century Hertfordshire* (Oxford, 2004), p. 27; H.F. Killick, 'Memoirs of Sir Marmaduke Rawden, Kt., 1582-1646', *Yorkshire Archaeological Journal*, 25 (1920), pp. 315, 317-19; *Life of Marmaduke Rawdon of York*, (Robert Davies, ed.) (Camden Society, 85: London, 1863), p. 24.

15. Smith, *Hertfordshire Houses*, p. 98; Hunneyball, *Architecture and Image-Building in 17th-Century Hertfordshire*, p. 116; Cooper, *Houses of the Gentry*, pp. 136-7.

16. J.T. Smith *English Houses 1200-1800: The Hertfordshire Evidence (London, 1992)*, pp. 76-7.

17. Morden, *New Description and State of England*, p. 36.

18. J.R. Woodhead, *Rulers of London 1660-89* (London & Middlesex Archaeological Society: London, 1965), p. 133; Robert Clutterbuck, *History and Antiquities of the County of Hertford* (London, 1815-27), II, p. 306; Nicholas Maddex, *Brief History of Codicote* (Codicote, 1987), p. 25; *International Genealogical Index* (Codicote parish baptisms).

19. Smith, *Hertfordshire Houses*, p. 50; HALS, Buckler Drawings, IV, f. 154.

20. Smith, *English Houses*, p. 78; Hunneyball, *Architecture and Image-Building in 17th-Century Hertfordshire*, p. 112.

21. Chauncy (1826), 1, p. 535; National Archives, C54/4560/34; *IGI* (registers of St Andrew, Holborn); J.B. Whitmore & A.W.H. Clarke (eds), *London Visitation Pedigrees 1664* (Harleian Society: London, 1940), p. 47; W.B. Bannerman (ed.), *Registers of St Helen's, Bishopsgate, London* (Harleian Society Registers XXXI: London, 1904).

22. Chauncy (1700), p. 272; Elizabeth McKellar, *Birth of Modern London* (Manchester, 1999), pp. 168-70; P. & I. Vingboons, *Afbeeldsels der Voornaemste Gebouwen uyt alle die Philips Vingboons Geordineert Heeft* (Amsterdam, 1648), pls 45, 52; John F. Millar, *Classical Architecture in Renaissance Europe 1419-1585* (Williamsburg, Va., 1987), p. 189; Kerry Downes, *Architecture of Wren* (London, 1982), pl. 87; Smith, *Hertfordshire Houses*, p. 88.

Chapter 12 (Pages 206-222)

1. Richard Peats & Paul Drury, 'Forty Hall, Enfield, Conservation Management Plan, Part 1 – Understanding', (unpublished typescript, London Borough of Enfield, November 2005). I am particularly grateful to Paul Drury and Richard Peats for sharing their findings.

2. Daniel Lysons, *Environs of London, II: the County of Middlesex* (London, 1795), p. 299, referencing Survey of Enfield Manors, 1635.

3. Richard Gough *et al.*, MS notes for a history of Enfield, 1771-1809, held in the Bodleian Library, Oxford, Gough London 126; William Robinson, *The History and Antiquities of Enfield, in the County of Middlesex* (London, 1823), II, p. 237.

4. Valerie Pearl, *London and the Outbreak of the Puritan Revolution* (Oxford, 1961), p. 118.

5. The best source for the house's general history is Geoffrey Gillam, *Forty Hall, Enfield* (London, 1997).

6. Lysons, *Environs of London*, II, p. 299. The copy in the Guildhall Library, London, has additional plates, including a watercolour of Forty Hall reproduced in Robinson, *History and Antiquities of Enfield*, II, p. 237.

7. London Metropolitan Archives (LMA), ACC/801/37-51.

8. LMA, Plan of Forty Hall with the Manor of Worcesters, lot XVII, ACC/0696/0001.

9. Robinson, *History and Antiquities of Enfield*, I, pp. 234-9.

10. 1793 view published in John Harris, 'Classicism without Jones', in *Country Life,* 4 October 1990, p.153. See also 'Review of Dr Robinson "History of Enfield"', *Gentleman's Magazine*, 93:1 (June 1823), pl. II, no. 1, opposite p. 537; also LMA, SC/PD/EN/01.

11. Lysons, Guildhall Library edition.

NOTES to pp. 209-217

12. Robinson, *History and Antiquities of Enfield*, I, p. 239.

13. Royal Commission on Historical Monuments, *An Inventory of the Historical Monuments in Middlesex* (London, 1937), pp. 23-4.

14. English Heritage, Historic Buildings file HB 51807. LMA, ACC/3499/EH/02/124, contains proposals for the conversion of the stable yard, but the works carried out appear different from those proposed: information from Richard Peats.

15. Robinson, *History and Antiquities of Enfield*, I, p. 237. I am very grateful to Andor Gomme for sharing his thoughts on Forty Hall.

16. As part of ongoing investigations for the Forty Hall management plan, Paul Drury and Richard Peats have shown that the windows in the first-floor panelled room, directly below this, had a similar form – indicated by the insertion of later panels above and below the present windows. Drury and Peats have used the position of the partitions on the second floor, which continue into the roof where the order of construction – predating original lath and plaster ceilings – shows them to be original, to determine the position of fenestration on the north façade.

17. Held in Enfield Local Studies Library (former Southgate Town Hall).

18. Nicholas Cooper, *Houses of the Gentry 1480-1680* (New Haven & London, 1999), p. 231; Howard Colvin, 'Thorpe Hall and its Architect', *Essays in English Architectural History* (New Haven & London, 1999), pp. 177-8.

19. Peter Smith, 'West Dean House, Wiltshire', *Georgian Group Journal*, 9 (1999), pp. 87-90.

20. Annotations by Richard Gough to Daniel Lysons, *The Environs of London*, II, p. 299: Bodleian Library, Oxford, MSS Gough Middlesex 8-9 (information from Sir Howard Colvin). I am most grateful to Sir Howard for thus confirming the supposition made by the Society of Architectural Historians at its study day at Forty Hall on 2 November 1999.

21. 'Forty Hall, the Property of Eliab Breton Esq., Situate near Enfield, in the County of Middlesex', sales particulars, 1773, held at LMA, ACC/801/44, and at Enfield Local Studies Library.

22. Peats & Drury, 'Forty Hall, Enfield, Conservation Management Plan', pp. 12-13.

23. *Meyer's Local and General Advertiser*, 27 Aug. 1897: cutting held at Enfield Local Studies Library.

24. 'Forty Hall, the Property of Eliab Breton Esq., … .'

25. LMA, MR/PLT 71-97 (Enfield Land Tax Returns 1767-1806).

26. Rev. H. Fowler, 'Tyttenhanger', *St Alban's Architectural & Archaeological Society Transactions*, 1893 and 1894 (1896), pp. 30-45; *Gentleman's Magazine*, 1797:1, p. 10.

27. Jonathan R. Hunn, Tyttenhanger, excavation and survey in the parish of Ridge, Hertfordshire, undertaken by Archaeological Services & Consultancy Ltd (Oxford, 2004).

28. Nabil Matar, 'Blount, Sir Henry (1602–1682)', *Oxford Dictionary of National Biography* (Oxford, 2004).

29. *Country Life*, 11 October 1919, p. 457.

30. Hertfordshire Archives & Local Studies Library (HALS), D/ECd/F28.

31. HALS, F22-24 (Garden Accounts 1838-58).
32. HALS, D/ECd/P2.
33. HALS, D/3/Of (Henry George Oldfield, 'Hertfordshire Topography', *c.*1790), V, p. 344.
34. HALS, D/EB/2067B/P1.
35. *Country Life*, 4 October 1919, pp. 424-32.
36. I am very grateful to Anthony Cleminson for supplying background information about cruck rafters.
37. HALS, D/ECd/P2; D/EB/2067B/P1.
38. HALS, D/EB/2607/F34 (1697); D/EB/2067B/F35 (27 Nov. 1701, 21 Sep. 1702, 1 Dec. 1725).
39. HALS, D/EDd (Add.) E4 (estate papers 1778-1792).
40. J.T. Smith, *Hertfordshire Houses: Selective Inventory* (London, 1993), p. 148.
41. Lady Jane van Koughnet, *A History of Tyttenhanger* (London, 1895), pp. 53-4.

Chapter 13 (Pages 223-246)
1. Christopher Wren, Jnr, *Parentalia; or, Memoirs of the Family of the Wrens*, (London, 1750; facsimile ed., Farnborough, 1965); Lydia M. Soo, *Wren's Tracts on Architecture and Other Writings* (Cambridge, 1998).
2. The houses referred to are the châteaux at Vaux-le-Vicomte, Maisons-Laffitte, Rueil, Courances, Chilly-Mazarin, Écouen, Saint-Maur-les-Fossés, Sainte-Mandé, Issy-Les-Moulineaux, Meudon, Le Raincy, Chantilly, Verneuil-sur-Oise and Laincourt.
3. The château of Le Raincy was designed and built by Louis Le Vau for Jacques Bordier in 1643. It was demolished in the early 19th century. The plan and elevations were recorded by Jean Marot in his *Petit Marot*; see Jean-Marie Pérouse de Montclos (ed.), *Le Guide du Patrimoine; Ile-de-France* (Paris, 1992), pp. 537-9.
4. *Wren Society*, 17 (1941), p. 180.
5. Howard Colvin, *A Biographical Dictionary of British Architects, 1600-1840*, 3rd edition (New Haven & London, 1995), pp. 1091-2.
6. B.D. Henning (ed.), *The History of Parliament: The House of Commons 1690-1715*, II (London, 1983), pp. 453-5; Eveline Cruickshanks, Stuart Handley & D.W. Hayton (eds), *The History of Parliament: The House of Commons, 1690-1715*, IV (London, 2002), pp. 125-32; *Oxford Dictionary of National Biography*, vol. 24, pp. 329-30.
7. Henning (ed.), *House of Commons 1690-1715*, II, pp. 225-26; Cruickshanks, Handley & Hayton (eds), *House of Commons, 1690-1715*, IV, pp. 674-82; *Oxford Dictionary of National Biography*, vol. 34, pp. 600-3.
8. Henning (ed.), *House of Commons 1690-1715*, II, p. 454.
9. Ibid.
10. Kerry Downes, *The Architecture of Wren* (London, 1982), pp. 102-4; Gervase Jackson-Stops, 'Tring Park', *Country Life*, 25 November 1993, pp. 60-3; J.T. Smith, *English Houses 1200-1800, The Hertfordshire Evidence* (London, 1992), pp. 84-5; J.T. Smith, *Hertfordshire Houses: Selective Inventory* (London, 1993), pp. 192-3.

11. Two fine marble chimney pieces also survive, in the entrance hall and in the original state dressing room, which probably date from the late 17th century. Gervase Jackson-Stops attributes these to James Gibbs's remodelling of *c.*1725 for William Gore, though it is more likely that Gibbs moved them to their present locations and added the carved marble overmantels: *Country Life*, 25 November 1993, pp. 60-63, pls 7 & 9.

12. Roger North, *Of Building: Roger North's Writings on Architecture* (ed. Howard Colvin & John Newman, Oxford, 1981), pp. 73-4.

13 Ibid., pp. 62, 73, 124.

14. Ibid., p. 74.

15. Ibid., p. 62.

16. Cruickshanks, Handley & Hayton (eds), *House of Commons, 1690-1715*, IV, p. 675.

17. Arthur Oswald, 'Winslow Hall, Buckinghamshire', *Country Life*, 24 August 1951, pp. 572-6.

18. *Wren Society,* 17 (Oxford, 1940), pp. 54-75, pls LVIII–LXIV.

19. *Country Life*, 24 August 1951, p. 574. John Churchill was a carpenter employed on the royal palaces and at Marlborough House.

20. David Green, *Gardener to Queen Anne: Henry Wise (1653-1738) and the Formal Garden* (London, 1956), p. 125, n. 2. London & Wise sent fruit trees in 1695, 1696 and 1701. They also sent a gardener, Michael Bough, and they charged £20.7s.10d. for planting 'the largest Garden, ye kitchen garden and the Platts before ye house': *Wren Society,* 17, p. 75.

21. A photographic copy of this picture, painted around 1700, remains at Winslow Hall.

22. The only precedent for this type of plan-form is a group of houses or lodges built at the beginning of the 17th century such as Chastleton House, Oxfordshire, and Kiplin House, Yorkshire, both of which have external staircase towers at either end, though without a central linking wall. There is also a group of five plans amongst the Thorpe drawings for houses with flanking staircase towers which do have a central linking wall: John Summerson (ed.), *The Book of Architecture of John Thorpe* (Walpole Society, 40 1966), pp. 52-3 (pl. 15), pp. 56-7 (pl. 20); p. 78 (pl. 56); p. 96 (pl. 90); pp. 102-3 (pl. 105).

INDEX

Numbers in bold indicate pages with black and white illustrations.